About the author

Lisa Smirl was a lecturer in international relations at the University of Sussex. She worked previously for the United Nations Development Programme in Africa, Southeast Europe and Central Asia. A Rhodes Scholar at Balliol College, Oxford, she did graduate work at the London School of Economics and completed a PhD at the University of Cambridge in 2010. Lisa was from Manitoba, Canada. She died in 2013 at the age of 37.

SPACES OF AID

HOW CARS, COMPOUNDS AND HOTELS SHAPE HUMANITARIANISM

Lisa Smirl

Zed Books
LONDON

Spaces of Aid: How Cars, Compounds and Hotels Shape Humanitarianism
was first published in 2015 by Zed Books Ltd, 7 Cynthia Street, London
N1 9JF, UK

www.zedbooks.co.uk

Set in Monotype Plantin and FontFont Kievit by Ewan Smith, London
Index: ed.emery@thefreeuniversity.net
Cover image © Juan Vrijdag/Panos
Cover designed by roguefour.co.uk

A catalogue record for this book is available from the British Library

ISBN   978-1-78360-350-3 hb
ISBN   978-1-78360-349-7 pb
ISBN   978-1-78360-351-0 pdf
ISBN   978-1-78360-352-7 epub
ISBN   978-1-78360-353-4 mobi

CONTENTS

FIGURES

NOTE TO THE READER

This book is based on Lisa Smirl's PhD thesis, which was successfully defended at the University of Cambridge in 2010. She died before she could publish it. Lisa was a pioneering scholar of the spatial dimensions of aid and development work, an area of inquiry which has expanded considerably in recent years. Her illness and death meant that she could not make use of scholarship published after 2010, nor could she incorporate discussion of events since then. With assistance from Ken Barlow at Zed Books, and with the advice of Lisa's friends and colleagues, we have lightly edited the manuscript for style, grammar and repetition. Those interested will find additional papers, data and other material by Lisa at spacesofaid.word press.com.

Tarak Barkawi, London School of Economics
Anna Stavrianakis, University of Sussex

FOREWORD

When Tarak Barkawi and Anna Stavrianakis asked me to provide a foreword for Lisa Smirl's book, *Spaces of Aid*, I was both honoured and humbled. To enthusiastically greet the posthumous publication of a young scholar's brilliant PhD thesis is not enough. The eloquence and prescience of Lisa's book constantly reminds us of our loss. Praise cannot recoup the intellectual riches that would have been. That Zed Books is publishing *Spaces of Aid*, however, has to be warmly acknowledged. That which Lisa did achieve is now here for all to see, enjoy and learn from.

I first met Lisa in March 2009, when I gave a talk at the Department of Politics and International Relations (POLIS) at Cambridge where she was completing her PhD. The title of my seminar was 'Aid, Architecture and Security in Sudan'. I had been in South Sudan about nine months earlier completing a consultancy for UNHCR. While I had been a fairly regular visitor during the civil war, this consultancy was the first time I'd been back to South Sudan for nine years. Although peace had been declared in 2005, the most striking thing in 2008 was the withdrawal of international aid workers into fortified aid compounds and the restriction of their movements. Paradoxically, during the war years, internationals had moved around a lot more freely. My Cambridge talk was a first attempt to make sense of this counter-intuitive experience through a tentative exploration of the spatial dimensions of humanitarian aid. It was a great delight therefore to find Lisa in the audience. As *Spaces of Aid* shows, through her research she was already there, in full command of this overlooked but vital intellectual terrain. In the pub afterwards, I learnt more from Lisa than I could give in return. Although I only knew her for a tragically short period of time, it was clear from the first that I'd met a warm, challenging and strong woman.

Spaces of Aid is an important book. It's about the spaces, environments and material objects of aid. While neglected and taken for granted, the built environment and material infrastructures that support international aid - the gated office and accommodation complexes, the four-wheel drive vehicles, and the exclusive bars and hotels that international aid workers frequent - circumscribe experience and influence policy. *Spaces of Aid* is the first book-length treatment of the closed environment that has been euphemistically summarised as Aid Land or the Aid Bubble. Not only does *Spaces of Aid* give this ignored but essentially subversive field of research visibility and coherence, the trend toward securitization that Lisa describes has, if anything, continued to deepen. International aid workers are physically remote from the societies through which they endlessly rotate. By showing how a culture of separation preceded the securitized hardening of the aid world's built and engineered environment, *Spaces of Aid* is an original and invaluable contribution to a debate that, in many respects, is only now beginning.

Mark Duffield, Emeritus Professor
Global Insecurities Centre, University of Bristol

ACKNOWLEDGEMENTS

It was not until I came to reflect on these acknowledgements that I realized how many people have contributed to the researching and writing of this thesis. Above all, I need to thank my supervisor, Tarak Barkawi, for his unflagging encouragement and advice both intellectually and professionally. I really cannot thank him enough and consider myself lucky to have been his student. I would also like to thank Charles Jones, my secondary supervisor, for his guidance and enthusiasm, tsunami comics and oxtail stew. Other members of the Centre of International Studies at Cambridge were incredibly generous with their time and advice, notably Duncan Bell, Devon Curtis and Mette Sangiovanni. Thanks also to Gerry Kearns and David Nally from Geography; Wendy Pullan and Peter Carl from Architecture; Jude Brown from the Gender Centre; and Ludmilla Jordanova from CRASSH. The research and writing of this thesis were supported by grants from the British Council (Chevening Trust), the Social Science and Humanities Research Council of Canada, the Smuts Foundation, the Centre for International Studies, and Emmanuel College's Carslaw Fund.

I am deeply indebted to all the people in 'the field' who took the time to talk to me about their experiences and to facilitate my research. Particular thanks go to Auguswandi, Azwar Hassan, Su Lin Lewis, Imogen Wall, Zoe Keeler (and her love of Emergency Sex), Murray McCullough and the Australian doctor who stitched up my eye! Over the course of this thesis, I have published and presented drafts of the various chapters and benefited greatly from the comments and discussions. Thanks to two anonymous referees for advice on a version of Chapter 4, which appeared in *International Political Sociology*. The opportunity to present a version of Chapter 5 at the

UCSB conference 'Spatial Americas' allowed Stella Nair to point me towards shotgun houses. Thanks also to Harald Wydra for forcing me to think about liminality and aid work by inviting me to present a version of Chapter 1 at the 'Liminalities and Cultures of Change' conference at CRASSH.

I feel fortunate to have been part of the welcoming and stimulating environment of the Centre for International Studies (now POLIS). Thanks to Joey Ansorge, Alex Anievas, Roxane Farman-farmaian, Sarah Nouwen, Miriam Anderson and Eric Schuldenfrei. Throughout the PhD, I had the opportunity to work as a research fellow at SOAS. Special thanks go to Steve Hopgood, Mark Laffey, Stephen Chan, Leslie Vinjamuri and Louiza Odysseos for their support. From my previous life at the UN, sincere appreciation goes to Ben Slay, Dorothy Rosenberg and Robert MacIntyre. Thanks also to friends and family for proofreading, and in particular Ellen Smirl, Mary Hunter, Samantha Martin and Henriette Steiner for food, references, inspiration, encouragement and style guidelines. And finally, heartfelt gratitude goes to Arran Gaunt, Austin Kneedy and Anna, Bruce, Jennifer and Ellen Smirl. I couldn't have done this without your support.

This book is dedicated to my parents Annamarie and Bruce Smirl.

Lisa Smirl

PREFACE

Aid workers will tell you that the spaces and experiences of working in 'the field' often sit uneasily with the goals they've signed up to. Aid workers visit project sites in air-conditioned Land Cruisers while the intended project beneficiaries walk barefoot through the heat. The aid workers check their emails from within gated compounds, while the surrounding communities have no running water. But the longer they work in 'the field', the more normalized these experiences become. Instead of living and interacting with the communities they have come to assist, aid workers are drawn towards other internationals or 'expats' and rarely move beyond a small number of hotels, restaurants, offices and compounds. While these observations are intuitive and much bemoaned within aid circles, no concerted academic or policy study has dealt with the impact of these factors on theory or policy.

This book begins with these observations about the *spaces*, *objects* and *environments* in which aid work occurs. It provides the first book-length description and analysis of what has colloquially been referred to as Aid Land. By looking at three of its main sites – the grand hotel, the SUV and the compound – the book uncovers the history of what has become an endemic, expected yet unexamined part of the aid landscape. The book develops a model through which scholars, practitioners and policy-makers can understand the impact of spatial considerations and material culture on aid work. It also maps out the unintended outcomes of the trend towards increased securitization and the consequences this has for the environment in which aid work is done. In drawing on spatial and material theory, the book provides a novel and rigorous theorctical grounding for the intuitions and casual observations within the aid community that 'space matters'. It does so in part through two case studies which show how lack of reflection about objects and spaces leads to perverse consequences for aid policy: the responses to the tsunami in Aceh (2004) and to Hurricane Katrina in New Orleans (2005).

The physical environment of the aid world – the hotels, planes, cars and compounds – has been a fundamental yet overlooked aspect of aid relations since the advent of contemporary humanitarian response. Each one of these built forms has played a key role in the evolution of development practice. Consider, for instance, how the Land Rover has normalized the use of high-cost, petrol-guzzling SUVs and the way this has impacted on town planning and pedestrian safety in places where most people walk; or how the highly guarded humanitarian compound has drawn upon colonial architecture to maintain hierarchical spatial divisions between the aid workers and local residents. Taken together, this landscape of aid has been a key driver in how the West has collectively understood aid and for the kind of policies that have been pursued.

The influence of these spaces of aid has increased in recent years as security considerations and reliance on abstract planning technologies, such as logical frameworks, have led to policy being heavily based upon the views of a select group of individuals: experts, international field staff or consultants who live in or visit the field. This book shows how these individuals' understanding and exposure to a situation will often be bounded and secured. Their experience of the field will rarely extend far beyond the hotel conference room or humanitarian compound. The resulting policy made at headquarters is therefore also spatially constrained by an overly narrow understanding of the place that is being assisted.

But this claim raises the question of how the physical and material experiences of aid workers in the field affect their perceptions and behaviour. By examining the experience of aid practitioners through the lens of contemporary theory on space, spatiality and materiality, this book investigates how material objects (places and things) have influenced aid work. It identifies a series of factors – the symbolic, the affective, the temporal, and social networks – which, taken together, influence how the development 'problem' is conceptualized and what solutions are put forward. It is only through the maintenance of this separate culture of aid that abstract solutions continue to be accepted as a logical and appropriate way in which to undertake development.

To develop these observations, the book progresses in two stages. After a brief introduction, outlining the theoretical approach, the first part of the book details the built environment of aid work: providing a material and cultural history through three key objects – the hotel, the SUV and the compound – while examining how these spaces and objects have had an effect on aid policies and outcomes. Historically these 'things' have been seen as nothing more than a functional and inert backdrop to the delivery of projects and programmes. However, the application of material and spatial approaches to novel archival and ethnographic research reveals that they are an active, constitutive part of aid relations.

The second part of the book turns to two case studies from 2005 – the Acehnese tsunami and Hurricane Katrina – to demonstrate how the spaces of aid shaped humanitarian reconstruction. In the case of Aceh, the short-termism and confinement of the international community meant that an inappropriate strategy was adopted and over a hundred thousand doll-like houses were built for the Acehnese populations, many of whom refused to live in them.

For Hurricane Katrina, reconstruction along the Gulf Coast is shown to be more about the humanitarian imaginary than about the beneficiaries. The superficial and the ornamental became metaphors for the inability of external actors to address the underlying causes of the disaster, namely race and economic disparity. The emphasis on the form of the shotgun house removed the centrality of the beneficiary from the reconstruction effort, which became all about form — making it more difficult for survivors to address their own problems. The final chapter synthesizes the three aspects of intervention: humanitarian imaginary; auxiliary space; and project (lived) space. The central claim of the book points to the need to fundamentally rethink the way in which we do aid.

It is important to stress that this book is not a moral tirade against the luxurious lifestyles of aid workers. Almost every aid worker comes to 'the field' with the intention to improve other people's lives. But as aid dollars become ever more scarce and aid workers are increasingly the target of violent attacks, a careful examination of why it seems so difficult to merely 'do good' is drastically needed. What is it about the way in which aid is delivered that continues to reproduce situations where aid money is wasted, projects are left unfinished and aid workers are themselves under attack? This book points to the elephant in the room: the way in which aid workers work and live.

ABBREVIATIONS

ADB	African Development Bank
ASEAN	Association of Southeast Asian Nations
ASF	Architecture Sans Frontières (Architecture without Borders)
AWSD	Aid Worker Security Database
BAPPENAS	(Indonesian) *Badan Perencanaan Pembangunan Nasional* (National Development Planning Agency)
BBC	British Broadcasting Corporation
BRR	(Aceh and Nias) Rehabilitation and Reconstruction Board
CHF International	Cooperative Housing Foundation International
CNU	Congress for New Urbanism
CRS	Catholic Relief Services
CUCSD	China US Center for Sustainable Development
DAC	(OECD) Development Assistance Committee
DBO	design-build-operate
DBOT	design-build-operate-transfer
DfID	(UK) Department for International Development
DRC	Democratic Republic of Congo
DSS	(UN) Department of Safety and Security
ECHO	European Commission's Humanitarian Aid Office
EU	European Union
FEMA	Federal Emergency Management Agency
GAM	*Gerakan Aceh Merdeka* (Free Aceh Movement)
GC	gated community
GoI	Government of Indonesia
GTZ	German Technical Cooperation (*Deutsche Gesellschaft für Technische Zusammenarbeit*)
HQ	headquarters
ICRC	International Committee of the Red Cross
ICTR	International Criminal Tribunal for Rwanda

IFI   international financial institutions (the International Monetary Fund and the World Bank)
IFRC   International Federation of the Red Cross
IHL   international humanitarian law
INGO   international non-governmental organization
IOM   International Organization for Migration
KC   Katrina Cottage
KKN   *koruptsi, kolusi, dan nepotisme* (corruption, collusion and nepotism)
KPA   *Komite Peralihan Aceh* (Aceh Transitional Committee)
LEHI   Fighters for the Freedom of Israel
MAF   Mission Aviation Fellowship
MAIP   Malicious Acts Insurance Policy
MDF   Multi Donor Fund
MDG   Millennium Development Goal
MEMA   Mississippi Emergency Management Agency
MIR   Make it Right
MORSS   Minimal Operating Residential Security Standard
MOSS   Minimal Operating Security Standard
MoU   Memorandum of Understanding
MRF   Mississippi Renewal Forum
MSF   Médecins Sans Frontières (Doctors without Borders)
NATO   North Atlantic Treaty Organization
NFI   non-food items
NGO   non-governmental organization
NOLA   New Orleans, Louisiana
NU   New Urbanism
OBO   Overseas Building Operations (US State Department)
ODA   Official Development Assistance
OECD   Organisation for Economic Co-operation and Development
OSCE   Organization for Security and Co-operation in Europe
PDI-P   (Indonesian) Democratic Party of Struggle
RAN or RAN-D   Recovery Aceh-Nias Database
RC   Red Cross
SUV   sports utility vehicle
TNA   *Tentara Negara Aceh* (Armed Forces of the State of Aceh)
TNI   *Tentara Nasional Indonesia* (Indonesian Army)

TRIP (report) Tsunami Recovery Information Package
UK   United Kingdom
UN   United Nations
UNAMID   United Nations Mission in Darfur
UNAMIS   United Nations Advance Mission in Sudan
UNDP   United Nations Development Programme
UNDSS   United Nations Department of Safety and Security
UN-HABITAT United Nations Human Settlements Programme
UNHCR   Office of the United Nations High Commissioner for
            Human Rights
UNICEF   United Nations Children's Fund
UNMIH   United Nations Mission in Haiti
UNMIS   United Nations Mission in Sudan
UNOCHA   United Nations Office for the Coordination of
            Humanitarian Affairs
UNOPS   United Nations Office of Project Services
UNORC   United Nations Office of the Resident Coordinator (in
            Aceh)
UNSECOORD   United Nations Security Coordinator
UNTAET   United Nations Transitional Administration in East
            Timor
USAID   United States Agency for International Development

INTRODUCTION

In his history of conflict between African-American workers and the plantation owners of the Mississippi delta, Woods (1998) uses the dialectical existence and development of two worldviews as an explanation of the conflict between the two groups. The Planter Epistemology that he describes is an all-encompassing worldview through which the plantation owners perceived not only their own interests, but those of their African-American slaves. By contrast, the slaves operated according to what Woods calls a Blues Epistemology, which interpreted their reality and defined potential solutions according to a narrative of suffering, endurance and (eventual) salvation. The two logics were not only incompatible, but ensured mutual miscomprehension in the way in which the two groups understood, defined and approached the issue of slavery.

In the context of post-crisis situations, a similar disconnect of epistemologies occurs between those 'external' humanitarian groups which come to assist, and those people who have experienced the disaster and its aftermath. Any solutions to a given problem, or how the problem is framed and identified, will be shaped by each group's epistemology. More specifically, in the context of reconstruction, it will be dramatically influenced by how each group thinks about and understands the space of the crisis. For example, architects, engineers and urban planners are taught to understand, use and believe in an established set of norms, rules and axioms unique to a given society or grouping. They will likewise be taught a certain way of conceptualizing, approaching and identifying a problem. Their design challenges will be formulated in relation to the perceived ills of a particular era (Ravetz and Turkington 1995). Consider how Howard and Unwin's nineteenth-century garden cities presented a rural, idyllic, quiet and organized alternative to the industrial, dirty and disorganized built environment of industrial capitalism (Kostof 1999). Le Corbusier's Radiant City put faith in modernist technologies and planning principles to transcend the misery, confusion, dirt and revolutionary potential of Parisian slums (Scott 1998; Le Corbusier 1967). Similarly, Costa and Niemeyer's plans for Brasilia were in response to the perceived "corruption, backwardness and ignorance of the old Brazil" (Scott 1998: 119; also Mehaffy 2008). So, when designing for a group that falls outside the group epistemology, assumptions will be made regarding the needs and nature of the second group. Historically, these assumptions are drawn from within the planner's *own* society, and parallels will be drawn between the problems and needs of the planner's immediate or known context and the problems that s/he encounters or imagines in the new environment.

Similarly, if we consider the way in which the 'international community' has provided humanitarian assistance after large-scale disasters, it is necessarily based on idealized assumptions regarding social organization and community: the 'humanitarian imaginary'. And while nominally global in its claims, the practice and lived experience of international humanitarianism firmly locates itself in the institutions, donors and regimes of the global North (Rubenstein 2007; Duffield 2001).

The idea of a humanitarian imaginary draws on Taylor's "social imaginaries", which he describes as "the ways in which people imagine their social existence, how they fit together with others, how things go on between them and their fellows, the expectations that are normally met, and the deeper normative notions and images that underlie these expectations" (Taylor 2002: 106; also Castoriadis 1987). It is both factual and normative, "carried in images, stories and legends" and shared by large groups of people, not just the elite (Taylor 2002: 106). It is also carried in the lived experience and built environments of societies (Bourdieu and Nice 1977) and practices of the everyday (De Certeau 1988). While metatopical in its locale, it is highly reliant on examples and practices, which may be referred to and called upon to legitimize its larger claims (Taylor 2002, 2005).

In their work on the nation, Jones and Fowler look at the importance of local spaces in the reproduction of the nation. They argue that this (re)production is done in several ways, including that "localized places" are used as "'metonyms' of the nation" and come to represent, "in a generic and abstract sense ... national messages, symbols, and ideologies" (2007: 336). Citing Penrose and Jackson (1994), they "stress the potential for localized places to be key sites for generating ideas and sentiments that can ultimately reproduce the nation" (Jones and Fowler 2007: 336). Taking these arguments to the level of the supra- or international reveals the potential importance of place(s) in the (re)production of international scale and in specific aspects of the international as a collective concept.

Read in this way, the reconstruction of a place following a natural disaster is not only of value for those who are the immediate recipients, but also for those who can claim it as an exemplar of a humanitarian or social ideal. Similar to urban planners who relish the opportunity to experiment with utopian plans free from the constraints of their day-to-day practice such as physical and regulatory frameworks or democratic and consultative norms (MacLeod and Ward 2002; Harvey 2000), for the international community the post-disaster site provides a blank canvas where idealized aspects of the international may be introduced and tested. Like Levittown in the 1950s or Letchworth before that, the contemporary post-crisis setting has become an environment where various ideas of the ideal society, family and even individual are proposed, contested and championed. And because of the nature of the post-crisis site, these aspects tend to embody a particular spatial epistemology – or way of thinking about space – which undermines the larger humanitarian project of remedying power asymmetries.

The argument

This book is concerned with the way in which humanitarianism at large, and post-crisis reconstruction more specifically, is influenced by spatial aspects on two mutually reinforcing levels. First, it explores how at the level of the field – the place where aid workers go to provide assistance – the physical and institutional underpinnings of providing humanitarian assistance manifest in material and spatial constraints for aid workers; and how, in turn, this influences the way in which the post-crisis situation is conceived at headquarters. In other words, how the space of the field, as the people who work there experience it, shapes the humanitarian imaginary. Secondly, it explores how from within the humanitarian imaginary, post-crisis solutions have strongly focused on the material and spatial aspects of the reconstruction which correspond to an idea of an ideal beneficiary, which has itself been constructed from within the enclosed space of the field.

This approach to understanding post-crisis dynamics in particular, and humanitarianism more broadly, stands in radical contrast to existing theories, which treat the experience of the aid worker in the field as unproblematic. Drawing attention to the experience of aid workers and their key position in interpreting, representing and reproducing local knowledge draws into question global claims regarding the figure of the 'beneficiary' and the relationship between donor and recipient. Specifically, this book shows, first, that the material and spatial practices of the international community in the space of the field need to be understood as an extension of their space of origin (headquarters, firms, countries) both spatio-temporally and increasingly in terms of securitization. Secondly, it demonstrates that the way in which the international community materially operates in the field has become a significant factor in the way in which humanitarian workers think about the places and people that they are assisting. And thirdly, it suggests that the spatio-temporal aspects of humanitarian assistance are such that there is a tendency towards an asymmetric temporal relationship between those individuals who come to assist (and then leave) and those people who are being assisted (and who stay). This leads to different ways of thinking about the reconstruction, and ultimately to conflict between different spatial epistemologies.

All three factors have contributed to a dynamic which sees the space of the field becoming more and more distantiated from the places in need of assistance, with aid workers interacting with beneficiaries in highly securitized or ritualized ways. The representation of the field that is reported back to headquarters, and upon which policy and programmes are based, is therefore not based on society at large, on the nation as it really is, but upon the bounded and increasingly securitized spaces of international aid workers.

There is the need to briefly address, at the outset, the way in which some of these terms are used. Given the focus of the book, spatially oriented terms such as 'local', 'global', 'international' and other terms designating location or 'context' are not used unproblematically. However, for the ease of the reader, I have made the stylistic decision to indicate these problematic terms, in the first instance only within single quotation marks. Double quotation marks are used for direct quotations or terms taken from a particular author. In the case of the field space of humanitarian work, a distinction needs to be drawn between the field, as locale of humanitarian assistance, and 'the field' as it is imagined and constructed through the process of aid work. This distinction is addressed in Chapter 1. The term reconstruction sites refers to geographic locations that have been or are being physically reconstructed with external assistance, after experiencing a crisis that overwhelms the ability of the affected society to respond. External assistance, as a term, refers to the provision of physical and/or financial resources by individuals and agencies that normally reside outside the geographic boundaries of the reconstruction site and have been brought there specifically by the event of the disaster. While for the majority of the book external actors will be agencies, organizations or individuals that comprise the humanitarian enterprise of the global North, this spatialization does not directly correlate, as is often assumed, to a North/South, rich/poor, developed/underdeveloped geography. While South/poor/underdeveloped places do, generally, experience a higher vulnerability to natural disasters (Smith 2006; Oliver-Smith 1996), this does not apply uniformly. Just as such blanket, binary categories have never applied uniformly, it will vary, with levels of wealth, development and security mapping themselves on to cartographies the world over.

One of the purposes of this work is to challenge the existing narrative of post-disaster assistance. Rather than looking at the already existing cartography of disaster and vulnerability as it is understood within the humanitarian imaginary, this book examines the way in which the relationship of assistance is spatialized between those who are assisting and those who are being assisted. Doing so incorporates the institutional spaces and places of assistance and the way the cartography of disaster and vulnerability is thought about within them. This allows for a better understanding of how the response strategies are conceived, who they are intended for, and why they so often fail.

To apply a spatial lens to the case of post-crisis reconstruction is not new. The mapping of disaster is often one of the easiest and best-executed aspects of a post-disaster intervention (Davis 1978). Careful attention is generally paid to the location and categorization of victims and beneficiaries and the types and location of damaged buildings and infrastructure. However, it is almost exclusively from a Cartesian perspective: of space as flat, mappable and static. This is consistent with the dominant approach to space within international politics, where Agnew's "territorial trap" (1997) assumes that physical geography and political territory are coterminous and can be mapped out, carved up, bordered and defended. In few situations are these assumptions as visible as in the reconstruction after a large-scale disaster (Helmig and Kessler 2007). As is shown in the case studies, despite the recognition that post-crisis geographies are not *tabulae rasae*, such thinking continues to inform the spatial epistemology with which external actors approach post-disaster reconstruction, as evidenced by planning schemes adopted in places as diverse as Sri Lanka, Pakistan, New Orleans and Ecuador (Mehaffy 2008).

Similarly, while there is widespread informal acknowledgement among development practitioners that the rapid influx of hundreds or even thousands of foreign workers has feedback effects (Collier 2007), these are dramatically under-examined. This is partly explained by the fact that the reconfiguring of space and the reconstruction of the built environment are not seen as politically and socially transformative in themselves, but just a basic and largely neutral component of any reconstruction process (Graham and Marvin 2001). This overlooks the way in which post-disaster reconstruction evolved. From its modern inception following the Second World War, international humanitarian assistance was conceived in spatial terms (Slater 1997). The categories and binaries by which it defined itself as an activity were fundamentally geographic: First, Second and Third Worlds; developed and underdeveloped countries; the global North/global South.

Direct links to the process of European decolonization can also be found (Duffield 2007). Fred Cuny (Cuny and Abrams 1983) attributes the rise of disaster response as an industry within the global North to the rapid post-1945 decolonization process, which left the former colonies without either the human or financial capacity to respond to their own crises. The international system of non-governmental organizations (NGOs) and multilateral agencies was seen as relatively apolitical and therefore preferable to the reassertion of control by former colonial powers. However, through the application of spatial considerations, it is possible to see how contemporary material and spatial practices of humanitarian response may continue to invoke and reproduce colonial power relations. If the social imaginary is interlinked with the material practices of the everyday, it is necessary to consider the impact of the material expression of particular places and practices (Bourdieu 1990; De Certeau 1988; Merleau-Ponty 1962).

The need to take material and spatial considerations into

account stemmed from my own experience working in international development and the endless search for 'the field'. There was an impression among fellow aid workers that it was impossible to ever reach 'the field' as it truly was. That instead, the experience was always mediated through the processes, rituals, practices and built environments of the international aid community (for more on rituals, see Kertzer 1988). While this observation may seem obvious to anyone who has worked in the field and to many who have not, within the realm of international development studies the built and material environments of the international community are hardly considered. The existence or agency of a field space is largely ignored. This is the result of two lacunae within international development studies which this book seeks to address. First, while most disciplines in the social sciences and humanities have undergone a process of self-scrutiny regarding the potential impact of spatial considerations for their key *problématiques* – the so-called spatial turn – development studies has, until now, avoided these challenges. Secondly, unlike the disciplines of sociology and anthropology, development studies has been remarkably unreflexive regarding the role of the aid worker as important component of humanitarian intervention. Each of these will be examined in turn.

Relevance of the 'spatial turn' for post-crisis reconstruction The 1990s saw the application of the spatial turn to a wide range of inquiry, from discourse analysis (Ó Tuathail 1996) to economic geography (Barnes 2003). The dissemination of work by Bourdieu (1990, Bourdieu and Nice 1977), Lefebvre (1991) and De Certeau (1988) highlighted the subjectivity and relativism in the designation and construction of particular physical and social spaces. This work contributed to and coincided with two major disciplinary shifts in the social sciences at large. First, in those disciplines that were already engaged with ideas of space and materiality such as geography and urban planning, it led to a re-examination and problematization of the ontological pre-eminence of an independent materiality that could be mapped, designed, shaped and built. Secondly, in disciplines such as anthropology and sociology, it contributed to the recognition of the need to consider space and materiality both as potentially causal variables in the societies under examination, and also as inextricable parts of the embodied experience of research and of the construction of knowledge itself (Crang and Thrift 2000). However, it did not have a significant impact on development or humanitarian studies, nor, by extension, on post-crisis relief or reconstruction, which all continued to focus on the level of the individual and its aggregate: society. Issues of governance, local livelihoods, civil society, capacity-building, human security and anti-corruption filled the agenda in the 1990s and 2000s (Pupavac 2005), an agenda that assumed that the solution to liberal, democratic, peace had already been found and only the instruments required perfecting (Paris 2006; Hoogvelt 2006).

An initial application of the spatial turn to the realm of post-crisis reconstruction points to several areas that are immediately problematized. First, the need to consider that the space of a reconstruction site is not a *tabula rasa*, and that what is produced is immediately and inextricably politicized and used in different ways by different groups and for different ends (Lefebvre 1991; Yeoh 1996; Gottdiener 1994; Harvey 1973; L. Liu 2008). Secondly, space is relative and relational. Spatial and material designations, mappings and representations of needs and responses may not be in keeping with other scalar designations or social categories such as the idea of the local in the policy designs of the international community; or the programmatic separation of certain categories of beneficiaries such as post-conflict versus post-disaster (Scott 1998; Escobar 2001).

Thirdly, knowledge is embodied: predicated upon "cognitive (mental) and physical (corporeal) performances that are constantly evolving as people encounter place" (Hubbard et al. 2004: 6). These geographies of embodiment are therefore implicated in the subsequent production and reification of categories of class, gender and, in the case of humanitarianism, of donor/beneficiary and of saviour/victim binaries (Grosz 1995; Teather 1999). In the case of post-conflict reconstruction, this embodiment is the result of the social and cultural environments that humanitarian workers have come from (their countries of origin) as well as the environments that they find themselves in during the reconstruction process. According to Bourdieu (1990), it is impossible to separate subjects from their habitus (the practices and games of their surroundings) either present, past and possibly future (Massumi 2002; Grosz 1999). This means that the responses of particular individuals and agencies are conditioned as much by previous experiences – both of their place(s) of origin and of previous reconstruction sites – as by the immediate emergency they are responding to. Further, the precise material circumstances experienced while in a reconstruction site may also be significant.

These linkages point to the fourth insight of the spatial turn for post-crisis reconstruction: that the presence of international humanitarian agencies in the country of intent must always be read contrapuntally with their space of origin (Inayatullah and Blaney 2004; Said 1995). The activities, practices and places of the international community in reconstruction sites are as (or more) closely networked to their spaces of origin as they are to their proximate physical environments (Castells 2000; Sassen 2000; Appadurai 1997) and may need to be considered as particular, embodied instances of larger global processes (Beck and Ritter 1992; Harvey 2001). As such, their representational consequences need to be taken into consideration. How are these international practices and spaces understood and interpreted by the groups and individuals in their immediate physical surroundings? Does this impact or affect the tactics that may be used in their interactions with the international donor community (De Certeau 1988; Scott 1998)?

A fifth area of consideration is: how are the spatial and material circumstances of humanitarian relief workers related to temporal considerations? How do differential spaces affect the way in which the time of response and intervention is conceived (Massey 2006)? The differential rates of mobility and speed between the international community and the target population are rarely examined, yet lie at the heart of some of the most problematic aspects of the ineffectiveness of humanitarian assistance, such as the mistiming of funding, the rapid turnover of international staff, and the recurrent nature of many disasters; aspects which are considered within the book.

Since the advent of the spatial turn, the theoretical focus has broadened to include the performances, rituals, affect(s), practices and ways of being that are produced by, and simultaneously constitute, space(s). These approaches have become subsumed under the broad class of what Thrift refers to as "non-representational theories" – theories which take as their leitmotif movement and which work "as a way of going beyond constructivism" (Thrift 2008: 5). Drawing upon radical empiricist and phenomenological philosophical traditions, non-representational theory differs from a "sense-perception or observation-based empiricism" (ibid.: 5), valuing the pre-cognitive as "something more than an addendum to the cognitive" (ibid.: 6). While any sort of serious engagement with this area of philosophy (Whitehead 1956; Whitehead and Frye 1960; James and Burkhardt 1981; Massumi 2002) is clearly beyond the scope of this book, it does benefit from a more narrow exploration of the sub-field of material studies (Miller 2005b; Carter 2004; Martin 1995), which emphasizes the iterative and transitive relationship between object and subject (Latour 1993). In the context of humanitarianism, the repudiation of "the privilege accorded to a humanity defined by its opposition to materiality as pure subject or social relations" (Miller 2005b: 41) challenges the underlying assumptions of Cartesian/Humean causation; unmitigated human agency; and, ultimately, the ability of the aid worker to assist the beneficiary.

The role of the physical presence of the aid worker in post-crisis reconstruction Within post-crisis reconstruction there is a growing acknowledgement of the externalities associated with aid. That is to say, that the provision of humanitarian assistance will result in unintended consequences. So far, these observations have largely been confined to the areas of economics and public health and have looked primarily at UN peacekeeping missions. For example, work by Carnahan et al. (2006) has looked at the effects of large peacekeeping missions on local economies and an increasing number of authors are looking at the gendered dimensions of peacekeeping missions, notably the exploitation and abuse of local women by male peacekeepers (Higate and Henry 2004; Whitworth 2004; Higate 2007). But the debate within policy circles, and development studies more generally, still concentrates on objective analysis and critique.

In international and development studies, the focus has been primarily on analysing policy outputs either in terms of pathologies (why they don't work) or in global terms: either through discourse analysis (Doty 1996; Escobar 1994), or theories of global capital (Gunder Frank 1971; Harvey 2001). The examination of the aid worker as an inextricable part of this process is largely omitted except in terms of their being part of institutional and bureaucratic processes and pathologies (Easterly 2002, 2006; Barnett and Finnemore 1999) or, as will be discussed in Chapter 2, in terms of staff security. This gap in development studies is beginning to be filled by work in anthropology on the ethnography of aid work, an emerging field of study (Rubinstein 2005; Kaufman 1997; Lewis and Mosse 2007).

Anthropologists benefit from a recognition of the significance of reflexivity in social science in general and more specifically in the process of 'field work', which is the dominant form of knowledge gathering within the discipline (Gupta and Ferguson 1997b). There is a long lineage of thinking about methodological and theoretical issues both surrounding the identification of the field site and regarding the role of the researcher, their methods and the feedback effects on a given research question. While theorists studying post-crisis situations within international relations and development studies do acknowledge the difficulties in conducting field research, it is largely from a positivist perspective, and clusters around questions of the correct unit of measurement, data collection methods or time interval (Barakat et al. 2002; Courtney et al. 2005; CSIS 2004; Fearon and Laitin 2003; Leach 2006; Smyth and Robinson 2001; Suhrke and Samset 2007). Turning the frame of analysis back upon the spaces and practices of the international aid community and the material and cultural aspects of the delivery of aid (De Certeau 1988) calls into question the programmatic claim that it is possible to "do no harm" (Anderson 1999) and problematizes such operational distinctions as relief and development planning. Most importantly, it reveals how the practices of the international humanitarian community involved in post-crisis reconstruction are inseparable from the production and reconstruction of global relations and identities (Barnett 2005). In a context where the visible presence of the international community and aid agencies is growing there is an urgent need for such an examination.

Methodology

It is important to mention the difficulties in undertaking this research. As the book will explore, aid workers are a closed tribe. Any insinuation that the project of humanitarian aid is flawed, not working or corrupt will be met, in the main, with a complete closing down of information provision. Conversations regarding the living conditions, expat lifestyles or the existence of a local–national divide are not topics to be discussed with 'outsiders'. This fact, of which I was aware from my own experience as a 'tribesman' with the United Nations, greatly influenced my choice of methodology for the case studies: an ethnomethodological approach which combined structured, in-depth interviews with participant observation. The insular and paranoid nature of the aid work circles under investigation also meant that if my informants were to speak freely, it was necessary to code my interviews and guarantee anonymity in the case of publication. This outside/inside divide will be further discussed within the context of the book.

The choice to focus on the reconstruction after natural disasters, instead of other forms of post-crisis intervention, was twofold. First, the perceived neutrality of humanitarian assistance in the wake of a natural disaster (Calhoun 2004; Rubenstein 2007) makes it an ideal testing ground for the hypothesis that all forms of humanitarian assistance are inherently politicized. Secondly, in both of my case studies, a clear event took place which mobilized a distinct humanitarian response, in contrast to more entrenched situations such as Sudan or Somalia where decades of overlapping crises and responses have made a discrete response narrative difficult to identify. A least-similar case study approach informed the choice of case studies (George and Bennett 2005). Two cases were chosen that were different in terms of all independent variables except for the fact that they involved a large-scale natural disaster and accompanying post-disaster response. The first, post-tsunami Aceh, was a more traditional humanitarian response – with aid flowing primarily from the international institutions of the global North *to* the global South. The second, the post-Hurricane Katrina Gulf Coast, was *within* the global North. This allowed me to test the theory that an imbalance occurs between those who are deemed to be in need of assistance and those who arrive to assist *in all cases*, not only in the context of North/South relations.

A quick word on definitions is also necessary. In the context of this book, 'humanitarian intervention' is used to refer to the full spectrum of international responses following a large-scale disaster, from emergency relief to long-term development programmes. In practice there is significant blurring and overlap between the categories of relief and development, particularly from the perspective of the beneficiaries. Also, in humanitarian response and reconstruction terms there is significant conceptual overlap between categories of post-disaster and post-conflict. This complexity spurred on the development of the category of 'complex humanitarian emergencies' in the 1990s: a term used to describe those emergency situations which display a multiplicity of causes, narratives and past and potential response trajectories (Keen 2008; Duffield 2007), including histories of conflict and/or natural disaster. Other matters of definitional clarification include the use of the term international community. Through the book I use the term to denote collectively those organizations, institutions, agencies and individuals which claim to operate – either overtly or implicitly – according to the tenets of international humanitarian law (IHL) and which have as their objective the assistance and betterment of international society according to universal principles as enshrined in the UN Charter. Somewhat controversially, I suggest that this definition needs to include those organizations that, while not humanitarian in themselves, operate as implementers for other recognized, international organizations – for example, the use of Dyncorp to implement programmes for the UN. This is because the material practices and environments of both organizations, in this context, are similar, and from the perspective of the beneficiaries are seen as interchangeable.

The structure

The first three chapters of this book examine the material and spatial environments of the international community; identify its characteristics and implications; and propose that these are essential, although under-studied, aspects of any intervention (Pandolfi 2003, 2002). The application of a spatial lens to post-crisis settings allows for the identification of characteristics of 'auxiliary space' which are common across post-conflict and post-disaster reconstruction sites alike (Kleinfeld 2007; Hyndman 2009; Le Billon and Waizenegger 2007). These characteristics are derived from the spatial and material practices, techniques and approaches used by the international community in post-crisis settings (De Certeau 1988) and contribute to how the international community is perceived by its beneficiaries, and to how the international community itself conceptualizes the reconstruction effort. They may lead to unexpected or unanticipated consequences. Contained within the auxiliary approach is the overarching assumption that places can be reconstructed; that space is malleable and static and that the production of new places can be disconnected from the techniques and processes used to produce it.

Chapter 1 begins the investigation by looking at how aid workers themselves experience the space of the field. While vernacular and autobiographical writings are rife with well-established visual tropes of the white UN Land Rover and the gated humanitarian compound (Cain 2004), they remain largely unstudied. Theoretical work by Yacobi (2007), Elden (2006) and Hyndman (2000, 2007) has drawn attention to the unique spheres created by NGO and humanitarian agencies. However, any potential causal impact of this auxiliary space has not been seriously examined (Yamashita 2004). Using the rich, and hitherto unexamined, resource of aid workers' memoirs, a close reading of three of the best known strongly suggests that the aid workers have a clear understanding of the space of the field as a distinct, bounded and separate place. Using work by Van Gennep (1960) and Victor Turner (1969), this chapter establishes that both the field itself and the process of coming to and from it constitute unique and bounded spaces. In the vein of Turner, it suggests that these spaces are liminal – that is, they are caught between both their spaces of origin (where they came from) and the wider space of the field. That the memoirs are select representations of reality – that the authors have chosen to include certain visual descriptions while excluding others – makes them all the more valuable because it allows for the identification of a series of spatio-material themes that recur in all three books, and which characterize what I have called auxiliary space. The themes are securitization and enclosure; mobility and temporality; exceptionalism; and links to the site of origin. The themes are reinforced through the use of material tropes that recur throughout the memoirs and include compounds, hotels and sports utility vehicles (SUVs).

Chapter 2 explores the first theme of securitization and en-closure. It looks at the trend in humanitarian aid work over the last two decades, at the increased physical securitization of aid work(ers) and, based on an examination of field security manuals and reports from leading international humanitarian agencies, establishes that the organizational push towards increased field security is based on a largely false perception of increased risk. While recent analysis (Stoddard et al. 2006, 2009) shows that between 2006 and 2009 there was a very slight increase in the targeting of international humanitarian field staff, it was only in a small number of countries (Afghanistan, Somalia, Sudan). However, the trend towards the increased securitization of (mostly international) humanitarian staff is occurring on a worldwide basis, as institutional policy. The chapter concludes by raising two questions that are to be explored in Chapter 3: first, what is the relationship between the increased enclosure and securitization of aid workers in the field and their perceptions of risk? The second question is: what is the broader impact of the built environment of aid workers?

Chapter 3 picks up on the questions raised in Chapter 2 and is divided into two parts. The first examines different theories on how material and spatial practice can be considered to be mediating factors in the experience of the field. The second part then looks at these theories in the context of case studies of two material tropes identified in Chapter 1: the hotel and the SUV. Through these iconic material objects the themes of mobility and temporality, exceptionalism and links to site of origin are explored.

The remaining chapters of the book move on to examine two case studies where external actors assisted other individuals who had been affected by large-scale natural disasters: Aceh after the 2004 tsunami, and Mississippi and Louisiana, after Hurricane Katrina in 2005. In both cases, the form of the house is used as a material anchor to explore the relationship between the humanitarian imaginary, the international community and those being assisted. While the first part of the book was focused on identifying, describing and understanding the auxiliary space of international aid work in the field, the second part looks at what happens in the physical and material encounter between the international aid worker and the local beneficiary.

Chapter 4 considers how the material circumstances experienced by aid workers in the field – the 'auxiliary space' of aid – shape the way in which the international community influences action and thought. It examines the reconstruction of Aceh after the 2004 tsunami and the way in which the different sets of actors involved in the reconstruction conceptualized the object of the reconstructed house in two different and quite distinct ways. Using Mauss's concept of 'the gift' and the contrasting concept of 'the commodity', the chapter examines the idea that the material and spatial characteristics of the international community's environment structure the way in which it conceives of the problem and the beneficiary. In other words, it contributes to a distinct way of thinking about 'the other' and to a spatial epistemology (Bourdieu and Nice 1977; Giddens 1990). Through the experience of the reconstruction, the dominant spatial epistemology of the gift was challenged by the actions of other actors: the beneficiaries, the Government of Indonesia and the Free Aceh Movement. However, I argue that the nature of auxiliary space led to an outcome where the fundamental assumptions regarding the giving and receipt of humanitarian assistance were *not* challenged. Rather, the dissonances and problems that arose through the process of implementation were kept separate from the core humanitarian process (i.e. from the humanitarian imaginary), guaranteeing that the imaginary is preserved and the process likely to be repeated.

Chapter 5 looks at the reconstruction following Hurricane Katrina along the US Gulf Coast. It examines how two different attempts to provide 'cutting edge' architectural solutions were met with difficulties in their respective contexts. The first example is that of the attempts to introduce so-called green architecture into New Orleans, and specifically the actor Brad Pitt's work in the Lower Ninth Ward. The second is the initial planning approach advocated by the Mississippi State Government, which stressed a New Urbanist ethos. Both cases demonstrate the pragmatic and ethical difficulties involved in planning for the other and how the dynamic of local versus foreign comes into play in situations that bring together people from "across the city", as one interviewee put it, as well as from across the world. This recognition of the spatialized nature of power dynamics provides a powerful insight into both the limits and possibilities of humanitarian assistance following a large-scale disaster.

The book concludes by proposing a tripartite model that may be of assistance in theorizing the spatial dynamics at play following a reconstruction: auxiliary space – the space of the humanitarian imaginary – and the space of tactics.

1 | STORIES FROM THE FIELD, STORIES OF 'THE FIELD': HOW AID WORKERS EXPERIENCE THE SPACE OF THE FIELD MISSION

This chapter starts from the perspective of the aid worker to establish, first, the overall spatial structure of the humanitarian field mission and, secondly, the spatial and material characteristics of 'the field' as perceived by those that are in it. Drawing on the work of Victor Turner and Arnold Van Gennep, it suggests that the act of being in the field, as a humanitarian, creates a unique and liminal space. While the term liminal has previously been used by a handful of theorists to describe international development and humanitarian work, it has generally been done in the context of post-colonial analysis, which considers the emancipatory potential of a hybrid 'third space' where boundaries and divisions blur and the emergence of new and potentially emancipatory subjectivities and relationships is possible (Bhabha 2004; Khan 1998; English 2005; Barlow 2007). Through an analysis of aid workers' memoirs, this chapter challenges the third-space reading. Instead, it interprets the process as a highly structured, codified and predictable 'rite of passage' (Van Gennep 1960).

Within this rite of passage, the transition or liminal phase provides a useful theoretical tool with which to develop the idea that the space of the field has unique qualities and characteristics for the aid worker. Through the aid workers' narratives, I identify recurrent material tropes and themes which (re)produce what I term the auxiliary space of the field. In particular, the metaphor of enclosure stands out in its various guises: the compound, the border and the gate. So do threshold spaces of the airport, the car and the border crossing. Taken together, they provide insight into the humanitarian imaginary: how international humanitarianism is understood, narrated and performed.

Aid work as rite of passage

Liminality or 'third space' in humanitarian assistance The term liminality in its contemporary usage in humanities and social science is usually attributable to the anthropologist Van Gennep (ibid.). It refers to a state in human society of being between two phases. In his original description, Van Gennep identifies a series of liminal or transitional events including pregnancy and childbirth, marriage and funerals, as well as the physical transition from one place to another. Although originally published in 1909, the concept did not gain widespread attention until the 1960s, when it was rediscovered by Victor Turner, who applied and developed the concept in a variety of anthropological settings, from the Ndembu tribe of north-western Zambia to "Western hippies" (Turner 1969). Turner developed and expanded the concept, which has subsequently been further elaborated through its use in a variety of disciplines from pilgrimage studies (Coleman 2002; Eade and Sallnow 2000; Yamba 1995) to management consultancy literature (Sturdy et al. 2006; Czarniawska and Mazza 2003). Turner himself was never extremely rigorous in his use of the term, and this ambiguity continued to plague the term in the way in which it was adopted and applied by subsequent theorists. Specifically, later theorists would concentrate their attentions on the liminal space as a unique space separated from the spaces on either side (for more on the origins and evolution of the term, see Martin 2007).

In theorizing the personage of the aid worker, liminality allows for the experience of the field to be considered as a unique and self-contained space: removed from the constraints and embedded power relations of late capitalist society. In this reading, new forms of development assistance could provide the opportunity to deconstruct historically oppressive binaries such as colonizer/colonized, teacher/student, donor/recipient, North/

South by providing the opportunity for new, hybrid relationships and subjectivities to emerge (English 2005; Barlow 2007). For example, ideas of partnership or participatory development imply a fluidity of exchange and dismantling of power relations through personal interaction between the aid worker and the beneficiary. This exchange is considered by some theorists to not only transform the beneficiary for the better, but to change the way in which the (First World) aid worker understands the (Third World) other. For example, English (2005) found that adult educators from the global North who take up positions in the global South consider themselves to be "nationless figures who inhabit a global community" and are able to "move away from the binaries that limit them, including those of geography and gender" (ibid.: 94). Similarly, Barlow (2007) found that Canadian social work students undertaking a practicum in India occupied and negotiated a third space where their beliefs, identities and preconceptions both about themselves and the other were challenged by what they saw and experienced. While there is the assertion, based on work by Bhabha (1990) and Spivak and Harasym (1990), that these spaces hold the potential for alterity and emancipation for aid worker and beneficiary alike, concrete examples are noticeably absent. Further, little (or nothing) is said about development work and liminality within the context of its more structured and common permutation: that of workers for multilateral organizations such as the UN and the World Bank and for international NGOs (INGOs) such as Médecins Sans Frontières, Oxfam or Save the Children.

While it can be said that the field is heterotopic, filled with vernacular globalizations (Bhabha 2004) and palimpsestic vistas (Tomlinson 1999), the ironies, juxtapositions, themes and tropes are remarkably similar from experience to experience. These experiences are nominally liminal, in the sense that they encompass multiple and competing allegiances, claims, identities, languages, cultures and expectations. For example, the African-American UN lawyer educating Liberian civil servants on human rights; or the

British doctor in Somalia assisting women with sanitized genital suturing upon their request. However, the experiences are also highly structured and predictable.

Interviews and analysis with third-space practitioners reveal a structured cycle of interaction that occurs when experts from a host country move to a target country to provide assistance (Heron 2008). This cycle is so predictable, in fact, that it has been distilled to provide the basis for staff training modules which describe the process that the practitioner will experience through the course of his/her assignment, including initial exuberance followed by fatigue and, upon return, re-entry syndrome (Government of Canada 2009). Rather than a post-colonial third space, the experience described strongly echoes Van Gennep's original formulation of a liminal space that is closely connected to the spaces on either side. In other words, while the field may be a liminal experience, it is only so for the aid worker, and only in the context of a processual trajectory whose beginning and end points are the aid worker's country of origin. Neither Van Gennep nor Turner was unaware of the processual nature of the liminal state. Particularly Van Gennep considered the liminal state as part of its larger, and generative, rite of passage.

The rite of passage in the memoirs of aid workers Van Gennep describes a rite of passage as a tripartite process consisting of, first, separation from an initial or equilibrium state, followed by a liminal or marginal state, and concluding with a reaggregation with the original society (also referred to as (re)incorporation; Bowie 2006: 149). Each stage has its own set of accompanying rites (Van Gennep 1960). Of the three stages, the liminal – signifying 'threshold' in Latin (Turner 1969: 94) – is distinct from the other two and involves spatial, temporal and social and moral separation (Yang 2000). In contrast to 'normal society', the liminal state is one of anti-structure, where established hierarchies and rules are inverted or suspended and transformative processes take place. Here, work and play blur, experimentation and novelty are encouraged and carnivalesque and ludic qualities manifest themselves (Turner 1977). The initiates are considered as simultaneously sacred and polluting to society at large and must be kept separate and distinct: confined to designated spaces and identifiable by new or bizarre clothes, masks or face paints, and possibly made to adopt new homogenizing behaviours or languages. Stripped of their previously defining characteristics such as clothes, insignia or property, they may form strong and rapid bonds of solidarity with the other initiates (Turner 1969: 95). Such ties of friendship or *communitas* often endure throughout life (Turner 1977). Once the transformation is complete, the initiate may return to society, to be reintegrated in his/her new role. While, in the broadest sense, we are all, at some point and necessarily, liminal figures, the application of the concept to the practice of international aid work offers unique insight into the possibilities and constraints for its broader structures.

In order to bring together the process of aid work and the theoretic perspective of Van Gennep and Turner, I turned to the untapped resource of the memoirs of aid workers: first-person narratives based on personal journals, notes and recollections (on autobiography and life writing, see Smith and Watson 2001; De Man 1979; Marcus 1994). These memoirs present the personal experiences of individuals who went to the field as an employee of an aid organization and subsequently returned home to resume normal life and to tell their stories.

Through an analysis of three of the best known of these memoirs, it became evident that the views, interactions and relationships of the field, as described by the authors, constituted a rite of passage, and the space of field a liminal space. As memoirs, they are by definition subjective and for that reason their consistency is remarkable, not only with regard to the personal trajectories and experiences of the characters, but also how the spaces in which they find themselves are described and what the authors consider to be worthy of documentation. This chapter uses these memoirs to analyse the experience of international humanitarian assistance on two levels. First, it identifies, in all three texts, the narrative structure of a rite of passage. Chronologically, the authors tell the tale of coming *from* their country of origin; moving *to* the field; and *returning* home, irrevocably transformed in the process. The second level that will be considered is the liminal quality of the space of the field: what metaphors and tropes recur within this space and how the space affects the aid worker. In a challenge to advocates of third space the chapter argues that while the space of the field may be transformative, it is only so for the perspective of the visiting aid worker, rather than for the beneficiary.

To ensure a wide range of coverage and balance, the texts were chosen for analysis based on several criteria. The authors represent a cross-section of organizations: both United Nations and INGOs on a variety of scales. They are both men and women and all the authors use their real names and claim that their stories are based on real events. The time period ranges from 1991 to 2004. While the time span covered by the books is quite short – thirteen years in total – it captures the long decade of increased multilateral activity following the fall of the Berlin Wall. While the choice of these memoirs as the subject of analysis can be critiqued on the basis that they, through their very existence as a personal post-mortem, are biased in an anti-aid direction, they are nonetheless valid for the significant population that they represent, and the use of oral narratives was encouraged by Turner himself (1975: 167). They are also some of the most readable and best-known examples of a much wider genre of 'aid memoirs' that, to date, has received minimal critical attention. Equally, the books analysed in this chapter are also some of the most controversial of the genre. I learned about two of them (Minion 2004; Cain 2004) while in the field myself, where the books and their authors were regarded with a mix of disdain and jealousy. The books were madly read, circulated and then dismissed, not on the grounds that they were untrue or misrepresentative, but that they broke the code of the field.

Within international humanitarian assistance, an important

structural divide exists between the physical space of headquarters, located in a (usually) First World country, and the field. The historical structure of international aid is such that traditional donor countries are primarily located in the global North. For example, Official Development Assistance (ODA) is primarily calculated by looking at the contributions from the OECD's Development Assistance Committee (DAC) members, all of whom are located in either Europe or North America, with the exception of Japan. The field, by contrast, is where the projects or interventions are located – away from headquarters or the main office, and, by definition, in 'less developed countries'. While headquarters define policy, the objective of their policy can be reached only by undertaking a physical voyage *to* the space of the beneficiaries: the field. Working in the field (sometimes referred to as a 'mission') is considered to be a hardship and is often remunerated accordingly.

The three books in question are all concerned with the act of the field mission which produces a narrative structure that replicates a rite of passage. Each of the memoirs follows the same format. The characters all undertake a sudden departure to far-off lands in an attempt to escape unstable, boring and/or unfulfilling lives. An unsteady (but pleasantly exciting) beginning is followed by a steady descent into increasing political, personal and institutional chaos. The characters become exhausted and frustrated with their persistent inability to have a significant or positive impact on their surroundings. They reach a crisis point where the character feels the need to make a decision regarding their future, at which point all but one of them choose to return to the First World (not necessarily home) to resume so-called normal life and to write their memoirs. In the case of one of the books – *Emergency Sex (and Other Desperate Measures)* – the chapters are named according to increasing levels of UN security classifications, moving from Condition Alpha (safe) to Bravo, Charlie, Delta, Echo (evacuate immediately) … and finally Return to Normal (Cain 2004).

Overview of the memoirs In *A Cruel Paradise,* Leanne, a nurse from Canada, receives an offer to work for Médecins Sans Frontières (MSF), an international NGO that provides "emergency medical assistance to populations in danger" (MSF n.d.). She is deployed to run a feeding centre in rural Liberia during the first Liberian civil war. After being evacuated back to Winnipeg, nine months later, owing to increased hostilities, she is almost immediately redeployed to Bosnia, where she meets Rink, a logistics officer with whom she starts a romantic relationship. Based in the Republika Srpska, their team is responsible for providing non-partisan medical supplies to hard-to-reach areas such as the infamous Bihac enclave. After being evacuated again, in June 1995 (after seven months), she rejoins Rink in Burundi, where she is in charge of renovating and managing a seventy-bed hospital in the north of the country. Dissatisfied with the MSF programme in Burundi, she and Rink hand in their resignations after only three months to join their friend working in Goma, Zaire (now DRC), "where nobody in their right mind wants to work" (Olson 1999: 153). In mid-May they leave Zaire, fearing for their lives. After a brief time in Canada, France and Holland, they join the international medical NGO Merlin and are deployed to a series of countries as short-term consultants: Rwanda, Angola, Albania and finally Liberia. After coming full circle, they returned to Holland to resume (in their words) normal life. The narrative spans from December 1993 to May 1997 (three and a half years).

In *Emergency Sex,* three interweaving narratives tell the stories of Andrew, an Australian doctor; Ken, an American law student-cum-human rights adviser; and Heidi, an American social worker-cum-UN secretary-cum-elections monitor-cum-jack of all trades. They meet on their first mission, in 1993, in Cambodia. After overseeing the country's first democratic elections they immediately depart for new missions. Heidi and Ken go to Mogadishu, "the 'dish'", Somalia, as part of the UN peacekeeping mission, Operation Restore Hope, while Andrew goes to Haiti with UNMIH to document human rights violations in prisons and hospitals. After the UN (and US) withdrawal from both Somalia and Haiti in early 1994, the authors rotate missions once again. Ken takes an assignment in Rwanda, collecting evidence on the genocide for the UN Criminal Tribunal in Rwanda (ICTR); Heidi joins the next UN mission in Haiti; and Andrew goes to Bihac, in Bosnia-Herzegovina, to "set up a forensic team to investigate massacres" (Cain 2004: 223). Unable to work owing to continued fighting, Andrew is almost immediately redeployed to Rwanda to collect forensic evidence by exhuming mass graves. Ken leaves Rwanda to meet Heidi in Haiti. Heidi, in turn, has fallen in love with a Haitian man and plans to stay in Haiti when the UN mission leaves. But in November 1998, her partner dies in an accident and she returns to New York to start her life "anew" (ibid.: 295). Ken takes up his last mission in Liberia documenting human rights abuses in the middle of the first Liberian War. Then they all return to New York, where Andrew gets married to another expat aid worker and decides to live in Cambodia.

In the case of *A Cruel Paradise* and *Emergency Sex* the characters undertake several tours or postings, whereas the third book, *Hello Missus*, documents two subsequent missions in East Timor by the Australian freelance journalist Lynne Minion. Lynne arrives in East Timor just prior to the official handover of the new country's administration from the UN transitional administration, UNTAET. Although she has no job, she does have one powerful acquaintance: the then foreign affairs minister and Nobel laureate José Ramos-Horta, who helps her get a job working as a UN adviser to the local TV station. After Timor Leste receives its independence[1] in May 2002, she is offered a job as media adviser to the then prime minister, Dr Mari Alkatiri. But her contract takes a long time to finalize, leaving Lynne to occupy herself with a series of unsuitable romantic liaisons, moving from house to house in an effort to find sanctuary. When her contract finally

---

1 The choice to use the work 'receives' rather than 'declares' or 'becomes' is intentional based on the way in which East Timor moved from a UN adminis-tered territory to an independent country. See Power (2008).

comes through, she is given neither a job description nor a place to work; crammed behind a child's school desk in the lobby of the perpetually absent prime miniature's (as she calls him) office. Stonewalled, and eventually sacked from her advisory position owing to her affiliation with Ramos-Horta, she is preparing to depart when the December 2002 riots break out. Following the riots, she decides to return home for good, although not before initiating yet other relationship with a peacekeeper, this time a Serb. The book ends with Lynne flying up and out of Dili, her capacity built.[2]

Rites of separation: leaving 'home' According to Van Gennep (1960: 11) rites of passage can be subdivided into rites of separation (or "pre-liminal" rites), transition rites and the rites of incorporation. According to Turner (1969: 94) the separation phase "comprises symbolic behaviour signifying the detachment of the individual or group either from an earlier fixed point in the social structure, from a set of cultural conditions (a 'state') or both". In all the memoirs studied, clearly identifiable rites of separation take place. The pre-departure state is characterized by a frustration with the inauthenticity or superficiality of the authors' own Western culture. In *Emergency Sex* the characters are openly dissatisfied with the perceived amorality of Western society and bored with a normal existence. When presented with the chance to leave, they jump at it. In both *Emergency Sex* and *A Cruel Paradise* the departures are whirlwind, rapid and unexpected. In Ken's case (*Emergency Sex*), after a fifteen-minute interview with a human rights organization, he is told that he has a week to "get shots, a visa, and on the plane" (Cain 2004: 33).

The inoculation of the aid worker against the unknown of the field is a common theme and includes the vaccination of the

---

2 The term capacity-building is often used within development discourse to refer to the transfer of skills in a particular area from external technical advisers to local beneficiaries – see Eade (1997). For critical perspectives, see Smillie (2001), Kenny (2005).

aid worker against fabulous, rare and potentially deadly tropical diseases, often without consideration for the real risk of coming into contact with, for example, rabid monkeys. Prophylactics are taken. Packing is done, often in a hurried and badly conceived manner. For example, Lynne, after a boozy going-away lunch, packs bikinis, frocks, hipster slacks and a tiara: "just because I'd be living in a Third World country I didn't have to *look* as though I was living in a Third World country" (Minion 2004: 3). MSF HQ warns Leanne about the impact of stress resulting in drinking, risk-taking behaviour and mood swings: "[w]e were also warned about the dangers of beginning relationships between the national and expat teams, primarily because in case of an evacuation, only the expat staff leaves, and bringing the national staff along is out of the question" (Olson 1999: 13–14).

The narrators admit an almost complete lack of knowledge about where they are going, or even where the missions are located. "To say that I was a bit naïve when I first started working as an international relief worker would be an understatement of monumental proportions! I knew nothing," said Leanne (ibid.: 9). "I was probably the only Canadian who didn't really have a clue about what was happening in Bosnia ..." (ibid.: 77) . Similarly, in *Emergency Sex*, Heidi signed up for the UN mission as a secretary, "without a second thought, didn't even know where Cambodia was" (Cain 2004: 29), while Ken admits to having thought about Somalia exactly once before landing there (ibid.: 109). The field is romanticized, compared with Hollywood movies (*The Killing Fields*) or the Discovery Channel (ibid.: 30). Admiring the idea of living in a war zone, Ken says, "[t]here are none of the subtleties and nuances of ordinary life; you're at the core of every feeling ... And that's how I want to feel" (ibid.: 13).

The transition from one stage of a rite of passage to the next requires traversing a threshold. This may be, quite literally, a passageway, a stairway or a door through which initiates must pass and is itself the quintessential liminal place. While in the threshold, initiates are suspended between two states: neither here, nor there. These transition states are often guarded by gatekeepers who determine who is allowed to enter into the next phase. The sacred status of the aid worker is communicated through dress (for example, the uniform of the MSF T-shirt, the "Smurf blue" of UN peacekeepers). This makes the uniforms attractive to expats and locals alike, as they confer a degree of inviolability to the wearer. As liminal, sacred and inviolable beings, the aid workers are allowed to pass through border zones that would, without the blue passport, and the international law that it represents, be off limits.

The liminal space of the field Once the characters have crossed the threshold, they pass into "a cultural realm that has few or none of the attributes of the past or coming state" (Turner 1969: 94). They are amazed at the degree to which the new countries differ from their previous situations: extreme poverty, razed buildings, all alongside the comparative luxury of the international community. Says Lynne upon first meeting members of the international community in Dili, "these humanitarians have eclipsed my most affluent fantasies" (Minion 2004: 15). Badly or inappropriately attired in the clothes/attitudes from a former life, they quickly make an effort to assimilate. In Heidi and Ken's cases, more in keeping with the international jet-set aesthetic of the UN; in Lynne's case more in keeping with what her third-space patron, Ramos-Horta, feels is appropriate. Taken literally, this shedding of clothing corresponds to Turner's description of the liminal state (1969: 103). By creating a *tabula rasa*, the neophyte's or initiate's individuality is erased and she or he becomes part of the larger group of expats. Leanne joyfully exclaims after five months in Liberia, "I felt like a real expat. I was an actual relief worker, and I was loving it" (Olson 1999: 47). Describing her experience in Cambodia, says Heidi, "[w]e're foreign and free and obnoxious and have dollars, so stay out of our way. We're immortal and nothing can touch us" (Cain 2004: 76).

Within the space of "us" of the expat community, privacy

is at a premium, and "there was no such thing as a personal private relationship" (Olson 1999: 51); everything is shared, including bathrooms (Cain 2004: 213). Close-knit living situations lead to the formation of rapid and close bonds with their expat co-workers: "[h]as it been six months already? Already? I love these people. I don't even want to think about saying goodbye" (Olson 1999: 68). Speaking of the situation in Banja Luka, Olson says, "[w]e have our little community here of MSF, ICRC and UNHCR, so it's nice to be back in my little family again" (ibid.: 108). This space also presents the opportunity to remake oneself in ways that would not be possible within their normal societies. It also presents the opportunity to live at an incredibly high standard compared to local populations. Lives prior to the field are downplayed and previously important markers such as "career or money or ... social class, the currency of social intercourse at Harvard" disappear (Cain 2004: 15). Among the expats, distinctions of race or background fade away. Admiring a female African co-worker on the dance floor of a party in Cambodia, Ken muses:

> I went to school with African-American girls during my entire
> adolescence in Michigan and never noticed them as potential
> girlfriends, never even wanted to meet them. How did that
> happen? I'm nine thousand miles from home and a pernicious
> wall of segregation I never noticed in high school suddenly
> materializes before my eyes, ten years after the fact. (Ibid.: 66)

For some of the initiates this is shocking. One Bangladeshi UN worker is horrified by the lack of funeral rights for Muslims in the field (ibid.: 73). In all the memoirs, drugs and alcohol play a prominent role and are frequently mentioned as a tool that gets them through the horrors they face. As a group they are separated from their previous lives through distance, both physical and emotional, and from their immediate surroundings. They are separated from their families and friends "at home" by a "distance of experiences, of time, of tragedy" (Olson 1999: 9–10).

Their inability to speak the local languages also creates a barrier between them and the local population, and security concerns (ostensibly) precipitate the maintenance of physical barriers (a point discussed in more detail in Chapter 2).

While Leanne insists that "[n]othing about this kind of work is typical" (ibid.: 10), it is this unpredictability which structures the narratives and characterizes their authors' experiences. The bizarre, the heterotopic, the unpredictable, the anachronistic and the politically incorrect are recurrent themes. All the characters express their amazement at the dreamlike or surreal quality of their life and work conditions in the field. Part of this is attributable to the places where they work, war zones, refugee camps, prisons, but also because they are witness to violent events while remaining untouched and outside of the structures that created these events. Leanne often speaks of being "in a dream" or "on holiday" (ibid.: 110) while Ken insists that "none of this is real" (Cain 2004: 132). They often use imaginary nicknames to refer to their situations, for example Blue Lagoon for Banja Luka – a tendency also observed in the military when serving on combat operations in the field.

In contrast with their previous lives, the space of work and play blend into one. In Cambodia, parties at Ken and Heidi's house become a place to exchange information on the political situation in the country. Conversely, their spaces of work become the places in which they celebrate. Leanne describes the unreal experience of spending New Year's Eve on the front line of a war, wearing "bulletproofs and drinking champagne to the sounds of shelling a few hundred meters away" (Olson 1999: 102). This feeling of unreality lends itself to ludic, verging on bacchanalian, activity. Exclaims Ken, "[w]e're on the roof of our mansion in the middle of Indochina, no parents, no boss. Everything everyone does is funny and perfect ... we're young and immortal and together and drunk and stupid and in Cambodia" (Cain 2004: 37).

While this is not asceticism in the way sometimes described by Turner (1969: 106), by engaging in bacchanalian and politically incorrect behaviour, the laws of Western society (as the characters know them) are suspended. Heidi, normally socially conscious and anti-elitist, goes to the beach in Cambodia with her fellow UN secretaries to float "in inner tubes in the steamy waters of the Gulf of Thailand. We signal to the waiters, who wade out to us fully clothed, carrying trays of beer and cigarettes already lit ... We decide this must be what it's like to be rich, to be entitled" (Cain 2004: 76). While in their normal lives she would condemn conspicuous consumption, here she partakes of it.

Part of the significance of such activities is that they occur in places that are simultaneously "cutting edge, dangerous, lonely, urgent" (Olson 1999: 175). In this context, experimentation, trickery and ignoring laws of normal society become the norm. Working on human rights law, Ken muses, "I'm not actually a licensed 'lawyer' in the US, but who's splitting hairs about that in Cambodia?" (Cain 2004: 32). Similarly, Leanne comes to accept that if one were to play by the rules of normal society, nothing would get done. She describes how MSF works with the Merhamets and Caritas, two local NGOs that supported unofficial and highly illegal medical clinics. These clinics were run by medical staff of the Croat and Muslim minorities, in Republika Srpska. The Merhamets served the Muslim population and Caritas the Croatians. By law, the minorities had no right to work. Their licences had been revoked, so no medical personnel were legally allowed to carry out their professional duties. To be caught doing so meant punishment by fines, imprisonment or delegation to a front line (Olson 1999: 91). She and her partner and lover, Rink, become valued by the organization, for their risk-taking and illegal behaviour.

Rink and I became quite famous [within MSF] for scrounging materials from whomever we could. Roel had christened us 'the vultures', and the name stuck. My natural talents expanded in unusual ways; I learned to lie with impunity, cheat, steal, negotiate with and manipulate anyone, to beg, borrow, stretch facts, bend truths and get what I needed by any means necessary. I worked hard to earn Roel's nickname … We developed quite a ruthless reputation but, considering the circumstances, one could say that necessity drove us to it. (Ibid.: 118)

Such 'abnormal' methods are sometimes justified by the juxtaposition of First World goals with Third World circumstance. For example, Heidi describes trying to set up polling stations in a mud field beside pigs (Cain 2004: 82), while Ken attempts to collect human rights abuse testimonies in a context where he does not know the language and can offer no protection to witnesses. The quality of pushing the boundary creates a euphoric atmosphere among initiates: "[i]t was terrifying, it was exciting, it was insane. We were living on the edge – and you should have seen the view!" (Olson 1999: 10).

Another way in which the structure of normal life is suspended is through sexual relations. Prostitution is openly accepted. Ken notes that around the perimeter of the French UN battalion are

hundreds of shacks hastily constructed to house young Cambodian and Vietnamese taxi girls. French soldiers exit the base and saunter openly to one or another of the whorehouses. The guys we are waiting for climb into the car and everybody's hugging and kissing. (Cain 2004: 76)

Two of the three female characters engage in a string of emotionally or physically promiscuous relationships. According to Turner, "[i]n liminality, the underlying comes uppermost" (Turner 1969: 102) and in *Emergency Sex* Heidi describes her need to have sex in the face of death as a way of reconnecting with her humanity. Heidi and Lynne also both find themselves in inverted sexual positions compared to their normal lives. Both women are excited by the "smorgasbord" of men. Crows Heidi,

[w]ith so few women available, the men have to try harder, offer more of themselves. … In the permanent emergency of the mission, I suddenly don't have to play by the boys' rules.

Which only proves that the boys' rules were bullshit to begin with. (Cain 2004: 133)

However, they both find themselves being bound by yet another set of rules. Stripped of their normal human agency as independent beings, they become pure women. In Heidi's case, she fights against this by trying to use sex to assert herself. In Lynne's case, she allows herself (and admittedly enjoys) becoming a classic "Dili Princess", wearing a tiara to serve dinner to her male expat housemates, and is then shocked because her sexualized relationships endanger her physically and ultimately get her fired from her job.

While initially the characters express exuberance about their jobs, they all eventually descend into despair. This transition occurs as they begin to realize that they are all in a state of ineffectual limbo, where none of their efforts has any impact, and where they seem to be constantly waiting for someone else to take action. Lynne's entire time in Timor is spent waiting: first for the independence celebrations working in an office where she is not wanted (hated, according to her colleague); then waiting for a job in the PM's office promised to her; then waiting for the PM to give her work to do. This leads to a sense of temporariness and uncertainty. "[E]veryone keeps a bag packed for emergency evacuation if we need it" (Olson 1999: 47); "I feel like a yo-yo" (ibid.: 98), complains Leanne.

People arrive and leave incessantly. The state of constant movement is also reflected in the characters' inability to effect any change. Andrew sighs, "[m]y dreams of being useful here are vanishing" (Cain 2004: 173). The characters see that their activities are directed towards their *own* liminal state, the space occupied by the international community: "all they [the UN] do is bring supplies into their own UN bases for their own staff, and certainly nothing gets to the population" (Olson 1999: 94). Many of their jobs are by definition observation posts, documenting the situations they are put in. And while "we do some essential work now, the minute we leave it will all fall apart" (ibid.: 151).

This results in frustration, followed by despondency and cynicism, in the narrators: "I managed to convince myself to believe in this work again. But I don't. It's a lie. We are the only beneficiaries of our righteousness" (ibid.: 226). The liminal situation loses its appeal, the narrators begin to crave private space and isolation. This is often preceded by a period of getting sick, when their inoculations, both medical and emotional, can no longer protect them from their surroundings. Or by an evacuation where it becomes clear that their presence in the Third World can only be temporary. Discussing the UN's evacuation from Haiti, Andrew says: "[n]ow that they're at their most vulnerable, we're abandoning them, ... flying out, clutching our precious blue UN passports and bags full of Haitian art" (Cain 2004: 174). Leanne ruminates,

> [w]hen things get really bad and we are needed the most,
> that's the time when we have to leave. It wasn't possible to
> take any of the national staff with us ... I think the evacuation
> of the expat team was far less traumatic for the national staff
> than it was for us. Expats come and go, and the staff had seen
> these evacuations before. For me, it was my first evacuation,
> but it certainly wouldn't be the last. (Olson 1999: 61)

Ultimately, the characters break down, psychologically and physically, and make the decision to return home. Says Leanne: "I just wanted to go home ... Frankly, I was sick and tired of the whole thing" (ibid.: 192). "I'd been at aid work for nearly four years and was beginning to feel too far removed from 'the real world'. I didn't know if we could truly ever return to the world but it was time to try" (ibid.: 234).

Rites of reaggregation: returning to 'normal' When the characters try to return to their previous ordinary lives, they find the reaggregation difficult. Heidi concedes,

> [w]e've all tried to make new friends here in New York, and
> to reverse the alienation we feel from our peers. But the

conversation doesn't usually go far once I say we lived in Somalia for two years, or Ken says that Andrew dug the graves of Srebrenica. (Cain 2004: 286)

Similarly, Leanne complains that, upon return, "I found out that my friends and family, for all their good intentions, shared little interest in what I had to say" (Olson 1999: 9). And later, "[e]veryone wanted to hear my stories and see my photos – for about five minutes … I was a little bit removed from everyone, and had just a little less to say" (ibid.: 135). They try to relocate normalcy as 'civilians' (as they call themselves) and find it difficult. Observes Leanne, "[w]e led one life that our regular friends and family saw and one that we saved for our friends from the field. We couldn't seem to get the two lives to merge" (ibid.: 221). This is arguably due to the fact that they have been irrevocably changed by their experiences in the field. In all three memoirs, the liminal phase is described as a transformative and quasi-religious experience. "Life as an international relief worker changed me profoundly," states Leanne (ibid.: 9). Even where it is not overly religious, there is the voiced desire on the part of Ken and Andrew to be part of something bigger than themselves (Cain 2004: 10).

The writing of the memoirs serves a duel process. First, it is a cathartic process that allows the narrators to come to terms with their experiences. Declares Ken, "I am a witness. I have a voice. I have to write it down" (ibid.: 292). But the act of writing such a memoir is the ultimate act of transgression and betrayal for those who remain in the field. By telling the story as they see it – "the story of what it's *really* like to be an international aid worker" (Olson 1999: 10) – they break the unwritten code of the field, they separate themselves out from its *communitas*, from its liminal state. Such an act is the ultimate rite of separation and can only be performed by someone who, at least temporarily, feels that the passage is complete.

Liminal spaces, affective constraints

The field mission for international aid workers resembles a classic rite of passage with the space of the field representing the liminal space of transition. Who are the people for whom this is a rite of passage, and what do the memoirs reveal about the material and cultural environment of this liminal situation? And what are its possibilities and constraints for aid work? In what follows, I argue that through their repeated deployment of the tropes of the enclosure and the threshold, the memoirs suggest that the aid workers are much more constrained in their inter-actions and choices than is suggested by third-space advocates, or understood by international policy-makers. And while the space is potentially transformative, it is primarily so from the perspective of the visiting aid worker, rather than for the beneficiary.

Whose rite of passage? If we consider the field mission to be a rite of passage it is important to establish exactly to whom this transition applies. Is it merely for the aid workers themselves, or for the societies that 'send' them? Arguably, the answer is both. The aid workers' decision to go to the field, to contribute to something bigger than themselves, is individual and global, and yet the structures and process that facilitate their journeys are products of their respective societies. Although only the aid worker can go through the rite of passage, the act of doing so has significance for society at large. But within their societies the aid workers are simultaneously revered and abhorred. People 'back home' respect their decision to undergo the hardship of the field and their contribution to the humanitarian imaginary, which ultimately relies upon them and their voyages to sustain itself. At the same time, their societies of origin (where they came from) seem to regard them as slightly threatening to the generally established life trajectory and associated societal norms.

As the act of aid work is, in some ways, a critique of normal Western society, it may be seen as potentially polluting to that society at large. According to Douglas (2002), liminal figures by

Turner's definition (1969: 109) are "almost everywhere regarded as 'polluting' and 'dangerous'", and this seems to be supported by the aid workers' experiences. As Andrew exhumes bodies in Gisenyi, Rwanda, he thinks to himself, "I have my UN passport and my air ticket out. But I don't smell so good, I have human flesh under my nails, and I spend my days arguing with priests and governors about corpses and money" (Cain 2004: 246). Sitting on the plane back to Winnipeg, Leanne remarks, "[n]o one wants to sit next to a skinny orange woman who has obviously been out in the bush too long" (Olson 1999: 58).

But just as they are regarded as profane, they are simultaneously sacred: untouchable, protected. Leanne voices a feeling of invincibility, that "if anything bad were to happen, it wouldn't be to me" (ibid.: 14). As codified under international and humanitarian law, the buildings, vehicles and bodies of international humanitarian actors are protected, neutral spaces. This "untouchability", however, goes beyond the juridical. For example, Leanne refers to the quality as "having 'it'".

> 'It' is the belief you have, you must have, to do this work. It is the feeling that nothing *really* bad will ever happen to you, and that you will be able to deal with whatever happens, that you will be able to talk your way out of it … You must have 'it', or you would never go into the countries that people are running out of … (Ibid.: 201)

It is worth keeping in mind the possibility that this quality of 'being apart' that the characters express may be symptomatic of the characters' marginal, rather than liminal, positions within their own societies. Turner distinguishes a marginal character as someone who is permanently on the outskirts of society, while a liminal figure is someone temporarily in a liminal state for the purpose of transformation. For example, even in her own society, Leanne did not have a secure nursing job (ibid.: 11), and in *Emergency Sex* all of the characters were dissatisfied with their regular existence: Heidi was escaping a broken marriage,

Ken was avoiding a 'real' job in corporate law. Similarly, Lynne gives the impression of being rootless. Although she claims to be there to contribute to the rebuilding of East Timor, she is badly shaken by an argument with a peacekeeper who, among other things, accuses her of running away from something at home (Minion 2004: 254).

Whether they are liminal or marginal figures is important to our investigation in two respects. First, if they are marginal figures, does this affect the experience that they have in the field; and secondly, what does this tell us about which types of people are attracted by aid work? The books suggest that all the narrators, with the possible exception of Lynne, are liminal not marginal figures. While they all voice the feeling of being outsiders in their normal existence, this feeling is repeatedly counterpoised with their secure integration into the expat community of the field. They also express solidarity with their larger home community, and that they are doing this to be part of something larger than themselves. This connection to something larger than themselves is an important feature of humanitarian work, as compared to the motivations of extreme tourists or travellers more generally. Still, it is worth considering the possible connections with extreme or so-called dark tourism, as there are certain commonalities that are important to our understanding of the humanitarian rite of passage.

Ansell (2008) examines the recent increase in what is being called gap-year tourism: the tendency for a young adult to take a year away from an established middle-class life trajectory of high school, university, career to spend between a few months and several years travelling and/or working/volunteering in the Third World. According to Ansell, middle classes in the West seek to differentiate themselves from those who engage in mass tourism by going to places in the Third World which may be seen as risky or unusual (ibid.; also Mowforth and Munt 2009). The valuable aspects of this type of tourism are that it conveys certain messages about the traveller (not tourist) to the people back home.

For example, they are seen to be worldly, experienced, adaptable and strong. Much like the characters in the aid memoirs, Ansell suggests that gap-year travel is primarily valuable when conveyed as an experiential narrative to audiences back home. However, unlike aid work, such travel is much more about *individual* experience, and although fellow 'gap yearers' may have experiences in common, they do not consider themselves as a like-minded group of initiates.

Similarly, the recent identification of the phenomenon of dark tourism – seeking out sites of genocide, disaster and war zones (Hughes 2008) – supports the ongoing demand for risky, unique and extreme experiences. But, for an individual, the events are all the more valuable for being solitary undertakings (see Stewart 2007). In sum, the rite of passage, identified in the aid memoirs, does have characteristics of adventure-seeking and thrill-taking. However, the aid workers' experience is not solely explained by theories of extreme tourism and needs to be considered as part of a larger, social process: it contributes to a particular humanitarian imaginary. One way in which this is done is through the constant presence of certain material tropes. The space of aid has a liminal nature that, unlike the previously mentioned postcolonial third spaces, is clearly demarcated and enclosed. Within these enclosures, the initiates are cordoned off from the societies in which they are supposed to be assisting.

Describing the liminal space The claim that the rite of passage is focused exclusively on the aid workers and their countries of origin is made on the basis that all three of the narratives are almost totally concerned with elements of the international. Staff and citizens of the host country make only select appearances. The spaces, places and situations in which the authors find themselves are almost always spatially contained, enclosed or set off from the wider population. For example, the space of the hotel is prominent in all the narratives. With temporary populations, this is inevitable; however, the significance of the hotel goes beyond a place to sleep and eat. It is also used as a place of First World refuge in the face of the surrounding discomfort.

Similarly, the space of the SUV or iconic Land Rover is prominent in the memoirs. There is a feeling of impenetrability within the vehicle, and of being above the land through which they travel. Riding around East Timor in a UN Land Rover, Lynne feels like "Queen Betty acknowledging her subjects" (Minion 2004: 80). In the context of the memoirs the Land Rover gives the impression of being an extension of the other spaces of work, life and play. In the case of Ken and Heidi in Somalia, their entire existence is spent in or being shuttled between fortified, enclosed spaces. The characters move from one enclosure to the next, to the point where Lynne has the impression that her life is nothing but a series of restaurants. Walking, especially for white women, is seen not only as bizarre, but dangerous. Outside of the expected and established spatial modes of interaction, they are considered fair game for trickery, harassment and abuse both by other expats and by local populations. This causes a retreat back into the established expat spaces, and a reinforcement of the divides. The aid workers become affectively constrained in how they conceive the other. This should not necessarily be seen solely as the product of 'international agency'.

Local populations may consider aid workers as potential contaminants to the larger society or a threat to local elites, and accordingly push the aid workers back into their spatial and social categories. During Lynne's time in East Timor, the bars and restaurants frequented by the expats are quite literally kept offshore, where boats have been converted into floating bars. As late as 2008, the international community is kept on permanent stand-by, by the refusal or inability of the Timorese government to provide long-term working visas for internationals. At several points the characters attempt to break out of the 'expat bubble', only to be met with resistance both from other expats and from the local communities. For example, Heidi, on 'rest and relaxation' near Mombasa, tries and fails to escape her tourist hotel to find the 'real Kenya' (Cain 2004: 95). Lynne attempts to enter into the daily routines of her Timorese patrons, but is met with a lack of understanding as to why she, a *malae* (foreigner, usually white), would want to. As international workers, they are protected by international accords of immunity. This translates not only into different laws, but different lifestyles within the compounds. In the case of the Australian compound in East Timor, the degree of wealth is so great that Lynne feels as though she's fallen down the rabbit hole (Minion 2004: 233).

Lynne often mentions the Timorese who crowd outside the gates of the restaurants and bars to stare at the *malae*. This is hardly surprising, as the *malae* (which Lynne translates into "scab foreigner") are not there to help the ordinary Timorese but rather to work with other liminal personae. In each one of the memoirs, the "logic of the mission" is theirs not the local community's (Cain 2004: 174). As the mandate of many international organizations is to work with those sectors of a local population which fall outside the jurisdiction of their national governments (i.e. by definition liminal populations), their spatial foci will be quintessentially liminal zones: prisons, hospitals, grave sites, enclaves. The memoirs give the impression of the expats moving from their own self-made enclosures to other zones of enclosure that they also have defined. Even when the project or intervention is intended to be for an entire population, such as the independence celebrations for East Timor in 2002, the beneficiaries end up being excluded: linguistically, culturally and physically. Lynne describes how the grandiose celebrations to celebrate the handover of the UN transitional administration to the Timorese, in May 2002, were aimed almost exclusively at the international community. She says, "despite the dark skins of some of the visitors, the host country has very few of its own in attendance, other than those who carry the trays" (Minion 2004: 114).

Beyond the material trope of enclosure is that of threshold spaces: of planes, cars, airports, helicopters and border crossings. While in the threshold, initiates are suspended between two states

– neither here, nor there – and protected by their sacred status as liminal beings: recognized by common logos and insignia. They are also protected through physical demarcation. Says Andrew, "I push through the seething crowd to the UN car. The driver takes me past the slums by the harbour, up the hill to the lush suburbs where the rich, light-skinned Haitians live, far above poverty" (Cain 2004: 109). When Leanne arrives in Liberia: "[u]nable to speak a word of French, I tried to fend off persistent taxi drivers and prayed to see *any* NGO car arrive. Finally a driver with an MSF T-shirt did show up. Chatting away in a language I couldn't understand, he whisked me off to a comfortable house in the suburbs" (Olson 1999: 19). Upon departure, the threshold also marks the end of the sacred zone of the liminal. Ken, leaving Mogadishu, says, "[w]e deplane and walk together across the tarmac, the UN has a special landing field in Nairobi just for us. But when I leave their company and cross the threshold of the main terminal alone, I'm a regular civilian again, a tourist" (Cain 2004: 199). These threshold spaces are similar to what Marc Augé (1995) refers to as "non-spaces" or *espaces d'autres*: spaces of super-modernity, as he calls it, such as airports, where one's identity is left at the door, and within these spaces all occupants are the same. Within the spaces, place loses its power, and time (schedules, departures, timetables) takes over.

Conclusion: setting the stage

In his article on the development of the American Red Cross movement, Kevin Rozario contends that contemporary humanitarianism is a "creation of a sensationalistic mass culture" (Rozario 2003: 418). Says Rozario, "it was only when philanthropy became a marketing venture and when donors began to be treated and courted as consumers who had to be entertained that philanthropy could become a mass phenomena" (ibid.: 419). He considers this to be part of the rise of the "spectacular society", when suffering could, through technological advances, be represented in ever more graphic detail. Turning to the experience of the narrators of the memoirs, it would seem that they were seeking the opposite of the spectacle. Rather than merely gaze upon humanitarianism, they wanted to viscerally experience the act of being a humanitarian, and through this experience to undergo a rite of passage that would fundamentally change them. However, the experience that they seek is always outside of the zones of exclusion – the enclosures and threshold spaces that they find themselves in.

This chapter has introduced, identified and described a liminal space which offers unique and distinct characteristics and material tropes for the aid workers who come to it. Several shared themes are prominent. First, securitization and enclosure run throughout the memoirs. The experience is one of being set off from their surroundings both through social behaviour and through the material buildings and vehicles that they live in. The second theme is that of mobility and of temporariness. The third is that of remaining linked to, but not fully at home in, their countries of origin in the West. There are, of course, exceptions. Some aid workers speak the language of the place they are going to, others will stay in a given country for the majority of their lives. However, these memoirs represent a view from the inside of the aid industry, and of thousands of aid workers just like them. That within these pages the same places, locations and objects recur over and over – the hotel, the Land Rover, the gated compound – deserves further attention. And it is to these places that the following chapters will now turn.

2 | EXPLORING THE HUMANITARIAN ENCLAVE

> Obviously, in a lot of these insecure countries your staff are either not going there or they are in heavily protected environments, in cantonments, and they are not actually going out into the field. (Chairman of the UK Public Accounts Committee, 2009)

This chapter provides an overview of trends in the securitization of humanitarian assistance and suggests that the current direction of humanitarian policy is moving towards an increased physical enclosure of humanitarian staff and assets. Through an examination of staff security manuals from ECHO, the UN, DfID and the IFRC, and interviews with security personnel in Aceh and East Timor, it explores this trend, highlighting the evolution of one dominant spatial typology: the humanitarian compound. The chapter proposes that the increased focus on securitization has been driven by the *perception* of insecurity for humanitarian work in general, which is not supported by existing evidence. It will explore how the two trends are related but not in the way that is normally presented; that is, increased insecurity leading to increased physical securitization. Rather, it will examine the opposite direction: an increased physical securitization leading to an increased fear of attack and perception of being under threat. The work in this chapter provides a theoretical basis for the intuitions and anecdotal evidence that the behaviours and symbols of aid workers matter. Further, it contributes to an understanding of how the material environment has an impact both on aid work *in situ* and on the evolution of global humanitarian policy.

Perceptions of insecurity among aid workers

There is a perception among humanitarian workers and policy-makers that insecurity in the field is increasing and that their bodily safety is increasingly endangered by their work (Stoddard et al. 2006; Buchanan and Muggah 2005; Fast 2007; McFarlane 2004). At first glance this is supported by the data, which shows that, in absolute numbers, deaths of humanitarian workers have increased since the 1990s. According to the most comprehensive (public) data collection system to date, the Aid Worker Security Database (AWSD), the number of "attacks in which aid workers were killed, kidnapped or injured has risen significantly since 1997", with a particularly sharp increase between 2006 and 2008 (Stoddard et al. 2009: 2). The average number of major incidents for the years 2006, 2007 and 2008 was 127, which represents an 89 per cent increase from the prior three-year period (2003–05) and a 117 per cent increase from the annual average between 1997 and 2002. The AWSD and the associated reports (ibid.; Stoddard et al. 2006) have become the most widely cited quantitative analysis of violent incidents against aid workers and, superficially, they do reinforce the claim that violence against aid workers is increasing. For example, a 2008 report by the UK National Audit Office, intended to inform future DfID policy, states that a

> 2005 study by the Overseas Development Institute found that almost 500 aid workers ... have been killed between 1997 and 2005 and another 500 kidnapped or injured. The number of aid worker deaths per year from violent incidents has increased from 34 in 1997 to over 70 in 2005. (National Audit Office 2008: 27)

What the report does not say is that this figure needs to be weighted against several factors, including the overall increase in aid workers in the field during this period and the incomplete coverage of the monitoring systems used to collect data. It also needs to be corrected for the conflation of military and humanitarian mandates in Afghanistan, Iraq and Sudan, where the majority of the casualties occurred. That is to say, that the recorded casualties arguably occurred in a context that was an active combat situation rather than in a humanitarian context (on the issue of providing humanitarian aid in combat situations and the conflation of military and humanitarian mandates, see Lischer 2007). For example, the ECHO 2004 *Report on Security of Humanitarian Personnel* states that:

> [d]espite a perception of increased insecurity for humanitarian workers, the few statistics that are available appear not to confirm this. Conclusions cannot easily be drawn from available statistics, because of inconsistencies in definitions and lack of information about the overall number of humanitarian workers. (European Commission Humanitarian Aid Office 2004b: 1)

The report continues,

> [t]here is no hard evidence to suggest that there has been a significant increase in the number of security incidents either in numbers of incidents, or in numbers of people affected. Numbers fluctuate from year to year for a number of reasons including the size of operation being undertaken, the level of insecurity where operations are happening, and other random factors. (Ibid.: 19)

The next section will examine why it has been so difficult to establish a clear, statistical picture.

The end of the Cold War saw the increased use of the United Nations (UN) as an instrument to address intranational conflict. This meant an overall increase in the number of peacekeeping missions and staff sent to the field (Wheeler 2000; Stoddard et al. 2006; Chesterman 2004). This coincided with an exponential increase in aid workers after the Cold War, as well as raising the visibility of international humanitarian work in the public consciousness, be it through the UN or other multi- and bilateral agencies (for more on this, see Chapter 3). According to Stoddard et al., the 1990s saw many aid workers have "their first experience of high-risk, militarised humanitarian relief efforts, where their aid commodities were treated as spoils of war and they themselves were frequent targets of combatants" (Stoddard et al. 2006: 4).

This 'high-risk experience' was the result of several new trends in aid work. First, as already mentioned, there was the overall increase in the number of aid workers going to the field, which meant more aid workers in all locations, dangerous or not.

Secondly, funds and agencies previously focused on narrow areas such as child health or population control now expanded their mandates to include situations designated as hazardous; and bilateral donors began to reallocate funding towards programmes focused on conflict prevention and management. Since the 1990s, this trend has only become more pronounced, and between 2003 and 2008 DfID more than doubled its support to insecure countries and plans further increases. It has also diversified its expenditure in insecure environments away from humanitarian relief and into longer-term development projects. This also relates to the increase in the high-profile blurring or rapprochement of humanitarian and military interventions, namely in Iraq and Afghanistan, which has meant that humanitarians are working not in post-conflict or so-called normal development settings, but alongside active combat missions. Although such situations were what led to the establishment of international humanitarianism in the 1800s (Hutchinson 1996; Kent 1987), this history is often forgotten, and since the 1990s humanitarians have largely perceived themselves as operating independently of political objectives (Rozario 2003; House of Commons 2009; Weiss and Collins 2000; on the politicization of aid, see Rubenstein 2007; Drury et al. 2005; Alesina and Dollar 2000).

Thirdly, changes in how humanitarian (narrowly defined) and development missions in insecure locations are recorded have changed. For example, according to the Office of the UN Security Coordinator (UNSECOORD), the number of UN staff deployed in hazardous missions increased from 0 in 1990 to 40,062 in 2003 (where "hazardous" is defined as a mission where "prevailing security conditions require the application of security measures under UN security phases") (Independent Panel on the Safety and Security of UN Personnel in Iraq 2003: 19). This obscures the fact that prior to 1990 there *were* staff deployed in countries that would be classified as hazardous according to 1990 metrics. However, circa 1990 saw the introduction of new classification systems for personnel and missions. This has arguably contributed to the skewing of numbers of aid workers in a post-1990 direction.

Nor were the UN alone in their absence of comprehensive pre-1990 figures of deployment in hazardous (broadly defined) missions. According to Stoddard, "[i]t is generally agreed that reporting and record keeping on security incidents ... was scanty and uneven across international aid agencies up until the mid-1990s" (Stoddard et al. 2006: 7). This lack of a centralized data collection system continued to plague the international humanitarian system throughout the 1990s and 2000s. In response to this dearth of empirical evidence, in 2006 Stoddard et al. undertook the most comprehensive study to date on the violent targeting of aid workers in the field. This study, as well as its 2009 update and associated database, have become the baseline for assessing trends on aid worker fatalities and other serious incidents. Their most cited finding is that there has been a steady increase in violent attacks against aid workers since 1997: moving from 34 violent attacks in 1997 to 155 in 2008. This statistic is accompanied by an increase in the overall number of victims: from 77 in 1997 to 260 in 2008. While a remarkable and thorough study, this central claim that violence against aid workers is increasing is problematic both within the terms of the study and on data collection grounds.

The authors use the term "aid worker" to

describe personnel working for humanitarian or multi-mandated aid agencies that operate in humanitarian relief contexts. The term 'humanitarian operations' is used to define the work primarily being implemented in relief contexts, including life-saving, basic welfare and protection-related activities. (Ibid.: 5)

It does not count incidents that affect "peacekeeping or human rights personnel or UN personnel outside of the UN aid agencies", but does "count individuals that have been contracted to undertake work for an aid agency, such as drivers and guards" (Stoddard et al. 2009: 2). Incidents were included which fell under the categories of killing, kidnapping (if held for more than twenty-four hours) and wounding. The overall number of incidents was calculated using public sources such as news reports and websites and augmented with other information provided to the study by international organizations. Other sources included US State Department reports (US Department of State 1997–2005b, a), UN Department of Safety and Security (UNDSS) reports and other UN documents. From this, they created the previously mentioned AWSD, which has been running since 2005. The six countries or areas that were identified as having the highest incidence – Somalia/Somaliland, Sudan, Afghanistan, Iraq, the DRC and the north Caucasus – were also subjected to in-depth research in their own right.

Each of the recorded incidents was coded for the number of aid workers affected; institutional affiliation (UN/Red Cross/ NGO/other, such as IFI, donor government); method of violence used; country or context of incident; and, where possible, motive, "although this was only possible for a limited number of incidents" (Stoddard et al. 2006: 5). The year 1997 was used as a baseline as the authors made the assumption that "reporting and record-keeping on security incidents ... was scanty and uneven across international agencies up until the mid-1990s, when staff security and security coordination became an organisational priority" (ibid.: 7). They also felt that starting in 1997 provided a control for the population explosion in aid workers post-1990. That is to say, that by 1997 humanitarian trends had regularized sufficiently to ensure the data was not skewed by the sudden post-1990 jump in field staff numbers. Overall, the quality of the data appears to be good, with incidents being cross-checked for accuracy, and the choice of categories, as well as estimates, sound. However, certain problems exist.

In most cases, the authors are aware of the problems and limitations of the data, but downplay their significance in the report. For example, an accurate counting of field staff numbers is essential to obtain a real estimate of increases in violent incidents. While it was widely accepted that there has been an exponential increase in the number of staff field numbers over the last two decades, the lack of any type of centralized accounting system both pre- and post-1990 makes it almost impossible to know by exactly *how much* the numbers have increased. Even within individual agencies, exact counts of field staff at any given time are very difficult to obtain owing to the high staff turnover and wide array of contracts within a given agency or programme. In order to obtain the aid worker denominator, Stoddard et al. approached ten UN agencies, fifty-four INGOs and the IFRC/ RC and ICRC to provide staff numbers for the years 1997–2005. "Of these organisations only 32% were able to provide full, disaggregated data for all or most years; 26% provided partial data and 41% provided only very minimal figures" (ibid.: 8).

For those organizations that provided only partial figures, the authors used inference based on proportion of staff to programme expenditure, and previous numbers of international staff members, to estimate numbers for the years that were not provided. From this they estimated that the aid worker population had grown by 77 per cent between 1997 and 2005, from 136,204 to 241,654. When the 2006–08 figures were added on, the total of aid workers in the field "topped 290,000 in 2008" (Stoddard et al. 2009: 21). While this number certainly under-reports the number of field staff, it may be considered to be an accurate estimate of trends. However, the lack of inclusion of several key agencies, notably the World Bank, the IFRC and UNOPS, all with large field-based presence and/or foci on large infrastructure projects that required extensive staffing requirements, mean that Stoddard et al.'s denominator may be *much less* than the real number of field staff working in hazardous environments.

The same criticism cannot be directed at the numerator, the number of violent incidents, as these are collected using data from a wide range of sources, including news reports. This becomes particularly significant when the trend changes are minimal because the under-reporting of the denominator compared to an accurate numerator would positively skew the figures. This would demonstrate an upward trend, when perhaps the trend is decreasing or remaining static. For example, the key change between the 2006 and 2009 reports is that the number of incidents involving internationals sharply increased from the three previous years. However, it is conversely possible that the number of violent crimes is actually under-reported (Fast 2007). Either way, the magnitude of the number of incidents is too small, and the time frame too short, to provide any reliable indication of long-term trends.[1]

Similarly, while acknowledging the paucity of reliable data pre-1990, they still use one of the few available studies (Sheik et al. 2000) as a "baseline for aid worker fatalities to compare against the later time period" of 1997–2005. The incomplete and vague coverage of the Sheik et al. report means that accuracy of the original baseline is questionable. For example, they do not provide a comprehensive list of agencies surveyed, saying only that "overall 32 organisations and their affiliates provided data" (ibid.: 166). It is not clear what the scale of the organizations are, what countries they work in, or whether they were able to provide records for all the years. When compared with Stoddard et al.'s significantly more comprehensive study, there has been a "considerable increase" from the earlier period of 1985–98

---

1 The average number of incidents against internationals between 2003 and 2005 inclusive was 24.34. In this case, an increase of even five incidents could be considered to be a sharp increase. The precise number is not given in the 2009 report (Stoddard et al. 2009).

(Stoddard et al. 2006: 9), which is to be expected given the variation in the scale of the respective studies.

Even taking Stoddard et al.'s data at face value, the claim that aid worker casualties have increased overall is accompanied by several significant caveats. The 2006 report saw an overall increase in the targeting of aid workers; *however*, national staff represented 79 per cent of the victims, and violence against international staff actually *decreased* by 41 per cent relative to overall aid worker presence in the field. Also, remarkably, even in the six countries with the highest incidence of events (identified above), "the number of incidents per staff member actually went down ... the total number of staff members deployed in field positions in these dangerous environments grew faster than incidents of violence against them" (ibid.: 17).

In the 2006 report, the authors identified a trend towards protective and defensive approaches to security and away from acceptance strategies. This translated into an increased reliance by many agencies on "remote management" techniques for projects and a disproportionate transference of risk on to local staff. This is reflected in a 108 per cent increase in national staff victims relative to overall aid worker presence. The report came at a time when there was a demand for empirical evidence regarding the status of field security. But, by the time it came out, most of the major agencies had already undertaken their own internal reviews of staff security. They were also already in the process of implementing the recommendations from those reports that included increased attention to physical security of staff and premises; the increased use of strategic risk assessments; and staff training programmes (European Commission Humanitarian Aid Office 2004b, a; National Audit Office 2008; International Federation of the Red Cross and Red Crescent Societies 2007). As described in the introduction, the message of the report was generally interpreted post hoc as empirical evidence to support these institutional changes and as evidence for the widespread 'feeling' that security for aid workers was decreasing. The report's caveats were rarely included.

The 2009 report provided an update on the numbers from the period of 2006–08. In this report, the first key message is that "[a]ttacks against aid workers have increased sharply since 2006" with the number of victims counted as 235 over the 2006–08 period as compared with 147 for the preceding three-year period of 2003–05 (Stoddard et al. 2009: 1). Farther into the report, they state that 75 per cent of all attacks on aid workers occurred in one of seven countries with ongoing armed conflict: Sudan, Afghanistan, Somalia, Sri Lanka, Chad, Iraq and Pakistan. A "closer examination of incident rates reveals that the spike over the past three years was driven by violence in just three contexts: Sudan (Darfur), Afghanistan and Somalia" (ibid.: 4). When these three contexts are controlled for the "long-term overall major attack rate for humanitarians is actually declining" from an average of 2.4 aid worker victims per 10,000 in 2006–08, down from 2.7 over the preceding three-year period (ibid.: 4). It also gives the impression that, unlike the previous report's findings, *this* period found that international fatalities in particular were increasing.

On the surface, this is true: the number of international victims almost doubled against the previous three-year period, from 65 to 110. However, again when the numbers are disaggregated, they reveal that attacks against the UN's international staff actually declined slightly, although attacks against their national staff and contractors, most notably truck drivers, rose. Looking at the numbers in this way provides an alternative story that reveals that outside of a handful of highly dangerous countries, it is actually becoming slightly safer, or at the very least no more dangerous, to be an aid worker. At 2.4 deaths per 10,000, a person is more than twice as likely to be in a fatal or serious car crash in the UK than to be killed or seriously injured as an international aid worker working in the field.

That aid work, in the main, has become statistically no more dangerous over the last twenty years sits uneasily with the deep-seated conviction among policy-makers and aid workers themselves that circumstances have changed. This conviction also obscures the historical record that the UN's staff have been the target of violence almost since the organization's inception. As early as 1948, only three years after the formation of the UN, the UN Mediator, Count Bernadotte, was assassinated by the Fighters for the Freedom of Israel (LEHI). His assassination led to discussions in the International Court of Justice which focused largely on whether reparations should be paid by the offending state (International Court of Justice 1949). But after this high-profile case, the issue of the international and violent targeting of aid workers did not become the subject of sustained high-level, international attention until December 1980, when the first reference to the safety and security of aid workers can be found in the General Assembly Resolution A/RES/35/212.

The resolution appealed

> to all Member States to respect the privileges and immunities accorded to officials of the United Nations and specialized agencies by the Convention on the Privileges and Immunities of the United Nations of 13 February, 1946 and by the Convention on the Privileges and Immunities of the Specialized Agencies of 21 November, 1947. (United Nations 1946)

Although the General Assembly continued to pass resolutions on the safety and security of staff, they tended to concentrate on international legal protection and immunity rather than on the material or physical conditions of protection. The matter did not receive sustained attention again until 1994, when the UN General Assembly Convention on the Safety of United Nations and Associated Personnel was adopted by seventy-nine state signatories (United Nations 1994). It is not clear how many humanitarian workers were killed during this period, since, as already mentioned, there was no centralized system of record-keeping. As a result, many deaths were apparently not reported back to headquarters in any systematic way (Stoddard et al. 2006). And although "agency level incident reporting has improved considerably over the past decade" (Stoddard et al. 2009: 2), the lack of a comprehensive overview is perhaps the most important contributing factor to the perception on the part of the agencies and staff that humanitarians are under increased threat.

According to Stoddard et al., this "widespread perception of new and growing threats to aid workers, to their operations, and to access to beneficiaries" (2006: 3) has put pressure on governments and organizations to increase staff security. However, it is possible that there is a circular relationship between the increased perception of insecurity and the trend towards increased physical enclosure of staff. For example, according to the EU, "the increased fear of attack can itself be considered a significant challenge in humanitarian agencies' efforts to maintain the security and well being of the personnel" (European Commission Humanitarian Aid Office 2004b: 1).

A 2005 study by Buchanan and Muggah found that

> while fatal and non-fatal injuries among workers may have stabilised or even declined in comparison with the mid-1990s, there is a *perception* that victimisation is nevertheless on the rise. In the words of one UN security specialist, 'what has increased may not be the figures, but the fear' (Buchanan and Muggah 2005: 12)

The issue of perception will be addressed in more detail in the next chapter. For now, it is sufficient to accept that there is a "general sense that the dynamics of security have somehow changed" (Stoddard et al. 2006: 3). This 'general sense' has become widespread among the humanitarian community and is reflected in the marked increase of attention paid to security in the 1990s and 2000s, both by the UN and other NGOs.

The evolution of physical securitization in the field

Since the mid-1990s, international aid agencies have consistently invested more resources, year on year, into ensuring the physical safety of their staff (Report of the Secretary General 2000, 2003; Eide et al. 2005). For example, in 2007 DfID found that security expenditure increased by 100 per cent compared to the previous year, excluding Iraq, where in one infamous project £5.1 million out of £7 million went to security of staff (National Audit Office 2008). The increased focus on security has manifested itself in the increased production of security manuals for staff; the undertaking of internal reviews; organizational revamps and the creation of dedicated staff positions for security. Several organizations have begun to allocate dedicated programme funds for physical security upgrades, equipment, new staff positions, and training. While the UN continues to reaffirm that the responsibility for the safety of humanitarian personnel lies with the host state, it independently began to introduce instruments to mitigate the risk of violent attack against its staff, most notably through the introduction of the Malicious Acts Insurance Policy (MAIP), security phases and minimum operating standards for offices and residences.

The need for the UN to ensure that it was insured, at a global level, against both reputational and financial implications of attacks against its personnel saw the adoption, circa 1990, of the Malicious Acts Insurance Policy: a policy covering all "eligible individuals in designated duty stations for death or disability caused by a malicious act" (UNDP 2003: 3). It is "administered by the United Nations Security Coordinator (UNSECOORD), through Willis UK Limited of London, a broker representing Lloyd's of London, the Underwriters" (ibid.: 3). To ensure eligibility, a field office must be seen to comply with the minimum operating standards as determined, to a large degree, by the security phase in effect.

The security phases were introduced at roughly the same time as the MAIP. They range from No Phase to Phase Five, "each denoting a different level of insecurity, and requiring different security measures" (European Commission Humanitarian Aid Office 2004a; Independent Panel on the Safety and Security of UN Personnel in Iraq 2003: 34–5). No Phase means that no exceptional security measures need to be taken. As described in Annex 40 of the ECHO Generic Security Guide (European Commission Humanitarian Aid Office 2004a: Annex 40), Phase One is Precautionary. Staff should exercise caution and all travel into the area requires advance clearance by a designated security office (DO). Phase Two is Restricted Movement. Staff and families should remain at home and no travel into or within the country is permitted unless authorized by the DO. Phase Three is Relocation.

> Internationally recruited staff and their families are temporarily concentrated or relocated to specified sites/locations and/ or eligible dependants are relocated outside the country ... locally recruited staff may leave the duty station on special leave without pay, or be relocated to a safe area within the country with up to 20 days Daily Subsistence Allowance ... (Ibid.: Annex 40)

Phase Four is Programme Suspension, where "all internationally-recruited staff who are not directly concerned with emergency or humanitarian relief operations or security matters are relocated outside the country" (ibid.: 145). Phase Five is Evacuation, where "all remaining internationally recruited staff leave" (Independent Panel on the Safety and Security of UN Personnel in Iraq 2003: 34–5). The options for locally recruited staff are the same for Phases Three through Five.

The application or change in a security level is often a highly contested issue. Host governments see an increased security phase as adversely affecting a country's economic and social stability: increasing its cost of investment for foreign firms and inflating insurance premiums. Conversely, lowering a security level may be equally disputed, as it may result in a decrease in peacekeeping troop levels; lower staff salaries; and less frequent recuperative leave for field staff. Despite the notoriously problematic use of security phases as a measurement of true security, they remain key determinants of the Minimum Operating Security Standards (MOSS) and the Minimum Operating Residential Security Standards (MORSS).

EXPLORING THE HUMANITARIAN ENCLAVE | 61

Introduced after the establishment of the first UN Security Coordination Office (UNSECOORD) in 1988 (Stoddard et al. 2006: 22), the MOSS and MORSS provide guidance for UN duty stations to: "review the various country-specific threats and their associated risks, using a standardized threat-assessment system to help determine the safety measures undertaken to enable staff to operate effectively and safely at the location" (Currier 2003).

They include guidance on "Protective Equipment and Facilities", which covers the use and storage of body armour, blast protective film for windows/windscreens, ballistic blankets, and bunkers and reinforced rooms. However, more specific guidance on type, specification and installation procedure is left up to a competent authority (United Nations 2002: Annex A) – this may be a member of the security team or an external consultant.

Throughout the 1990s, the dominant approach to field security was considered to be best determined by the field offices themselves, and beyond the MOSS and MORSS, headquarters provided little guidance on more standardized approaches to security. As security tended to be generally underfunded and falling under the purview of the host government (which often did not want to share sensitive information), there was little push on the part of UN field offices to increase security measures. Further, unless the field office was under a Phase One or higher security phase, no MOSS or MORSS existed (ibid.). Since 2002, MOSS and MORSS are now specified for all phases including No Phase and are required if the MAIP is to be valid. There has been an increased standardization for MOSS and MORSS and a move towards, and increased reliance upon, Strategic Risk Assessments. An intensification of system-wide staff training among most major agencies can also be observed.

Benchmark training programmes such as the UN and the IFRC's draw upon the 'security bible': Van Brabant's recommendations for risk mitigation through a knowledge and understanding of one's environment (Van Brabant 2000). This security awareness should then be integrated into "project design, implementation, monitoring and evaluation" (European Commission Humanitarian Aid Office 2004b: 8). The objective is to effectively incorporate security awareness into all aspects of humanitarian assistance. And while there are attempts to include national staff in security trainings, historically such training has been primarily targeted at international staff (Brahimi 2008). Even when national staff are included in the training, recommendations to avoid walking around the local environments or to refrain from eating local food can only be aimed at international staff.

Such internationally targeted security training may contribute to an increased consensus within the international staff (as compared to local staff) of what constitutes risk. For example, the EU openly acknowledges that it adopts a Western perspective over security. Its 2004 report states that "the view [on security] is rooted in Northern – particularly US and European – perspectives" (European Commission Humanitarian Aid Office 2004b: 8). Even when there are no explicit material constraints, staff will be bound together by a joint understanding or consensus over what is safe and what is not. Further, this will be institutionalized through regulations which will impose restrictions over where and when staff can travel – for example, through the UN security phases.

In general, the UN's unique role in humanitarian affairs has meant that it has been at the forefront of codifying IHL around humanitarian personnel (Alagappa and Inoguchi 1999). The UN is often more constrained than bilateral or other multilateral organizations, such as the IFRC, in instituting formal security guidelines which could be interpreted as undermining the social or economic stability, or political authority, of a member state. However, as explained by one interviewee, it also tends to be more conservative in its staff policies, issuing curfews or curtailing field visits, when other agencies are actively working in those areas. Particularly in contexts where there is a strong UN presence, either a peacekeeping mission or a visible humanitarian programme, it will tend to set the standard for what is considered to be an acceptable risk for humanitarians and insurers alike. For example, DfID defines "insecure environment" as a composite assessment based on the number of reported deaths due to political violence ("general security") and the UNDSS's security phases as a proxy for "personal security" (National Audit Office 2008). Duffield (2009) has referred to this as the centrifugal force of the UN in the field, and this rapprochement of NGOs and the UN over the issue of security has been codified in a series of documents, most notably *Saving Lives Together* (IASC Working Group 2006). Donors are also increasingly encouraging implementing organizations to ensure that their modalities incorporate security awareness (European Commission Humanitarian Aid Office, 2004b: 8; 2006).

It is important to stress that the trend towards overall securitization has occurred iteratively between the UN and other INGOs and bilaterals. One of the most important catalysts for thinking on operational security came out of a 1993 forum of informal experts called the Security Advisory Group. Initiated by programme staffers from CARE, World Vision, Save the Children and the IRC – all INGOs active in dangerous settings – this group would prove to be an incubator for the ideas on security developed by NGOs during this period and which would influence the humanitarian community at large, including the UN. According to Stoddard et al. (2006: 21), it paved the way for future work, including the drafting of the aforementioned field security 'bible': Koenraad Van Brabant's *Operational Security Management in Violent Environments* (2000).

In this publication, Van Brabant laid out the security philosophy that is still widely accepted by the majority of NGOs operating in violent environments: the identification of three major security strategies, also known as the security triangle of acceptance, protection and deterrence (European Commission Humanitarian Aid Office 2004a). Acceptance refers to "reducing the risk [to the mission] by increasing the overall acceptance of your presence and work" (Van Brabant 2000: 11). Protection refers to "reducing the vulnerability with protective measures", such as increasing physical security, imposing curfews, etc., while deterrence refers to "deterring the threat with a counter-threat", such as the use of armed guards or working alongside military personnel (ibid.: 11). Each strategy includes benefits and costs, and will be more or less appropriate in different environments. Traditionally, humanitarian actors have positioned themselves, sometimes intentionally, sometimes through default, on the acceptance point of the triangle. Among some groups, such as MSF, this continues to be the policy line (although in practice this is not always the case).

The last decade has seen a definite movement towards protective and even defensive strategies of protection, most noticeably in the form of physical securitization. While the 1990s had seen an escalation of staff awareness of security matters, and widespread codification of staff and security issues, it was arguably not until the August 2003 bombing of the UN and ICRC offices in Baghdad that humanitarian workers truly felt that their mandates were no longer adequate protection against hostile forces, most notably al-Qaeda and their sympathizers.

The 2003 Baghdad bombing, which killed twenty-two UN staff and visitors and injured over 150 others, led to a dramatic restructuring of UN security, including the establishment of the UNDSS, which was an attempt to streamline the various reporting channels under a single framework for accountability (Independent Panel on the Safety and Security of UN Personnel in Iraq 2003). This led to an increased focus within the UN on security training for staff and further elaboration of MOSS and MORSS to ensure field office compliance with HQ directives. In 2005, an Optional Protocol was added to the aforementioned 1994 Convention, but only a handful of member states signed it.

Nor was the UN alone in its drive towards security. As mentioned, during this time most of the other agencies, including ECHO, DfID and the IFRC, produced comprehensive security manuals for their staff. In all these reports, staff and management are urged to undertake security assessments and to take appropriate measures to mitigate risk and tighten their security arrangements (National Audit Office 2008).

Discussions of *physical* security also became more prominent. For example, ECHO's *Generic Security Guide* (European Commission Humanitarian Aid Office 2004a) stresses the importance of the physical security of offices and warehouses, and includes as its first Annex "Buildings and security". This is a checklist of physical security details that encourage staff to ensure that the walls of their buildings, including accommodation, are "strong enough to withstand likely threats" and to check whether the windows are barred (ibid.: 60).

With the August 2008 bombing of the Algiers UN building, building security jumped to the top of the agenda. According to the 2008 report by the Independent Panel on Safety and Security of UN Personnel and Premises Worldwide, "[i]f any single issue is now foremost in the minds of DOs it is the issue of safe office space" (Brahimi 2008: 55).

> DOs interviewed by the Panel reported spending a good deal of staff time on visits to possible alternative locations, chasing prime locations in expensive cities with a thriving real estate market, and trying, in the meantime, to negotiate improvement of perimeter security with the host government. (Ibid.: 55)

The report recommends that support is provided to field offices to "obtain technical advice and support to determine how to accept an imperfect location and improve it to an acceptable level of perimeter integrity" (ibid.: 55). Both the Brahimi report and the 2003 Independent Panel on Iraq identify the need for increased access to blast engineering expertise within DSS (ibid.: 56) and for "qualified professional expertise in the setting up of protective measures, such as the perimeter wall" (Independent Panel on the Safety and Security of UN Personnel in Iraq 2003: 24).

It is, of course, possible to see the recent decrease of international staff fatalities as a *result* of the increased security measures.

At first glance, this is supported by Stoddard et al.'s (2009) findings, which show that while the death rates of international UN
workers have gone down, those of international NGO workers
have gone up. This implies that those organizations with more
money to spend on securitization and training (the UN) are
better able to protect their staff compared to the less well-funded
NGOs. However, before drawing this conclusion, several factors
need to be considered.

First, NGOs is a very broad category, ranging in scale from
INGOs like Oxfam and CARE to very small, new and often
poorly equipped organizations. The latter will suffer from a lower
quality of information and less experienced staff. In other words,
even if there were no physical securitization, NGOs would be at
a disadvantage vis-à-vis the UN regarding the safety of their staff
from general criminal activity.

Secondly, as discussed, while there have been many and repeated attempts to increase the quality and scope of field security,
the physical results are often quite far removed from the bureaucratic rhetoric. For example, in their analysis of the problems that
had led to the bombing of the UN in Algiers, the Independent
Panel on the Safety and Security of UN Personnel and Premises
Worldwide notes,

> the Panel found a wealth of excellent recommendations in earlier
> reports and has benefited from the letter and the spirit of many
> of them during its work ... The Panel was also impressed by the
> amount of attention give to security by all parts of the United
> Nations: Member States, in particular through the General
> Assembly, the Secretary-General and several Departments in
> the Secretariat, Agencies, Funds, and Programmes, and Staff
> Unions. Much of this work has been very thorough and creative.
> *But it was surprising that many of those recommendations – even
> some that had been repeated again and again – have not been fully
> implemented over the years.* (Brahimi 2008: 31, emphasis added)

Nor is this observation restricted to the cases of Algiers and

Iraq. The high staff turnover of many of these organizations, and other factors such as unwieldy and contradictory bureaucracies (Easterly 2002), means that many of the security recommendations fail to materialize in any coherent manner. What is perhaps more remarkable than the two recent attacks on UN (and Red Cross, in the case of Algiers) premises is the general absence of attacks given the poor quality of any real security displayed by the majority of UN premises.

Thirdly, the trend of increased securitization did not emerge historically from the perception of staff insecurity. As shown by the discussions of the two trends, they occur almost in parallel. Further study of a wide range of international organizations would be required in order to establish with certainty which trend came first. However, within the context of the UN, the introduction of the security tools of the MAIP and MOSS/MORSS occurred in the early 1990s, prior to the widespread fear of attack.

Finally, a closer look at the location and tactics of many of the attacks is revealing with regard to the role played by physical security. Stoddard et al. found that the largest group of victims were truck drivers (2009: 3), an observation supported by Fast's work, which found that NGOs responsible for distributing material aid were definitely made more insecure by their actions (Fast 2007: 141). Stoddard et al. also found that the most frequently deployed tactic was kidnapping, which increased by 350 per cent between 2006 and 2008. Stoddard et al. emphasize that "[t]he most dangerous location for aid workers in 2006–2008 remained the road, with ambushes (including carjacking, banditry and other vehicle-based attacks) by far the most common context for violence" (Stoddard et al. 2009: 5).

These observations are important in two ways. They draw into question the widespread assumption that (the perception of) increased targeting is political; that it is linked to wider anti-Western trends and possibly to the 'global war on terror'. For example, despite the observation that the majority of attacks involved the targeting of truck drivers or the kidnapping of staff for ransom,

Stoddard et al. stress the political motives behind the observed overall rise in attacks. According to their data (of incidents whose motive could be determined), politically motivated incidents rose from 29 per cent in 2003 to 49 per cent in 2008 (ibid.: 5). However, Buchanan and Muggah's findings imply that the major factor behind the increased perception of insecurity among aid workers is the prevalence of civilians with small arms and light weapons and the increase in general criminality and lawlessness in the areas in which humanitarians are working (a point to be returned to in the conclusion) (Buchanan and Muggah 2005). The second way the targeting of mobile vehicles is important involves how it is interpreted by humanitarian staff in the field.

If the most dangerous place is on the roads, away from the known spaces of the neighbourhood, the safety of the office, then the most important safety technique becomes the enclave. The last part of this chapter examines the increased trend of enclavism in humanitarian work, towards the form (and metaphor) of the humanitarian compound. Building on Chapter 1, it will examine how the trend towards 'compoundization' is being reinforced through recent developments in aid practice.

The compound as the new archetype of humanitarianism

A familiar material aspect of international humanitarian assistance has become the walled and gated compound: an enclosure containing an assortment of offices, storage, medical and sometimes living and leisure facilities. This can be seen most clearly in countries that are perceived to be highly insecure (often Phases Two through Five). It is highly securitized and may have an extra buffer zone or checkpoint. There may be watchtowers on the walls where guards can be located. It can also have other oversight mechanisms such as security cameras or barbed wire on top of the walls. Compounds secure the vehicles, materials and delivery systems that are used to interact with the target beneficiaries and provide communications networks when others have been destroyed or are not working. Scale will be determined by the size and the mandate of the organization in question. For example, the World Food Programme and UNHCR require space to store the vehicles used for distribution and the items slated for distribution. This requires large warehouses, water and petrol storage facilities, and even hangars, while programmes that are involved in so-called soft projects such as training and capacity-building need less space. The level of required security will determine the degree of physical fortification of the compound as well as the degree of mobility and concentration of internationals' spheres of activity.

If a country is highly insecure, or is generally lacking in basic amenities, it is more likely that living quarters and offices will be integrated. From the perspective of an organization, it is necessary to provide an environment in which staff are able to carry out their tasks at a speed and level of efficiency required by their donor governments and funding agencies. This means high-speed communications systems and a common working language. In a development context, it may also be required for hygiene standards to be maintained at a level where foreign nationals are able to function and remain healthy. Food and water may be flown in or provided to a standard that reduces exposure to local pathogens and meets country-of-origin standards. Power generation facilities will also be required in most developing contexts. This is not to suggest that the archetype of the 'humanitarian compound' exists in all humanitarian contexts. However, increased physical securitization is becoming the default position for humanitarian work in the field.

It is worth noting that to talk of the international community as a homogeneous entity is itself an abstraction. Within the aid community there exists, in many large-scale reconstruction sites, a 'tiering of aid', as one interviewee described it, between the multilateral organizations, INGOs, and small-scale NGOs. Often each of these three groups creates its own spheres of dialogue and interaction, functionally separate from one another. However, within the context of securitization, this tiering serves only to reinforce the overall theme of exceptionalism, as the more 'elite' or prominent the international body, the higher the likelihood that it will have resources to invest in securitization, mobility and links to the space of origin. For these reasons, the next section will use the UN as the benchmark of securitization trends and look at four interrelated developments in physical securitization which support this claim: the drive towards "One Office"; the move towards integrated missions; the tendency to co-locate development programme premises with either diplomatic or military operations; and the increased use of "remote management" in projects. Each will be examined in turn.

The move towards One UN at the country level has set out One Office as a key feature of the programme, which is meant to streamline and consolidate the UN's work in the field (and overall). This includes a move towards joint premises and "a common security infrastructure" (United Nations 2006a: 13). A major plank of the strategy is the establishment of a UN House in several pilot countries which brings together the various funds, agencies and programmes working in a country in a single premises. While many different agencies will often be simultaneously present in a country at one time, they may be working out of different offices. *Deliver as One* and subsequent internal documents recommend the retrofitting of existing premises where possible. Where this is not possible, a DBO or DBOT strategy is being recommended (UN Development Group 2008b, a). DBO stands for design-build-operate and DBOT stands for design-build-operate-transfer. As defined on the UN House/UN Common Premises Programme website:

> A developer/financer will: 'Design' and 'Build' a building in accordance with UN specifications including security requirements, then 'Operate' and maintain the premises for a defined number of years, collecting rent from the UN Agencies. Finally, the developer may 'Transfer' the title or ownership of the building to the UN once costs are amortized. After the 'Transfer', the Agencies will no longer pay rent. (UN Development Group n.d.)

This implies that DBOs will need to be built by external contractors to certain specifications, particularly with regard to security.

As late as the Brahimi report (2008), the precise physical security specifications of field offices were left up to individual, country-based DSS officers. They in turn based their decisions on the Strategic Risk Assessments and the current security phase level. However, there appear to be moves towards standardization of physical security specifications both through default and design. For example, although MOSS directives are broad enough that specific engineering requirements were not included, the limited number of contractors and experts who are available means that similar design solutions will be repeated across an organization. In the case of security, the people hired tend to be from similar, often military, backgrounds owing to an absence of alternatively qualified candidates. The institutional approach of most humanitarian organizations with a significant field presence is to rely heavily on 'lessons learned' or 'best practice' for organizational development or strategizing, using an approach in a new context which has been seen to succeed in others.

All of these factors may contribute to a material and visual homogenization of the built environment of the UN and to the inclusion of subtly politicized assumptions regarding entitlements and access. For example, in their guidelines on "Standard Office Space", the UN Joint Inspection Unit offer space requirements for UN staff according to different grades. Staff of all grades are allocated 120 square feet per person, while general service staff are to be allocated between 60 and 90 square feet depending on function. This makes sense given that general service staff will not generally require space to greet visitors (i.e. they require less office space). However, the grades also obscure an implicit national/international divide as general service staff are almost always national staff, while the other listed grades are by definition international, with the exception of national professional-grade staff.

A second 'compound' tendency is illustrated by the movement

within the UN towards integrated missions. Originally developed for Kosovo in 1999, these have since been undertaken in a variety of contexts, including Timor Leste, Sierra Leone, Afghanistan, Liberia, the DRC, Burundi, Haiti, Iraq, Côte d'Ivoire and Sudan (Eide et al. 2005). The idea was initially put forward in the 1997 SG's report on *Renewing the United Nations* (UN Secretary General 1997) in an attempt to bring together the humanitarian, development and peacekeeping obligations of the various UN bodies, agencies, programmes and funds in a particular location. The report emphasized that "the reform process is designed to maintain and reinforce the distinctive nature of UN entities while seeking to facilitate their functioning in a more unified, cooperative and coherent framework as members of the United Nations family" (ibid.: para. 149).

Given that many UN peacekeeping missions are hybrid missions, integration may also be an attempt to bring together other cooperating organizations such as the African Union, the European Union, NATO or the OSCE. In the spirit of cooperation and transparency, the process seeks to integrate all relevant actors and provide mechanisms by which NGOs and other bodies may also become involved in the planning and execution aspects of a response.

Since many of the policy discussions surrounding integrated missions concentrate on the reporting and communication mechanisms (Brahimi 2000; United Nations 2006b), the physical implications of integration are often overlooked. In circumstances where there is an integrated mission, the physical requirements of a peacekeeping mission or peace support operation are such that they command a large material and spatial presence. This will take the form of a base and will be accompanied by the military aspects of a mission, such as armoured personnel carriers, barracks, etc. Given the size of the military component and its visually striking characteristics, such as high walls, guarded access points and surveillance towers, it tends to dominate the surrounding landscape. For example, in the case of the UNAMID mission in Darfur, each regional peace support operation is based in large, integrated compounds that have colloquially been named 'super-camps' by staff. The new super-camps are purpose-built compounds that contain both the peacekeeping operations and the civilian components of the UN operations. While in some cases the civilian component is restricted to Department for Peacekeeping Operations (DPKO) staff, there is talk of bringing together peacekeeping with humanitarian and development funds and agencies (Harmer 2008; Eide et al. 2005).

This physical rapprochement of the military/political and humanitarian sides of the UN has not been without its critics (Harmer 2008). For example, according to the Brahimi report, the integration of humanitarian programmes and activities with peacekeeping missions may necessitate "security arrangements that do not seek acceptance from local communities" (Brahimi 2008: 72). More generally, some humanitarians believe that the integration of the various functions of the UN compromises the neutrality of the humanitarian mandate, and in turn puts in jeopardy both their ability to deliver and the security of their staff and beneficiaries. The evidence is still too scanty to draw firm conclusions on whether this is the case. However, the process of integration can be seen as a clear example of the increased enclosure, or compounding, of the international community in the field.

A third tendency is the co-location of humanitarian workers with their associated governments. For example, in eleven of fifteen DfID offices in insecure countries the offices are now co-located with the Foreign and Commonwealth Office (National Audit Office 2008). When the offices have not been co-located as a purpose-built complex, the move is often the result of a security incident such as one that occurred to DfID staff in Kinshasha, in 2007, which led to DfID relocating "all staff to a residential area near the Embassy" (ibid.: 33).

While this co-locating of bilateral development agencies with their associated embassies is neither new nor surprising, given the increased securitization of many overseas building assets, the co-location has also meant co-securitization. In the DfID Kinshasa example, DfID now pays for half of all security costs for the joint compound, these costs being a major component. Between 2005 and 2007 DfID's security contribution to the joint premises rose from £116,000 to nearly £575,000, excluding staff accommodation (ibid.: 44). This reflects the dramatic increases in financial resources being directed towards material security of humanitarian field operations, particularly in the context of co-location.

In the case of USAID, the overseas development arm of the US government, security upgrades have led to many of their offices becoming literally barricaded from the populations they are supposed to be assisting. In Rwanda in 2004, meetings on explicitly and exclusively development issues were held within a windowless, bombproof room: a bunker. Even getting to the meeting required going through an extensive security check of your body and possessions, including a metal detector. In other locations, such as in Bishkek, Kyrgyzstan, in order to comply with spatial requirements such as being set back from major traffic arteries, the embassy may be built on a greenfield site, outside of the city centre, in places reachable only by car and in effect inaccessible to the majority of the target beneficiaries.

A final tendency is the increasing trend towards remote management in humanitarian aid work as a result of the (perceived) increase in the targeting of humanitarian workers, leading to decreased access and a move towards more protective and defensive engagement strategies, as defined by Van Brabant (2000). "Access" refers to the ability of aid workers to reach citizens in need. It may be limited by increased insecurity, lack of funds for security measures, or externally imposed restrictions by governments or other groups. Over the last twenty years, there has been an increased perception among aid workers that access has declined, although according to Stoddard et al. this is not necessarily supported statistically (2006). Regardless, this perception has resulted in the increased use of remote management techniques for projects.

Stoddard et al. describe "remote management" as all projects which use "arm's length" modalities "to ensure that aid continues to reach the beneficiary population despite security or access constraints" (ibid.: 38). Techniques include direct programming and management from a remote location; the devolution of decision-making authority to local staff; the turnover of project implementation responsibilities to a local NGO; the handing over of a project to government or a local partner; or "fee for service" arrangements whereby a private firm is paid to undertake basic provision (ibid.: 39). Stoddard et al. divide the remote approaches into two basic types: off-site programming, where the international staff are physically located at a distance, but manage the project on an ongoing basis either through sorties or local partners; and "one-off operations", which they describe as "hit and run" or "give and go" (ibid.: 38). They stress that remote project management is not new, and has been used in different formulations for decades. Examples include the experience of "long arm programming" used by agencies in Somalia in the early 1990s; the use of "aid on the run" by Operation Lifeline Sudan in Southern Sudan in the 1990s; and, as early as 1951, its use by Oxfam GB in Bihar India (ibid.: 38). However, according to one of the few comprehensive analyses of the phenomenon, because it is seen largely as a strategy of last resort, and therefore deployed in an ad hoc manner, there is a lack of systematic documentation on the various types of approaches and almost no evidence of evaluations or post hoc assessments (ibid.).

The rationales are numerous, including the faulty assumption that local staff face lower risks than internationals. Arguably, it is also because local staff are easier to blame. For example, in DfID's 2008 report on *Operating in Insecure Environments*, the assertion that "[w]eak partner capacity has undermined effectiveness in some insecure countries" (National Audit Office 2008: 6) was repeatedly cited as a key explanation for failure in these contexts. Despite the well-documented lack of post-crisis human capacity in post-crisis contexts, the report implied that this failure was the result of intentional mismanagement, fraud or negligence on the part of local counterparts. Contradicting these claims, oral evidence taken before the Committee of Public Accounts, UK, in November 2008 found that the success rates of DfID projects in fragile versus non-fragile states were roughly the same (House of Commons 2009). In summary, while the use of remote control programming has generally been restricted to non-permissive environments, its usage seems to be increasing across the development spectrum and contributing to a culture of enclosure among international humanitarian workers.

Conclusion

An examination of the major changes in field security identifies a causal relationship whereby major policy changes occur as a result of violent events. For example, in the case of the USA, following the Kenya and Tanzania bombings in 1998, the US State Department created the Bureau of Overseas Building Operations (OBO): "[i]n concert with other State Department bureaus, foreign affairs agencies and Congress, OBO sets worldwide priorities for the design, construction, acquisition, maintenance, use and sale of real properties and the use of sales proceeds" (US Department of State n.d.).

Through the development of their Long Range Overseas Building Plan, OBO were responsible for the massive security upgrades of US embassies worldwide (Weinberger 2007), which have included the construction of seven-foot-high steel periphery fences, additional entry screening procedures, and increased setback (Leapman 2004). Where existing locations do not permit the creation of additional setback, public roads and sidewalks may be blocked off with concrete barricades. For example, in London, UK, this required the installation of bollards in Upper Brook Street and Upper Grosvenor Street. Where existing embassies cannot be upgraded, entirely new compounds have been created in locations that could be more easily secured (such as the aforementioned complex in Bishkek). In the case of the

UN, the creation of DSS was in response to the bombing of the UN building in Baghdad, and the Algiers bombing led to further recommendations for building security, including perimeter upgrades and an increased focus on blast-resistant engineering and building. As these regulations are rolled out across a range of countries, they physically influence the way in which other countries operate, reinforcing the perception that all aid workers are at risk, not only those located in high-risk areas.

The relationship between one-off, high-profile targeting of humanitarian assets and institutional changes to security deserves closer scrutiny. A survey of the reports and interviews with humanitarian personnel indicates the tendency for a high-profile occurrence to generate an immediate flurry of activity, including investigative missions, reports and recommendations, but that eventually it all goes back to 'business as normal' (Brahimi 2008; Independent Panel on the Safety and Security of UN Personnel in Iraq 2003; and interviews). However, another reading of the changes to physical security implies a different trajectory.

As the institutional memory of humanitarian organizations has been notoriously poor and staff turnover very high, the perception of what is normal is often highly subjective and changeable. An 'old timer' may be someone who has worked in the industry for over five years: a short time in any other field. It is possible that operational changes to the physical environment have not been well documented and have occurred at a different pace to the rapid turnover. For example, the first recorded instance of the phrase "United Nations compound"[2] being used in a field context in the English-language press was in a news report by Thomas Friedman for the *New York Times* in 1984.[3] He was reporting

---

2 A similar search for "Red Cross" and "compound" reveals that its earliest use is in a *New York Times* newswire on 7 June 1975 (New York Times 1975). A Lexis-Nexis search for the phrase "UN compound" (or "United Nations compound") displayed 12,159 instances of the phrase post-1990 while prior to 1990 there were only forty-four recorded instances.

3 In October 1982, Jim Anderson referred to the UN premises in New York as the UN Compound (Anderson 1982).

on the UN-held talks between the Israelis and the Lebanese in Naqura, Lebanon, and devotes an entire paragraph to describing the built environment where the talks were held.

> It was in a prefabricated building made of corrugated iron at the headquarters of the United Nations Interim Force in Lebanon, in Naqura ... The meeting room was surrounded by fresh coils of barbed wire and dozens of guards wearing blue berets. Soldiers from the nine-nation United Nations force were posted on rooftops. Israeli troopers patrolled the roads outside the United Nations compound, and an Israeli patrol boat cruised up and down the nearby coast. (Friedman 1984)

While there is no mention of this occurrence in contemporary discussions of humanitarian security, the timing is worth noting because it occurred a little over a year after the first use of suicide bombs (in the current understanding) against US targets: in April and October 1983. That Friedman would have begun to include descriptions of UN defensive architecture for the first time soon after does raise questions as to the role that high-profile incidents have played in the increased securitization of humanitarian premises, only to be forgotten as a contributing force.

Stoddard et al. (2006) refer to this cyclical phenomenon as a "security spiral". The term describes a situation where a particular violent incident drives the humanitarian community towards a marked increase in physical and deterrent approaches and away from access-oriented approaches. Once acclimatized to more preventive and deterrent approaches, staff begin to lose touch with their beneficiaries, losing the "acceptance" of the community. They then adopt ever more defensive methods, which in turn decreases the community's "acceptance" still further (Van Brabant 2000).

An additional repercussion results from the networked nature of many humanitarian organizations that operate in a variety of countries. A security incident that occurs in one country will affect the security recommendations and restrictions in other countries. This has already been identified in the restructuring of the security systems and institutional procedures as a result of the 2003 and 2007 UN bombings in Iraq and Algiers. In the case of the USA, the August 1998 bombings of the US embassy in Beirut, and later the US embassies in Dar es Salaam, Tanzania, and Nairobi, Kenya, can be seen to have decisively influenced the material presence of the USA across the globe for years after.

This chapter has traced the recent trend towards increased physical securitization of humanitarian field staff by their respective organizations. It demonstrated that this trend has dovetailed with the increased perception of insecurity on the part of humanitarians worldwide. Establishing the causal relationship is less important than recognizing the tendency and determining the potential impact. That an increasing number of humanitarians are operating within a physically circumscribed space from which they are analysing, projecting and managing aid projects needs to be recognized not only for its impact on the success or failure of a particular project but also how it shapes the entire humanitarian imaginary and the view both of 'ourselves' and the other.

Chapter 3 will engage with the theoretical underpinnings of the proposition that the material environment can be understood to have agency or causality. It explores two questions that have been raised by this chapter: first, what is the relationship between the increased enclosure and securitization of aid workers in the field and their perceptions of risk? The second question is: what are the broader effects of the built environments of aid workers?

3 | HOW THE BUILT ENVIRONMENT SHAPES
HUMANITARIAN INTERVENTION

In the security manuals and policy recommendations for field staff, there is the implicit recognition that the built environment has a degree of agency. For example, aid workers are told not to live in luxurious houses as it may attract resentment from local populations: "[i]f local people perceive that humanitarian staff live in luxury, paying excessive rents on unnecessarily lavish accommodation, not only will it damage the organisation's reputation but it may lead to greater insecurity for its staff, as local opinion turns against them" (European Commission Humanitarian Aid Office 2004a: 19).

Similarly, Van Brabant is clear that, as part of an ideal acceptance strategy, material and spatial considerations are important. He writes that the location of a meeting may be important in forging positive relationships with the local community: "[s]ummoning local elders to your office, for example, conveys a different message from going to see them in their own environment" (Van Brabant 2000: 63). In his section on "Implicit Messages" he asks the reader to:

> consider the image that is projected by the use of mobile
> phones and VHF radios, the new 4-wheel drive vehicles with
> air conditioning and tall radio antennae, uniformed guards at
> compound gates, large desks of finished hardwood with two
> telephones and a secretary in attendance. Well organized, well
> protected, but well accepted? (Ibid.: 64)

Another example of the general sense that the built environment is significant in shaping social interactions can be seen in the lead-up to the 2003 bombing of the UN premises in Baghdad. According to the Independent Panel on the Safety and Security of UN Personnel in Iraq,

> To enhance the protection of the Canal Hotel compound, United States military personnel established an observation outpost on the roof of the hotel and placed a five-ton truck to block access to a service road that runs parallel to the western perimeter wall of the Canal Hotel compound ... *UN senior management was uneasy with this highly visible military presence ... [and] asked the Coalition Forces to withdraw their heavy equipment from the front of the compound, dismantle the observation post on the roof top of the building and remove the obstacle on the access road because the United Nations did not own the property.* (Independent Panel on the Safety and Security of UN Personnel in Iraq 2003: 11, emphasis added)

Here is an explicit acknowledgement that the built environment is significant in building relationships with local communities and that an over-reliance on physical security and deterrent approaches is counter-productive to the overall aim of assisting a population (Brahimi 2008; Stoddard et al. 2006). A similar line of reasoning was evoked more generally during the Iraq war when the USA's enclosure within the fortified green zone was considered a metaphor for their inability to win Iraqi 'hearts and minds' (Chandrasekaran 2006).

The architectural redesign of US embassies has also been the subject of significant negative commentary; the high modernist, slate-grey buildings drawing derogatory comparisons with prisons and fortresses (Leapman 2004). In his 2009 article, Jonathan Glancey considered the current trend in American embassy building as an "architecture of failed diplomacy" (Glancey 2009). He argues that embassies should balance functional concerns such as security with a cultural sensitivity for their surrounding location. But in all these arguments, the precise relationship between buildings and their contribution to insecurity remains unclear.

Often multiple logics are deployed simultaneously to support the intuition that, somehow, buildings matter.

This chapter investigates the relationship between the built environment and people with reference to material and spatial theory. It proposes that in order to understand the impact of the built environment in humanitarian intervention two reciprocal dynamics need to be considered: the way in which buildings structure social interaction and simultaneously how buildings come to embody social structures. While the last chapter concentrated on the physical form of the compound, this chapter examines how a bounded auxiliary space is created from the everyday performances and practices of the international community in the field. The chapter investigates the nature of this space and considers what its impact is on its 'inhabitants' through comparison with UK and US gated communities.

The second part of the chapter brings these two dynamics together by looking at how the privileging of certain humanitarian built forms structures and defines the humanitarian landscape. It does this through two case studies: the sports utility vehicle (SUV) and the so-called grand hotel, two dominant material tropes of the humanitarian experience in the field. Through these case studies, the chapter concludes that the built environment contributes to the maintenance of distinct spatial epistemologies and reinforces the divide between donor and beneficiary. This divide is not limited to the strict form of the humanitarian compound, but exists throughout the humanitarian landscape.

How the material matters: a framework for analysis

The use of the built environment to control human action is one of the fundamental tenets of urban planning and, more recently, of urban crime control (Minton 2009). It also underlies the improvements to humanitarian building security, as discussed in the preceding chapter. The intention of these security upgrades is to ensure the separation of two groups of people – the people who support a given humanitarian operation and those who pose a security threat. It rests on the assumption that these groups are static, identifiable and containable. This approach can be seen in the use of the security barrier to restrict Palestinian movement between the occupied Palestinian territories and Israel (Weizman 2007) or in the design of a classic prison, which relies on material restraints to ensure the restriction of prisoners' movements.

The uniting feature of this type of material control is that it is the planned outcome of human agency. The control is intentional and the built environment inviolable. But there are also unintended outcomes of spatial planning decisions that seek to curtail or control human movements. Theorists as distinct as Newman (2003) and Jacobs (2000) have observed the unintended impacts that spatial design has on community security through the various ways in which it allows its users to see, occupy and take ownership of their environments. By shaping patterns of behaviour, the built environment changes behaviour by making certain options more or less efficient, desirable, noticeable or palatable. Work on spatial syntax argues that the layout of buildings will influence all manner of human behaviour, from the efficiency of a daily routine; to the types and frequencies of interaction with other people and things; to the scenes and landscapes that are observed (Dovey 1999; Hillier and Rooksby 2002). While such observations are common to urban planners, humanitarians rarely take them into consideration in a conscious manner. But through the designation of certain areas of a city as secure, for example, a higher number and frequency of aid workers will be attracted to these areas' rental properties, restaurants, bars and services. Not only will this potentially reshape the city, but for the aid workers, where they go and how they travel through it will constitute their experience of that place. In the terminology of the social theorist Henri Lefebvre, these trajectories and places will structure the aid worker's *perceived space* and *lived space* (Lefebvre 1991).

Perceived space (or spatial practice) is the space of everydayness. It is how a place is commonly used in routine existence and contains the "routes and networks which link up the places set aside for work, 'private' life and leisure" (ibid.: 38). Lived space (or representational space) is the space of "the imagination which has been kept alive and accessible by the arts and literature" (Shields 2004: 210). It is

> space as *lived* through its associated images and symbols, and hence the space of 'inhabitants' and 'users' ... This is the dominated – and hence passively experienced – space which the imagination seeks to change and appropriate. It overlays physical space, making symbolic use of its objects. (Lefebvre 1991: 39)

These two spaces are connected, trilectically, to a third space: conceived space (or representations of space).[1] This is "conceptualised space, the space of scientists, planners, urbanists, technocratic subdividers and social engineers ... all of whom identify what is lived and what is perceived with what is conceived" (ibid.: 38) and is analogous to what I have been calling, in the context of humanitarian intervention, the humanitarian imaginary.

Applying Lefebvre's insights to the European Commission's advice to staff on "relations with local people" demonstrates that quotidian humanitarian practice severely limits the aid worker's exposure to local surroundings and creates a highly biased map of his/her environment. They advise managers and staff to "spend a considerable proportion of their time meeting and talking with a representative variety of local people" as part of an effective security strategy (European Commission Humanitarian Aid Office 2004a: 21). They go on to stress the importance of

> random visits to homes in a variety of geographical areas ...; visiting people living away from major towns and away from major roads. (There is a tendency for busy humanitarian staff to visit people near easily accessible towns and routes far more

---

1 Most theorists consider lived space to be the 'third' space (Soja 1996; Shields 1999, 2004; Saco 1998). My designation of it as second space is purely within the rhetorical context of my argument.

than those in areas off the beaten track); ... visiting areas inaccessible to vehicles, on foot if necessary. (Ibid.: 21)

The statement implies that even in the context of unsecurit-
ized, normal, everyday humanitarian practice, spatial patterns,
routines and rituals occur which influence the way in which the
aid worker sees and understands his/her environment. It is part
of the habitus of aid work.

Pierre Bourdieu pioneered the concept of habitus as a way of
getting beyond the problem of structure versus individual agency.
Bourdieu himself defines habitus as

> systems of durable, transposable dispositions, structured struc-
> tures predisposed to function as structuring structures, that
> is, as principles which generate and organisational practices
> and representations that can be objectively adapted to their
> outcomes without presupposing a conscious aiming at ends
> or an express mastery of the operations necessary in order to
> attain them. (Bourdieu 1990: 53)

Painter elucidates this famous definition by describing habitus as

> the mediating link between objective social structures and
> individual action and refers to the embodiment in individual
> actors of systems of social norms, understandings and patterns
> of behaviour, which, while not wholly determining action ... do
> ensure that individuals are more disposed to act in some ways
> than others. (Painter 2000: 242)

Habitus is a notoriously slippery concept (Hillier and Rooksby
2002). For the purposes of this discussion, the most important
element to note is that it questions the privileging of human
agency over material form. The place(s) surrounding the individual need to be considered for how they structure the thoughts,
actions, dispositions and preferences of individuals and, in turn,
attention needs to be given to how surroundings can be changed

through individual action (Bourdieu 1984). Bourdieu claims to transcend "the dualism between explanations that attribute social change and social reproduction to certain overarching structures and theorisations that privilege individual subjective intention or experience" (Bridge 2004: 59). In a similar vein, Giddens' structuration theory conceives physical place and the actions of the individual as "simultaneously determinant and mutually recursive rather than a simplistic dualism of opposing forces" (Warf 2004: 132; Giddens 1984, 1993, 1995). In both cases, there is no first instance of action, but a mutually constitutive relationship between the material environment and the individual.

More recently, drawing on work in the philosophy of science (Stengers 2000, 1997) and post-structural philosophy (Deleuze and Guattari 2004), Latour has also attacked the dualism of structure and agency, although from a more radical perspective. He claims that binary distinctions of people and things, of nature and society, serve only to obscure the underlying assemblages and networks which distribute power not only from human subjects to things but also in reverse (Latour 1993; Laurier 2004). According to Latour (1993), the distinction between things and people – the world of objects and the social world – has never existed. He urges us to resist the modern urge to superimpose this artificial distinction upon lived experience, and to recognize the co-constitutive relationship between human and non-human actors. Unlike the previous theorists, Latour does not espouse a Marxist underpinning, but rather positions himself in the anti-foundationalist tradition of Bergson (1988), James (James and Burkhardt 1981) and Whitehead (1956; Whitehead and Frye 1960).

The application of the insights of these theorists to humanitarian intervention reveals the urgent need to consider the co-constitutive relations between aid workers and their built environments. The next section of this chapter will examine this spatial dimension in more depth, first by looking at the spaces that aid workers create; secondly by examining the impact that these spaces have on those around them; and finally by considering the reciprocal impact of the spaces on the aid workers themselves.

Auxiliary space

The previous chapters have advanced the idea that through spatial practice in the field a distinct space is created that is offset from its immediate environment. Chapter 2 explored how the physical environment contributes to the maintenance of this space. But the argument that is being advanced is that there is a lived and perceived space of the field that exceeds the simple built form of enclosure such as the compound. This section both elucidates the qualities of such a space and explores how it might be constructed.

The term auxiliary space is evocative of the auxiliary forces of a Roman army (see Duncan-Jones 1990; Luttwak 1976; Holder 1980; Goldsworthy and Keegan 2000; Voegelin and Franz 2000). These largely volunteer forces were brought together from across the Roman Empire, in flexible groupings, to establish outposts of empire. Similarly, international humanitarian workers are drawn from a wide range of locations and brought together in a foreign land to promote shared values and cosmopolitan norms. While differing in their approach and personal relationship to the particular location, like auxiliary forces, aid workers all have the shared objective of assisting and supporting a particular strategic goal. They are also fluid: moving frequently from one theatre of response to the next. Without pushing the analogy too far, it is useful in illuminating a key spatial aspect of international aid workers in the field. Even when they are not explicitly a spatially constrained group, boundaries are formed which create and maintain divisions between various groups.

Randall Collins investigates how lifestyle rituals, which he defines as "natural rituals in the middle ground between formal ceremonial and low key unfocused social encounters" (Collins 2004: 297), create social boundaries which map out one group of individuals from another (also Tilly 2005; Nexon 2009). As applied to the concept of auxiliary space, it is plausible that the everyday lived experience of being part of the humanitarian community in the field creates and maintains social boundaries, which separate it, as a group, from the local community. In particular the principles of time, networks, rituals and velocity play key structuring roles.

An essential constitutive aspect of auxiliary space is the role that differential understandings of time play in its creation and maintenance, particularly when compared to its immediate physical surroundings. The temporal structure of the in-country workday, including holidays and working hours, for example, will be strongly influenced by the country of origin. Local customs such as prayer and fasting may come into conflict with competing temporal demands, such as fiscal and reporting deadlines from headquarters. The length of time that staff spend in a country also sets them apart from the local community. Much of the work carried out by an organization may be done by staff who come for either very short periods as consultants (a few days or weeks), or for slightly longer, but still temporary, assignments of six months to two years. To remain in a country longer than a few years is unusual in most agencies and particularly so in the context of emergency relief and reconstruction. The demand for such skills is high and workers are often quickly moved on to the next emergency. The significance of this is recognized by the agencies themselves. As described by DfID in a 2008 report,

> [b]ecause of the hardships and the stress involved, the contract length of postings varies between countries. In Iraq and Afghanistan, the standard initial length of a posting is 6 and 12 months respectively whilst for secure countries it is often 36 months. Shorter contracts are important to safeguard the welfare of DFID staff but the resultant staff turnover needs to be managed well if it is not to be harmful to DFID's development efforts. Our country survey found that 40 percent of teams believed that the standard length of overseas posting in their country was not long enough to promote staff development or

to operate most effectively. Developing country officials and DFID staff also reported that staff turnover has been disruptive to relationships with key stakeholders and contributed to a loss of institutional memory. (National Audit Office 2008: 3.8)

The relationship between constructions of space and understandings of time were addressed by the spatial theorists. Lefebvre proposed the idea of moments as the fundamental building blocks of affective, and ultimately spatial, experience, and later was intrigued by ideas of rhythm in everyday life (Lefebvre 2008, 2004; on the relation between time and spatiality, see also Kern 1983).

More recently, the relationship between the construction of place and time differentials has been taken up by globalization theorists, who see increasing velocity as a defining characteristic of late-stage capitalism (or of a new age, depending on their ideological bent) (Castells 2000; Beck and Ritter 1992; Giddens 1990; Massey 2006; Sassen 2000; Virilio 2006). Without entering into a discussion of the diagnostic utility of these theories, their descriptive power of networked relationships, which operate according to differential time requirements vis-à-vis their physical surroundings, is applicable to spaces of contemporary humanitarianism. Duffield has referred to this linked geography of humanitarian spaces as the "aid archipelago" (2009). The fundamental quality of this archipelago is its disjuncture with the local physical environment: temporally, socioculturally and in terms of mobility. As an exemplar, consider the description of the American base at Guantánamo:

in some regards modelled on a vision of small town America: the base has a Starbucks and a McDonald's; it has four wind turbines that generate enough energy for it to remain self sufficient; it has a scouts club; a bar and two traffic lights, the national anthem plays every morning; Miss Teen USA has even paid a visit. Through this sort of cultivation of a particular vision of American life in the base the claims of the homeland are asserted over those other bodies stationed

there: the guards. ... Via the conduct of the American part
of its population, therefore, the claims of the homeland are
re-iterated through the presentation of a particular vision of
American life in the base. (Reid-Henry 2007)

While UN bases do not have the financial wherewithal to
contain a Starbucks, the rituals of the enclave exist nonetheless.
Clothing is Western, the language is usually that of the previous
colonial power, the electricity, water and sanitation systems, and
communications networks, are self-contained. Certain exceptional
behaviour is also permitted within the confine. This applies not
only to the ability to drink alcohol in Muslim countries, for
women and men to work together or for women to bare their
heads, but also to the categorization of workers into pay scales
and privilege according to their place of birth. Within the UN
system, those workers categorized as local will earn a fraction of
what their international colleagues earn.

The distinction between local and international categories
of staff goes beyond pay grade. It also dictates status within
the organization, and the length of time spent in a place. While
international contracts tend to be quite short, as previously examined, local employees may spend their entire lives working for
one organization in one place. With reference to security phases,
"locally recruited staff members may be evacuated from the duty
station in only the most exceptional cases in which their security
is endangered as a direct consequence of their employment by the
organization of the United Nations" (United Nations n.d.: 10).

The priorities of INGOs and multilaterals are also strategically
and temporally more closely linked to their respective places of
origin than to that of the host government (Collier 2007). As the
source and location of primary funding, it is in their 'space of
origin' – the country or institution in which they are ordinarily
based – that field missions are approved and results are assessed.
While there is a stress in the programmatic literature on downward
accountability, the key stakeholders remain those organizations

and individuals which fund the intervention. The creation and oversight of contracting, procurement and assessment all happen in the space of origin, as does the recruitment and retention of staff. Employees' career paths are tied to their points of origin, or, through short-term contracts, they are tied to particular events or disasters and may be leveraged into working in other, similar situations. Current debates and policy models at headquarters will inform strategy and approaches where programmatic operating procedures are often based on best practice or lessons learnt from previous reconstruction efforts, and may be implemented in a new situation with minimal adaptation to local circumstances. In the case of post-tsunami Aceh, the larger organizations flew in their crisis response teams from headquarters and quickly transported those field staff who had been working on similar crises (Telford and Cosgrove 2006).

This often rapid circulation of staff between humanitarian missions and the links to headquarters are what Duffield is referring to in his term archipelago. Such velocity is logical from the perspective of the organization. In order to accomplish a quick and efficient intervention an organization needs people who are experienced with the instruments and processes of humanitarian response. An organization cannot afford to reinvent all its procedures at every new disaster. From a political perspective, however, the reification of a mobile space of response means that certain assumptions regarding the appropriate process of response become increasingly difficult to challenge and will develop into the de facto way of doing things in the event of a humanitarian crisis. Within the context of the humanitarian compound, in Chapter 2, this tendency creates an environment where "you can forget where you are and sip your latte", as one NGO worker interviewee cynically quipped.

The impact on 'others'

So far, the discussion has primarily centred on how the space affects its primary inhabitants: the aid workers. It is also necessary, however, to consider how this space affects those around it, namely the intended beneficiaries and associated local community.

The impacts of restructuring a built environment are well documented, most notably for its counter-intuitive and unintended consequences. Scott (1998), Ferguson (2006) and Hodge (2007) all look at the way in which large-scale development schemes have backfired. In the area of humanitarian response, work by Edkins (2000b), Keen (2008), Duffield (2001), Chandler (2006) and Marriage (2006) has demonstrated how the implementation of humanitarian interventions produces unintended and often negative consequences for the very people for whom the intervention has been designed. While ideas of the reciprocal causal relationship between subjects and their environments have been common currency in other, more spatially oriented disciplines, development studies and practice have not, in the main, stressed the importance of spatial concerns. Doing so reveals a whole set of ways in which the presence of the international community inadvertently changes its space of intent. For example, a well-documented phenomenon upon the arrival of a peacekeeping mission is the nearly simultaneous arrival of prostitutes (Higate 2007; Higate and Henry 2004; Spees 2004; Whitworth 2004), which will change both the social structure and physical topography of a locale (for an examination of this phenomenon in historical perspective, see Gillem 2007). Most of a slim body of policy work that looks at the impact of (mostly peacekeeping) missions concentrates on the negative externalities that are introduced into the local economy, such as inflation and the 'brain drain' of highly qualified local staff into menial but highly paid jobs with international organizations (Carnahan et al. 2006). But other, more subtle effects occur as well.

In his work on everyday life, Michel de Certeau distinguishes between strategies and tactics. He calls a strategy:

> the calculation (or manipulation) of power relationships that
> becomes possible as soon as a subject with will and power
> (a business, an army, a city, a scientific institution) can be

isolated. It postulates a *place* that can be delimited as its *own* and serve as the base from which relations with an *exteriority* composed of targets or threats (customers or competitors, enemies, the country surrounding the city, objectives and objects of research, etc.) can be managed. As in management, every 'strategic' rationalisation seeks first of all to distinguish its 'own' place, that is, the place of its own power and will, from an 'environment.' A Cartesian attitude, if you wish: it is an effort to delimit one's own place in a world bewitched by the invisible powers of the Other. It is also the typical attitude of modern science, politics, and military strategy. (De Certeau 1988: 35–6)

Such a description could equally apply to the contemporary humanitarian field mission. But according to De Certeau, any strategy *necessarily entails* the appearance of tactics that will be deployed by those whom the strategy is intended to control, or, in the case of humanitarianism, to assist. These tactics are inseparable from any strategy, and will arise wherever one is imposed.

De Certeau describes a tactic as the exploitation of the gaps in a strategy; as equivalent to "wile" (De Certeau et al. 1980: 6). It has its own type of mobility,

a mobility that must accept the chance offerings of the moment, and seize on the wing the possibilities that offer themselves at any given moment. It must vigilantly make use of the cracks that particular conjunctions open in the surveillance of the proprietary powers. It poaches them. It creates surprises in them. It can be where it is least expected. It is a guileful ruse. (De Certeau 1988: 37)

De Certeau particularly emphasizes the deployment of tactics with regard to differentials in time. While a strategy has schedules and routines, tactics have "heterogeneous rhythms" that can be used to destabilize the strategy (ibid.: 38–9). He calls these practices "making do". In a context of post-disaster reconstruction, tactics are manifested by the intended beneficiaries in the way in which they use, adapt or reject the houses, infrastructures or trainings that are provided for them by donors; in the way in which they 'make do'.

How donors' strategies are adapted through the tactics of their intended users will be discussed in more detail later. For the remainder of this section, I will concentrate on how the donors themselves understand their built environments to have an impact on the surrounding communities. Returning to the previous discussion of the potential impact of the compound, its effects tend to be understood within the international community in one of three ways: in terms of symbolism; exceptionalism; and formalism.

Traditionally, the baby blue of UN peacekeepers or the Red Cross of the IF/ICRC has been a form of security in itself. By marking those buildings, assets, vehicles as property of the international community they *symbolize* that they and their inhabitants and users are protected by international law. The implication was that if these assets were to be touched, a higher penalty would be invoked than a similar crime against a local civilian, as the workers of these organizations represented a higher, universal ideal. But the explicit targeting of humanitarian installations, such as in Baghdad and Algiers, has raised questions as to what else these symbols represent. An examination of the security manuals suggests that what is symbolized is a state of exception: a continued global inequality between North and South/rich and poor that the organizations' mandates seek to redress. In the case of the built form of the compound, it may be seen as a location where exceptional behaviour takes place, as compared with the behaviour of the local population. It thus may become materially and symbolically associated with this inequality, exceptionalism and, ultimately, hypocrisy, and may become the target of hostility from the local population.

This *spatial exceptionalism* has been the subject of much discussion over the last several years within the social sciences, particularly the form of the camp. Drawing (often loosely) on Agamben (Agamben and Heller-Roazen 1998), theorists such as Ek (2006), Minca (2006) and Edkins (2000a) have used the concept with reference to particular geographic locations or confined spaces where the established juridical order was arbitrarily suspended by the sovereign. However, recent scholarship has questioned the applicability of Agamben to these so-called unique spaces by positioning them within longer geopolitical narratives (Reid-Henry 2007; Kaplan 2005). Rather than a new and exceptional experience, these nested spaces, exempt from local laws and conditions, are the historical norm. Imperial cantonments, religious ghettos, elite suburbs have been a constant throughout the history of the built environment. The simultaneous presence of distinct cultural artefacts has been a recurrent characteristic of a moving and interdependent world (Bhabha 2004; Tomlinson 1999; Hirst and Thompson 1999).

This recognition challenges suggestions such as those from Glancey (2009) that foreign buildings such as embassies should pay tribute to local architectural traditions. If the local is a variant of the global, why is it preferable to yield to the style of the moment, and *which* 'local' tradition is to be considered the preferred one? Therefore, rather than assuming that the coterminous presence of different built forms is in itself a potentially disruptive force, there is the need to ask *how* this might be so.

Some development critiques, such as those of Duffield (2009) and myself in an earlier work (Smirl 2009), suggest that the form of the compound could evoke earlier forms of North/South relations such as the colonial enclave. A similar suggestion is also made by Hirst with regard to the military form of the fortress, which he says is a "vital part of the European experience of urbanism" (Hirst 2005: 180). Beyond its military objective, such a form would be a constant reminder to the citizenry of the ruler's elevated position, and their right and potential capacity to see and know all (Foucault 1995). If the built form in question is a European one, then its use in other contexts, even if benign, could result in an association with originating ideas of conquest and domination. However, this would require either the demonstration of the affective and universal significance of particular forms; or the demonstration that populations in one country are operating within the same semiotic frame of reference as the country of origin. In addition to assuming the perspective of local beneficiaries, it also ignores local settlement patterns, which in many parts of Asia, Africa and the Middle East are highly focused upon private, inward-looking space, the compound being a common spatial arrangement for all sectors of society, and not necessarily restricted to the elite or the military.

This is not to say that visual and formal associations should be dismissed out of hand. However, rather than proposing an essentialist assumption that certain forms imply certain reactions on the part of host populations, a deeper level of analysis is required that asks why certain forms seem to be associated with certain outcomes. Within the context of the political iconography of the city, a common assumption is that "axes reflect totalitarian tendencies, while less formal arrangements express democratic conditions" (Sonne 2003: 29; Sudjic 2005; Sudjic and Jones 2001; Walker 2003). A related idea is that buildings are characteristic of their producing societies, an idea that was explored by the artists Bernt and Hilla Becher, who dedicated their lives to the photo-documentation of industrial typologies, such as the winding structures of mines, processing plants, water towers, factory halls, silos and blast furnaces. Obsessed with both the form and function of these structures, they wanted to use classification to better explore their intuition that these so-called anonymous buildings had "landscape-defining characteristics" (S. Lange 2007: 28).

The Bechers were particularly interested in the association of particular forms with their social era and how the forms impacted on their landscapes and social environments. Applying this to the context of humanitarian field missions raises questions as to which era or society compounds are associated with and what they say about the society in which they are currently deployed. According to Lefebvre, "the spatial practice of a society is revealed through the deciphering of its space" (Lefebvre 1991:

38). He also proposed that different historical eras have different spatializations – different ways of thinking about space and also being shaped by it. This latter point brings the discussion back to the previous chapter, and a dramatically under-examined aspect of the increased securitization of humanitarianism: how living in an enclavic space affects the humanitarians themselves. With reference to compounds, it raises the question whether the form of the compound could itself be a contributing factor to increased perceptions of insecurity. This question will be explored in the following section with reference to so-called gated communities.

The impact on the aid workers: gated communities

Since the 1960s the defensive architectural technique of gated communities (GCs) has been studied as a identifiable and prevalent settlement type (Blakely and Snyder 1997). Atkinson and Blandy (2005) define GCs as a "housing development that restricts public access" symbolically and/or physically, "usually through the use of gates, booms, walls and fences. These residential areas may also employ security staff or CCTV systems to monitor access. In addition, GCs may include a variety of services such as shops or leisure facilities" (ibid.: 177). Most importantly, they represent an attempt by their residents to disengage with the wider social processes in an attempt to increase security, safety and comfort. They are "residential enclaves [that] in all times and places share a basic characteristic of setting themselves off from the urban matrix around them, through control of access, and the solidification of their perimeters" (Luymes 1997: 198). Work on GCs in the UK reveals startling similarities with international humanitarian compounds. Acknowledging the immediate difference – that the compound is established with the purpose of accomplishing a particular labour outcome, while the GC is established primarily for residential and associated purposes such as increased social cohesion and quality of life – comparisons may offer insight both in terms of material form, and in the ways they affect their residents' understandings of their local environments.

For many internationals, the experience of working in the field will have an effect much like that of Atkinson and Blandy's description of the inhabitants of so-called GCs in the UK, the USA and Canada. Consider Atkinson and Flint's description of connected "fortified residential and work spaces" which resemble "a seam of partition running spatially and temporally through cities" (2004: 877). Residents of GCs restrict their movement to a small and secure number of places, "… elite fractions seamlessly moving between secure residential, workplace, education and leisure destinations" (Atkinson and Blandy 2005: 180). Similarly, for many humanitarians in the field, movement is restricted between office, home and target project. Contact with the aid recipient is often limited, and when it exists it is a highly codified interaction – often within humanitarian or government space.

Significant research has been undertaken on the relationship between the form of a GC and the perceptions and behaviour of its inhabitants. The results raise similar questions for the inhabitants of humanitarian enclaves. In particular, three findings are applicable to this discussion. First, Low (2001, 2003) found that the process of living in gated communities may have actually increased residents' fear, even though fear of crime and personal insecurity is cited as a major reason for moving to a GC (Blakely and Snyder 1997). The first way that this would occur was through the general, overall increased attention to security, which heightens residents' awareness of anything that might seem abnormal. By surrounding themselves with constant reminders of the possibility of crime, such as CCTVs, guards and gates, residents begin to frame their existence in terms of secure versus non-secure situations. As applied to the case of international humanitarian assistance, a similar impact could be seen from the introduction of system-wide, standardized training programmes for staff; the mainstreaming of security concerns into programme design; and the introduction of increased physical security measures.

A second way in which GCs increase their residents' fear is through heightening the residents' distinction between the space of the GC, which is safe, and that which lies outside the gates, and is unsafe and threatening. Residents of GCs expressed the feeling of being threatened "just being out in normal urban areas, unrestricted urban areas" (Low 2001: 54). The process of gating a community is by definition about identifying those that belong and those that do not. The category that is used to define this belonging is spatial. Those that are outside are against us; those that are within are with us. Rationally, there is a recognition that not all the people who live outside of the humanitarian enclave are enemies. However, looking at the impact that gating has on its inhabitants, even within a normal civic setting, raises serious concerns as to the potential impact of humanitarian enclaves on the humanitarians who reside in them.

A security expert in Banda Aceh felt that within expat communities in the field a "siege mentality" can develop, whereby "you don't speak the language, don't read the local press so are completely isolated from what is going on around you. This can mean that you have the impression that everyone is incredibly nice, or that everyone is out to get you." He went on to say that, in an immediate post-disaster situation, internationals are particularly isolated; they "really don't have any contact with the local community". In this context, when an event that is actually part of the "normal chaos" happens, such as kids throwing stones at a passing car, or a mugging of international staff, it is seen as a huge aberration warranting (and requiring) stringent security measures. And unlike in most other places, where the longer you stay, the more comfortable you get, in an expat situation the situation is "highly charged", and because as a Westerner you are "highly visible" even in a neutral or positive way, you begin to think that everything is about you, and may interpret things in a skewed way.

At the time of the above interview, in June 2008, there had been an increase in recorded incidents of crime (World Bank/DSF 2008), which many expats in Aceh were anecdotally interpreting as proof of increasing anti-foreign sentiment among the Acehnese.

However, my informant proposed that this crime increase could actually be seen as evidence of things in Aceh "returning to normal"; that people were no longer in a state of "post-tsunami shock". Further, prior to and during the tsunami, crime figures were not published, so any statistical increase used an artificially low crime rate as its starting point. However, within the 'gated community' of the 'expat bubble', anecdotal experience (often second- or third-hand – see Chapter 4 on community-enforced negotiation for more on this) quickly turns into fact, resulting in increased security measures on the part of some international organizations.

A third way in which the spatial arrangement of the gated community affects its residents' perceptions is through path dependence. Low observed that once residents started to live within GCs they were unlikely to move out again (2001: 47). This is supported by Merry (1981), who found that a lack of familiarity with one's surroundings is an important contributing factor to residents' perception of danger. Again, as applied to trends in humanitarianism, the more humanitarians tend to enclose themselves, or adopt defensive or deterrent security strategies, the less likely they will be to revert to acceptance strategies. Even if the fear is not supported by empirical evidence, over long periods of time it may lead "people to unnecessarily secure themselves, remove themselves from social activities, and increase levels of distrust of others" (Wilson-Doenges 2000: 600; also Blakely and Snyder 1997; Taylor 1988).

This is supported by those who argue for a geographic basis for culture. For example, Wagner and Mikesell (1962) stress the importance of the "habitual and shared communication [that] is likely to occur only among those who occupy a common area" in the formation of a cultural identity (as quoted in Cresswell 2004: 17). Within this cultural identity are shared models of self and also shared models of the other. By increasingly using the compound epistemology as the basis for envisaging and understanding the place that they are in, both possibilities of thought and possibilities for action are shut off: dismissed as non-options or, worse, simply unimaginable. If we consider Tuan's (1977) view that as human subjects we get to know the world through our perception and experience of places, if the perceptions and experiences of humanitarian workers are confined to compounds, then there is little chance for humanitarians to get to know the world that they are assisting. If the objective of the humanitarian assistance is to better understand, relate to, assist and capacitate the 'other', is this not completely at odds with such practices of enclosure? If experience of space and place is fundamental to humans' understanding of the world, what is the impact of humanitarian enclavism on its inhabitants' understanding of the beneficiary that lies outside the gates? A counter-argument could be that the compound is just the extreme example of humanitarian assistance, used only in the least permissive of environments. In the majority of cases, humanitarian workers move freely within society. This criticism will be explored in the second section of this chapter by looking at two dominant material forms of 'the field' as identified in Chapter 1: the sports utility vehicle and the grand hotel.

Sport utility vehicles

The white sports utility vehicle (SUV) has become a symbol of international humanitarian presence; in many countries better recognized than the symbol of the blue helmet of UN peace-keepers. To humanitarian workers, it represents physical safety both in terms of its large frame and on-road visibility, and the protection that has historically been derived from its symbolic values of neutrality, impartiality and universality. However, to the Third World it has arguably come to represent the petroleum-fuelled inequality that has led to a situation in which a self-appointed few behave in a way which damages their surroundings and others. More recently, the SUV may also be seen as a symbol of hybridity and the co-option, by local power brokers, of Western elite dominance.

While the white SUV has become a ubiquitous part of aid work, any history of why or how this happened is lacking. In the late 1970s, Land Rover held 80 per cent of the aid market (Wernle 2000). While this translated into merely 40,000–70,000 vehicle sales per year, their importance "goes far beyond the numbers" (ibid.). As late as "the early 1980s, Land Rover was the vehicle of choice of aid organisations such as the United Nations, Oxfam and the Red Cross. There was even an old saying that, for 70 percent of the world's population, the first vehicle they saw was a Land Rover" (ibid.).

By 2000, Land Rover's share had fallen to just over 5 per cent, with new entrants such as Toyota, Nissan and Mitsubishi taking over (ibid.). The form and design of the vehicle, however, has remained remarkably unchanged since the introduction of the iconic Defender model in 1948. It is still a four-by-four, all-terrain vehicle, based on the model of a jeep (Campbell 2005). It has a gross vehicle weight of approximately 3,500 kilograms, a strong, rigid chassis often with an integrated front grille, and all-terrain tyres. It sits high off the ground and can pull a load equal to its own weight (Land Rover n.d.). In the context of humanitarian aid it is almost always painted all white, and bears the logo of the agency that owns it. The jeep itself was developed in response to the requirements of troop movements during the Second World War. As the jeep's heir, "[f]rom the outset then, the SUV has been marked by the military" (Campbell 2005: 956). Nor has the potential of this history been lost on the marketing teams of Land Rover and its competitors. Advertising and promotional material continues to emphasize the capacity of the SUV to protect its passengers from the dangers of the passing environment (ibid.; Glover 2000; Bradsher 2003). In the original 1940s and 1950s development context, Land Rover did present one of the few vehicular options for development agencies to transport staff in areas with poor or sometimes non-existent roads.

Just as the vehicles are associated with safety and refuge (Glover 2000: 364), they are also intentionally linked in their promotional material with ideas and images of adventure, individualism and the frontier. Speaking of SUV names (and therefore of marketing strategies), Glover says that a common theme is "the Western frontier, those most mythologised and culturally laden of times and places" (ibid.: 362). Likewise, according to Campbell, consumers of SUVs felt that through their purchase they expressed "a rugged individualism" emphasizing their connection to untamed nature and the idea of the frontier (Campbell 2005: 957). This is significant for the context of humanitarianism in two ways. First, with regard to potential viewing audiences in the First World, the image of a brand such as Land Rover or the Toyota Buffalo being used in humanitarian contexts will add to the appeal of their eventual purchase. As quoted in *Automotive News*, a management consultant named Ken Slavin, being interviewed for a report on Land Rover, said, "[w]hen you have disasters, you need 4x4s. There's nothing better for a 4x4 vehicle than to be seen with an emblem that says United Nations or Oxfam or the World Wildlife Federation. That's worth a whole lot of money to any manufacturer" (Wernle 2000).

This is supported by Koshar's research, which demonstrates that "a car's notionally unique national qualities depend in part on how ... other nations regard it as both artifact and image once it travels, literally and figuratively across national borders" (Koshar 2004: 123; also Edensor 2004).

The second way in which the association of the SUV with the frontier, rugged individualism and adventure is significant is with regard to the aid workers who use them. As discussed in Chapter 1, insofar as the aid workers can be seen to be part of the international community, and sharing a habitus of advanced-stage capitalism in their countries of origin, they will have common symbols and mythologies. Particularly with regard to OECD nationals, to step up into a (white) Land Rover is to simultaneously step *into* the myth of the First World aid worker assisting Third World populations in need. Furthermore, it allows them to step into it in relative comfort and, until recently, security.

The experience of being inside a Land Rover, or inside an automobile more generally, has been the subject of sustained attention in the area of the phenomenology of car use (Sheller 2004; Dant 2004; Thrift 2004). These theorists examine how the experience of being in an automobile – as either a driver or a passenger – has affective, and ultimately epistemological and ontological, impacts. Work by Miller (2001) and Michael (2001) has proposed the car as a social-technical hybrid with driver and vehicle operating as a co-constitutive assemblage. In line with Sheller (2004), I argue that the experience of being in a car, or in this case a Land Rover, "orient[s] us toward the material affordances of the world around us in particular ways and these orientations generate emotional geographies" (ibid.: 228). These emotional geographies (or, in Lefebvre's terms, perceived and lived spaces) shape the way in which aid workers see themselves *in* a place.

In the most basic of terms, it changes the experience that the aid worker has of the physical environment and climate. Instead of being exposed to heat, rain, dust, the aid worker can ride along in a climate-controlled environment. Likewise, it changes the noisescapes of a place, enclosing the rider in a sonic envelope (Bull 2004). It may allow the passengers to move at a higher velocity than the majority of other people around them, introducing a level of inequality of movement, and possibly making movement for those on foot, bike, motorcycle, horse or even lower, older cars more dangerous. This may also introduce an affect of privilege and/or guilt for this inequality.

Work on the social impact of the SUV in America suggests that the rise of the sports utility vehicle parallels a model of citizenship that values safety and inviolability of person above all else (Mitchell 2005; Campbell 2005). Similarly, the material practices of the international community may be seen to constitute an attempt at self-imposed exclusion from the wider neighbourhood, as well as the exclusion of others (Atkinson and Flint 2004), reinforcing the observations from local residents, as explained to me by one interviewee in Banda Aceh, that "the objectives of the international community are different from those of the community they are assisting". Just as the white Land Rover (or SUV) is associated with certain affective and symbolic resonances for the people who use it, it may evoke other, quite different things for those whom it is meant to assist.

Globally, the SUV's large petrol-guzzling body has increasingly become a symbol of the excess of the West and the exceptionalism with which the West is seen to regard itself. The vehicle is also a constant reminder of the underlying economic driver of much global conflict: unequal access to oil. In El Fasher, Darfur, home to one of the UNAMID 'super-camps' discussed in Chapter 2, the introduction of hundreds of humanitarian Land Cruisers (or Buffalos, in this context) has led to the streets being widened to avoid traffic jams. The example of Darfur also points to the destabilization of the myth of the SUV as safe haven. As of August 2009, "due to a spate of carjackings" all Toyota Land Cruiser (Buffalo) vehicles have been withdrawn from use by UN personnel (UNAMID 2009). This phenomenon is not restricted to Darfur, and increasingly SUVs are seen as valuable both for their resale price and as fighting vehicles for rebel groups, who would cut off the Buffalo's top and attach a gun, according to one interviewee. The increased frequency of carjackings is forcing aid agencies to look to other, less conspicuous modes of travel, such as local taxi drivers and minibuses. More dramatically, these trends are rendering car travel, as a mode of transport, effectively unusable outside of urban centres, and in Darfur travel by helicopter between cities and towns has become the norm for aid staff. Nor is the co-option of vehicles restricted to SUVs. In April 2007, the *New York Times* leaked a UN report that said the Sudanese government had been intentionally painting its planes white with UN insignia in order to ship arms to Darfur (Hoge 2007).

While carjackings have increased, they have not been associated with an increase in violent attacks against humanitarian workers. In general, the transaction is a purely monetary operation, with the vehicle being taken away and the passengers returned unharmed. However, returning to Latour's idea of hybridity (Latour 2005) and Miller's proposal of the car as an assemblage of worker and vehicle (Miller 2001), any assault on an SUV is seen as an assault on the aid worker, and ultimately on the larger humanitarian norms the vehicle has come to represent. Rather than an assault on the hybrid form of the Land Rover/aid worker, the capture of the vehicle is a bid for what it embodies: wealth, excess, greed, military might. It is a clear statement that what is wanted from the international humanitarian community is not their assistance, but their material assets and the associated power. Nor can this desire be interpreted in a simple, linear manner, which sees rebels groups or government militia capturing humanitarian assets in order to replicate Western material modes of existence. Rather, these actions need to be interpreted as a local response – a 'making do' – to the already existing, structuring material space of humanitarian assistance, informing "a new range of strategic military initiatives" (Hoffman 2004: 212) in contemporary Third World conflict.

The grand hotel

A second material trope that is seen as a key aspect of auxiliary space is that of the so-called grand hotel (Denby 1998; Sandoval-Strausz 2007). Technically, the term is used to refer to a large luxury hotel, usually dating from the nineteenth century and having a colonial heritage (Henderson 2001; Stewart 1988). But in the context of humanitarian work, it will usually refer to one or two large hotels in a given city or town which are used for the majority of diplomatic conferences, summits, press briefings, retreats and negotiations. They will often be left over from previous regimes, such as those of British colonialists in Singapore (Henderson 2001) or the Portuguese in East Timor. What makes it architecturally recognizable will be both the grandeur and scale of its physical form and its multifunctionality. It will usually have bars, restaurants, conference halls, travel agents, shops, swimming pools and health clubs. And while these may not be well maintained, at some point they would have been the height of luxury in their respective milieus. In the context of international humanitarian assistance, the grand hotel may be the only structure with adequate facilities in which to live and work.

The space of the grand hotel provides the setting for a remarkable number of political acts and performances. Particularly in the context of humanitarian assistance, the space of the grand hotel is central to both formal, high politics, and to the politics of the everyday: the informal meetings, chance encounters and daily rituals of both local political classes and visiting elites (De Certeau 1988; Bourdieu 1990; Vesely 2004). Not only is it implicated in local power structures and contestations, but, in the event of social and political collapse, it often provides sanctuary and enclosure for guests and local populations alike. As a site of perceived inequality and amorality it may equally be the target of outrage, vandalism and violence (Sandoval-Strausz 2007). But despite its centrality to international political interactions and events, outside of cultural (Jameson 1990) or tourism studies (Pritchard and Morgan 2006) it remains largely unexamined. Although its iconic or emblematic status is regularly invoked in the context of a particular conflict, with the single exception of Hoffman's radical ethnography of the Brookfields Hotel in Sierra Leone (Hoffman 2005), I have come across no work within international relations or development studies that seriously engages with the object of the hotel and its central role in international humanitarian intervention.[2]

As discussed in the context of aid workers' memoirs, the space of the hotel is a recurrent theme. In the context that aid workers can also be considered to fall into the related category of tourists or travellers, the hotel, as a temporary shelter, is a necessity. In the literature of tourism and travel studies, this is the way in which the hotel is most commonly considered: as a networked space of flows (Castells 2000); a transit space (Pritchard and Morgan 2006); a non-space (Augé 1995). The necessity for frequent refurbishment,

2 Martin Coward deals with it obliquely in the context of his theory of "urbicide" (Coward 2002, 2009, 2001).

novelty and (re)branding meant that high-end hotels also presented the opportunity for famous architects to experiment with ultra- (or post)modern designs. This arguably significantly influenced the framing of the object of the hotel in cultural theory (McNeill 2008; Davis 2006; Jameson 1990).

While the 1990s theories on hyper-modernity and globalization have since been amply critiqued for their hyperbolic claims regarding the ontology of a new age, certain aspects warrant a re-examination. In particular, the much-(ab)used work of Marc Augé deserves a second look. Augé assigned the term *non-lieux* to

> contemporary topographies characteristic of what he calls
> 'supermodernity' – namely those urban, peri-urban, and
> interurban spaces associated with transit and communication,
> designed to be passed through rather than appropriated, and
> retaining little or no trace of our passage as we negotiate them.
> (O'Beirne 2006: 38)

And as identified in Chapter 1, 'threshold spaces' made up a significant part of the humanitarian field experience. For Augé, these are not "just spaces to be analysed but manifestations and above all agents of a contemporary existential crisis, a crisis of relations to the other, and by extension a crisis of individual identity constituted through such relations" (ibid.: 38; Augé 1998, 1994).

This crisis of relations to others is particularly relevant in the context where the 'other' (or, in the humanitarian context, the beneficiary) only makes select appearances within the non-space of the hotel: as subservient waiters, porters, maids or prostitutes. In the ethos of contemporary hotel management, staff should neither be seen nor heard, melting seamlessly into the decor, effectively erasing themselves from the interior landscape. Katz claims that, in the context of twentieth-century US and European hotel construction, hotels

> came to resemble cities in microcosm, vertical cities housing
> laundries, valet services, barbers, gymnasiums, travel offices,
> drug stores, libraries, music rooms, baggage rooms, automobile

fleets, libraries [sic], swimming pools, clothing stores, banks, florists, gift shops, screening rooms, medical services, convention halls, newsstands, mail services, roof gardens, and ballrooms – to name only the respectable services that hotels provided. Like the self-contained superblock, the privatized space of the metropolitan hotel could be said to have turned its back on the city. (Katz 1999: 137)

While the 1950s and 1960s saw the global spread of these big, architecturally similar hotels (Ibelings 1998), many of which are still in use in the Third World capitals under discussion, by inhabiting these non-spaces, the international humanitarian community may be seen as turning its back on its constituents. However, the nature of the work is such that the beneficiary is at the centre of the imaginary and if the beneficiary is absent, then s/he must be invented. Inside the non-space, says Augé, "[t]here is no room ... for history unless it has been transformed into an element of spectacle" (Augé 1995: 103): into a meeting, conference or workshop where the problem can be distilled into so-called action points and plotted into a matrix.

The significance of the hotel as metaphoric stage for a wide range of humanitarian gatherings has been vastly under-emphasized. As a touristic enclave, hotels are "'purified' spaces, which are strongly circumscribed and framed, wherein conformity to rules and adherence to centralized regulation hold sway" (Edensor 2001: 6; also Sibley 1988; Schmid 2008). Moreover, the rules and regulations are geared towards the international clientele, immediately creating a power imbalance between those framing the discussions and those invited to attend. As security becomes more of an issue for the international community and mobility increasingly restricted, it is likely that the necessity of the hotel as a venue for conferences will not diminish in the near future. Nor are the 'performances' necessarily restricted to official gatherings.

The hotel lobby has long been regarded as a key site of social, cosmopolitan interactions (Berger 2005; Kracauer and Levin 1995; Cocks 2001), and in the context of the field its significance is amplified. This is the place where local and international businessmen, journalists, politicians, aid workers all come to unwind and to interact (George 2004; Courtemanche and Claxton 2003; Minion 2004). Information is exchanged, alliances publicized, and rumours spread. A further examination of the significance of these networks is undertaken elsewhere, but for the purposes of this chapter, I will now turn to how these non-spaces are seen by those outside the hotel.

As Tomlinson rightly points out, these non-spaces are only non-spaces from the perspective of the visiting travellers; for the hotel's employees and the local residents they are real spaces (Tomlinson 1999). From an external perspective – that is, not only from a perspective of someone standing 'outside' but also from the perspective of someone who is not a user of these spaces – the grand hotel is important in a number of ways. First, it may represent a space of opportunity: a place of potential employment; a locale to sell souvenirs; or from which to offer taxi rides. Secondly, it may be seen as a place of safety. In the context of Hotel Timor, in Dili in 2008, one of the three internally displaced persons (IDPs) camps in the city had grown up outside the hotel's front door. To the IDPs, proximity to the hotel was thought to confer safety, as well as potentially offering positive externalities such as running water, or leftover food. Similarly, in the context of the Serbian siege of Sarajevo, Martin Coward quotes from testimony before the US Congress in which gunners on the hillside overlooking Sarajevo apologized to BBC journalist Kate Adie for shelling the Holiday Inn where the foreign correspondents were known to live, "explaining that they had not meant to hit the hotel, but had been aiming at the roof of the National Museum next door" (Coward 2002: 30). During the 1994 Rwandan genocide, Hotel des Milles Collines became a refuge of last resort for internationals and Rwandan civilians alike as they attempted to barricade themselves against the Interahamwe's machetes (Dallaire and Beardsley 2003).

The imagined safety of the hotel is the by-product of the

association with not only international humanitarian law and humanitarian conventions, declarations and resolutions but also because of the hotel's association with inequality and privilege. These same qualities can also make the hotel a target, as seen most recently with the bombing of the Taj Hotel in Mumbai (Biswas 2008). What is being attacked, precisely, is a matter of debate. While it is sometimes seen as a direct targeting of the symbols of foreign interests (Wharton 2001), it could just as likely be seen as the targeting of domestic political dealings (Donais 2002), or its embodiment of the "essential common ground of togetherness" (Iveson 2006: 80). A hotel may also be seen as the site of immoral or amoral behaviour, which also contributes to it being perceived as a predominantly masculine space. More mundanely, as a high, often centrally located and well-built structure, it may offer a valuable strategic acquisition from the perspective of local military actors.

In summary, the hotel contributes to the shaping of humanitarian relations in the field in myriad ways and deserves additional research attention. In the context of this book, its impact is most noticeable in the way in which it shapes the perceptions and understanding of the local situation for the aid workers it houses. For the people that pass through it, it is a temporary non-space, but for its host community it is a part of everyday lived and perceived spaces. Considered in tandem with the SUV and other material forms of humanitarianism, the hotel creates a material landscape of humanitarian intervention. From the perspective of the internationals, this landscape is temporary, but from the perspective of local people it has become the permanent topography of assistance. The people in the hotel rooms, in the cars, in the offices will change but the built environment stays the same. If anything is symbolized by the compounds, the cars, the planes, perhaps it is first and foremost the repetition of the ritual of assistance. While the internationals each experience the field as a new, albeit enclosed, experience of the 'other', the material and spatial rituals of the interaction never change.

Conclusion

This chapter has discussed a variety of ways in which the material environment of humanitarian assistance impacts outcomes. The primary way in which this occurs is through the subtle framing of perception (Goffman et al. 1997), and the creation of spatial epistemology, particularly with regard to impressions and understandings of the 'other', the beneficiary.

By spatializing binary categories of good/bad and safe/dangerous, there is the tendency to regard those people who are located within the safe space of the hotel or compound as 'good' and those outside of the space as 'bad'. While the spaces discussed – the compound, the SUV, the hotel – ensure the virtual elimination of violent crime within their confines, their diplomatic space of exception may actually encourage other types of non-violent crime such as graft, theft and fraud. And while, according to one reading, the mobility and weightlessness of the internationals in these spaces are powerful resources, they also open up a space for the locals to exert power from below (Low 2003: 131). With a longer time horizon of employment, local employees may have the knowledge of local personalities, relationships and affiliations that may help direct projects or funds to the groups or agencies of their choice. Certain local workers may be in better positions to exploit loopholes in procurement systems, obscure nepotism, and act as informants to the host governments. These gated experiences will then contribute to how the internationals understand, interpret and report back upon the entire country. They may fail to recognize that their experience of a given country is dramatically mediated by their experience within the secure spaces, and that the actions of locals within these spaces are inevitably a response to the spaces themselves; a form of 'making do'. For example, in the UK government's reports on the failures of development assistance in insecure environments, the lack of capacity and implied dishonesty of local partners was often blamed for a lack of programme results (National Audit Office 2008).

The idealization of the beneficiary is equally common and

necessary for the continuation of the humanitarian project. Without a sublime beneficiary, in need of and grateful for assistance, the entire project is called into question (Žižek 1989). Interestingly, this process may be easier from within the confines of a secured enclave, as the reified abstraction of the beneficiary is not challenged by the contradictions and complications of a human subject. For example, DfID uses a theoretical model as the basis for determining aid allocations to various countries. It is based on World Bank data and other indicators that are fed back from country-level assessments. However, the circumscription of information and knowledge (which constitute these assessments) will be determined by the extent to which the international community is kept separate from the populations that it is meant to assist.

Both tendencies – the overly positive and the overly negative constructions of beneficiaries – are amplified by the short time span of internationals relative to nationals, which means that many internationals have a superficial experience of their 'surrounding' environment. Much like the gated communities' residents' disengagement "with wider urban problems and responsibilities, both fiscal and social, in order to create a 'weightless' experience of the urban environment" (Atkinson and Blandy 2005: 180), the internationals' ability to leave, to come and go at will, guards against anything but the most codified and superficial interaction with local citizens. While spatial divisions between humanitarians and beneficiaries have always existed, increased perceptions of risk and securitized building trends are reinforcing (and reifying) them in physical form. Similar to Hoffman's use of the barracks as a spatial metaphor for contemporary African cities (Hoffman 2008), the compound has become a metaphor for contemporary humanitarian intervention – at the level of individual, group and society.

4 | BUILDING HOME AWAY FROM HOME: POST-TSUNAMI ACEH, AND THE SINGLE-FAMILY HOUSE

This chapter demonstrates how material and spatial considerations shaped the post-tsunami reconstruction landscape of Aceh, Indonesia. In the vein of Appadurai (1986) and Latour (1993) it uses a single 'thing' as an anchor to guide the narrative: the single-family house. The house dominated reconstruction discourse in Aceh with far-reaching consequences for the province, for Indonesia, and for the future of humanitarian responses. This chapter establishes how this occurred. First, the material and spatial constitution of the post-tsunami response will be outlined. Secondly, the way each of the parties involved related to the house as an object will be critically analysed. Difficulties arose owing to a fundamental disjuncture over how the various parties involved in the reconstruction interpreted the response strategy and the place of the house in it.

The parties included the Government of Indonesia (GoI), the Aceh and Nias Rehabilitation and Reconstruction Board (BRR), the Free Aceh Movement (*Gerakan Aceh Merdeka* or GAM), the Aceh Transitional Committee (*Komite Peralihan Aceh* or KPA), contractors, and the beneficiaries themselves. While initially this disjunction was formulated largely along the lines of international donors and NGOs versus local beneficiaries/GoI, as the reconstruction wore on, the spatial imaginary changed, and with it, the modality by which the international community approached the situation. This chapter argues that initially, from within the humanitarian imaginary, the house was viewed as the Maussian ideal of the gift, while from the perspective of other parties concerned it was viewed as a commodity. However, through the process of reconstruction, the international community came to fundamentally alter its approach to housing reconstruction. In doing so, it laid the foundations for future processes of responses and reconstruction. The other parties changed their approach in the other direction: moving from the image of the house as pure commodity and incorporating a more nuanced understanding of the process of housing reconstruction. In doing so, they too were fundamentally changed by the process. The question that remains is whether these alterations will be permanent and transmissible to other contexts – both political and humanitarian – or whether the experiences will be consumed by the larger institutional cultures into which they were born.

The chapter is based on participant observation and in-depth interviews with international aid workers, government officials and local NGO representatives in Aceh, Indonesia, from May 2006 to June 2008. During this time, three field visits were undertaken and each visit was used to focus on a particular beneficiary group. The May 2006 visit concentrated on international aid workers, the December 2007 trip concentrated on BRR and the May/June 2008 visit concentrated on local beneficiaries. During the last trip, I was physically located within the Banda Aceh offices of an Acehnese NGO which worked with local survivors. All interviews were conducted with the promise of anonymity. Interviews were conducted in English or in Bahasa Indonesia or Bahasa Aceh with help from a translator. While I have a basic knowledge of Bahasa Indonesia, I would often use the services of a translator to ensure correct interpretation. Further, while many Indonesians involved in the reconstruction programme spoke Bahasa Indonesia in the Jakarta (or Javanese) style, local Acehnese have their own dialect of Indonesian, which may diverge significantly in terminology and accent.

Supplementary work on the tsunami reconstruction was also undertaken in Sri Lanka, where two field visits were made to the south coast in May/June 2006 and December 2008. While the timing of the re-emerging conflict meant that further research became impossible (my travel visa was refused by the Sri Lankan embassy in spring 2008) my work in Sri Lanka has informed my overall research questions and approach.

With regard to the reconstruction of Aceh, the time frame under discussion extends from 26 December 2004 (the day of the tsunami) to April 2009, when BRR closed its doors and the GoI declared the reconstruction phase officially over. With regard to housing programmes, the majority of the 'end of project' figures will be taken from December 2008. This date is significant for two reasons. First, December 2008 marked the four-year anniversary of the tsunami, and for publicity reasons many agencies and organizations, including BRR, wanted to be able to issue progress statements. For many of the organizations, such as the Multi Donor Fund (MDF) and the International Federation of the Red Cross (IFRC), three years after the tsunami was considered to be an appropriate length of time to have been able to fulfil programme commitments. Likewise, the GoI, in its original reconstruction time frame, had set out three phases: emergency, rehabilitation and reconstruction. They adhered to these phases, and the third anniversary of the tsunami was set, by BRR, as the date when all housing commitments (totalling approximately 120,000 units) needed to be completed.

Unless otherwise specified, within the context of this chapter, the term reconstruction will be used to refer to the entire forty-month period. For analytic purposes, this period can be divided into two qualitatively different phases. The first phase spans from the end of the emergency phase until approximately May 2006. The second phase covers the period from June 2006 to the end of the reconstruction. It was at this point in time that the way in which the reconstruction was conceptualized fundamentally changed, primarily on the part of the international community, but to a certain degree for all parties concerned. This shift hinges on the distinction between aid as a Maussian gift versus aid as commodity. This distinction has been previously applied to international assistance (Hattori 2001, 2003; Harrell-Bond et al. 1992). Here, it is used to introduce a spatialized way of thinking about the two concepts. The first part of the chapter will apply the idea of a bounded humanitarian space, as developed earlier, to the context of the post-tsunami response. It demonstrates how the development of an auxiliary space strongly influenced the disproportionately large focus on the single-family house. This contributed to a Maussian tendency to see aid as a gift on behalf of the international community. The second part looks at how this tendency was transformed, through local processes, into one of commodification: for the other actors involved – BRR, the GoI and the GAM – the house became a commodity. While during the first phase of the response these two positions emerged, solidified and clashed, the second phase saw a transformation of all parties and an uneasy consensus established around the commodified form of the house.

Mapping the 'second tsunami'

The rapid arrival of thousands of humanitarian workers following the 2004 Boxing Day tsunami has frequently been referred to as a second tsunami of aid (Vltchek 2005). The largest post-crisis reconstruction effort ever seen led to approximately $7.7 billion being pledged for post-tsunami reconstruction and hundreds of humanitarian agencies descending upon the province in a matter of months. There remains ambiguity over the precise number of agencies that participated in the reconstruction. According to Telford and Cosgrove (2006), the number of INGOs peaked at around 170 in mid-2005. This was in addition to 430 local NGOs that were also identified. In December 2007, the official government database (the Reconstruction of Aceh and Nias or RAN database) had identified 841 Donors and Partners that had participated in the response. According to Barron (2007), they initially numbered in the thousands. The GoI stated that 133 countries provided assistance during the emergency phase. In an official statement, the GoI claimed that "16,000 troops from different countries were deployed in what has been described by observers as one of the largest non-war military missions since the Second World War" (BRR 2007). The humanitarian actors ranged from the usual humanitarian organizations such as UNOCHA, UNHCR, the IFRC and affiliates to international NGOs such as Oxfam, CARE and Save the Children, to private sector organizations such as Shell and Bayer, to a myriad of tiny and unaffiliated concerns, many of which were operating for the first time.

According to the GoI, the official emergency phase lasted for three months following the disaster (Republic of Indonesia 2005: II-13), and according to most assessments, the emergency phase operated fairly well. The geography of the disaster facilitated relatively easy access to the disaster zone. This allowed for the provision of rice and water to the victims and for victims to rapidly and independently evacuate the disaster zone by moving a few kilometres inland. The climate of Sumatra, and the fact that the disaster occurred outside the rainy season, meant that no one was at risk of immediate climatic exposure. Initially, one interviewee explained, the responsibility for overseeing the entire response was given to BAPPENAS, the cross-cutting National Development Planning Agency. They convened, through the GoI, a high-profile conference in Jakarta to lay out a reconstruction strategy with all major donors and government agencies. The strategy that emerged was a comprehensive, well-thought-out approach to post-crisis reconstruction based on established international best practice (Consultative Group On Indonesia 2005).

Unfortunately, events on the ground quickly overtook BAPPE-NAS' ability to manage, leading to a supply-driven reconstruction. The direction of the reconstruction was largely informed by events that occurred in the first eight months. The most significant were the (default) decision to concentrate on the reconstruction of permanent houses as a reconstruction priority; the signing of the MoU between the GoI and the GAM; and more specifically, the lack of official integration between the tsunami reconstruction and the post-conflict reintegration processes (Smirl 2008). Without discounting the decisive role that the GoI, through BRR, would play in the ultimate outcome of the reconstruction, initially the main driver of the reconstruction was the overwhelming physical presence of the international community. While the amount of money was obviously what permitted such large numbers of people to physically come to the region, had the money been provided through alternative modalities, for example as budget support,[1] the outcome would have been completely different.

Drawing on the discussion of the material characteristics of a humanitarian response examined earlier, the 'second tsunami' of aid exhibited many of the classic characteristics of auxiliary space: differential mobility and temporality, securitization and enclosure, exceptionalism, and links to site of origin. In the case of Aceh, all of these factors came together to create an initially extremely strong and visible auxiliary space. Internationals descended upon the capital of Banda Aceh and quickly rented a significant proportion of the houses still standing, offering a quick source of income for those who had property to spare. It also heightened the demand for accommodation. With housing stock already depleted, this predictably drove up rental prices and the costs of associated commodities. While initially some of the money did flow into the local economy, this was primarily through the employment of drivers, translators, fixers, administrators and secretaries, rather than through demand for local goods. Most of what the aid workers needed was initially brought in through humanitarian supply channels. Informants from this period admitted that they knew little about Aceh, few spoke the language, many had limited experience in post-disaster situations, and most would not stay much beyond the emergency phase.

---

1 The term budget support is used to refer to the direct transfer of ODA to the recipient country's national budget. This provides the government with a larger degree of flexibility regarding expenditure. Project support, by contrast, means that donors provide their funds within the framework of specific projects or programmes.

Some international agencies initially built their own camps from which to operate logistically, including the UN Office for the Coordination of Humanitarian Affairs (UNOCHA), the International Federation of the Red Cross (IFRC) and Catholic Relief Services (CRS), particularly those that were working farther down the west coast. But many agencies remained in compounds long after the emergency phase was over. First, the fact that many of the organizations, such as CRS, were involved in rebuilding houses meant that additional security was required for building materials and associated non-food items (NFIs). Secondly, several interviewees expressed the sentiment that they "weren't sure if the locals wanted us there". A 'siege mentality', as mentioned in Chapter 3, was observed among the expat community in Aceh, fostering a feeling of 'us against them'.

This situation contributed to, and possibly resulted from, the clash of cultures that sometimes occurred between the internationals and the Acehnese locals, who generally practise an extremely devout form of Islam. As late as 2006, reports surfaced of Syar'iyah (sharia) Police harassing sleeping residents of the World Food Programme (Deutsche Presse Agentur 2006). A recent World Bank Conflict Monitoring Update reported that during the April 2009 election campaigning, some parties deliberately appealed to anti-foreign sentiment (World Bank/DSF 2009: 5). It continued,

> [t]he Chairman of the Aceh branch of the Indonesian Democratic Party of Struggle (PDI-P) declared that 'Aceh is not Kosovo', expressed his concern that foreigners were 'playing' in Aceh 'as they did in Palestine', and called on authorities to carry out sweepings to check on the documentation of internationals. (Ibid.: 5)

One construction specialist for an INGO, who had been in Aceh from the beginning of the reconstruction and who had worked in many different humanitarian responses, appreciated living in a compound, as it offered him security. In May 2008, he admitted, the people of Aceh are not so welcoming, because of the conflict ... everybody [international aid workers] felt not comfortable coming here ... everyone had a weapon ... maybe threats ... here people [the Acehnese] don't want to get mixed up ... and several people thought that these foreigners are making problems, are changing the culture.

When asked directly, he said he was not sure whether the Acehnese wanted the internationals there at all – referring both to the situation two years after the tsunami and to the two years preceding.

The GoI also contributed to the creation of a context where the distinction between locals and internationals was reinforced. First, the GoI was initially reluctant to let in foreigners. Unable to stem the tide, they demanded aid workers register with the military or face expulsion if caught outside the main cities of Banda Aceh and Meulaboh (BBC 2005b). This both created a sense of uncertainty among the humanitarian agencies (especially the smaller NGOs which did not have political or administrative support) and concentrated them physically in the capital of Banda Aceh and the provincial capital of Meulaboh down the west coast. In some cases, it meant that an inordinate amount of time was spent establishing political relations in Jakarta, prior to actually arriving in Aceh. A similar situation occurred in Bangkok after Cyclone Nargis, where aid agencies were kept waiting in Bangkok before being allowed into Burma.

In some ways this may help coordination, as it forces agencies to engage in planning prior to arriving at the disaster site, but it will usually also lead to wastage as many elements of an emergency response are time sensitive. It may also give rise to political lobbying which takes up politicians' time, and may lead to NGOs committing themselves to projects that are beyond both their own capabilities and the constraints of the target environment. This is done in an effort to gain government support and, ultimately, political capital. In the case of one architecturally oriented NGO, they spent the first three weeks post-tsunami lobbying the president's wife in Jakarta. They proposed an elaborate series of boarding schools for tsunami orphans that were never built. From within the humanitarian imaginary or auxiliary space of international aid, the idea of providing shelter for tsunami orphans made perfect sense. But once the practical difficulties of establishing who is an orphan and the legality and long-term status and maintenance of the schools were confronted, the plan was no longer viable.

A second way in which the GoI contributed to the creation and maintenance of auxiliary space was through its imposition of martial law in May 2003 (Schulze 2003). This effectively meant that any international NGOs working in Aceh left. Even prior to this, numbers had been very low owing to the protracted guerrilla campaign by the GAM against the GoI (Reid 2006; Aspinall 2007; Kell 1995) – according to two informal informants, the number of international aid workers present in Aceh prior to the tsunami was fewer than eight. Although a handful of agencies maintained a presence in the province, even fewer maintained international staff. Consequently, relatively little was known about Aceh as a province. This lack of information contributed to what has been called the orientalist fascination that many aid workers felt coming to this place (Kenny 2005). As Aceh was the site of an ongoing civil war, it was classified by the UN as Security Phase 3 and above, for the duration of the initial phases of the tsunami response. As discussed in Chapter 2, Phase Three and above severely restricts movement of staff, making a large-scale disaster recovery operation very difficult. It was therefore largely ignored in practice, according to one interviewee. Whether Phase Three and above was an appropriate designation or not (many informants thought not), it meant that the international community was generally uncertain as to the security situation in the province: unnecessary internal travel was either prohibited or discouraged and staff in some organizations were eligible for frequent recuperative leave.

Both the security situation and the devastation caused by the tsunami amplified the dynamic of constrained mobility, characteristic of an auxiliary space. In order to move up and down the approximately 300 kilometres of damaged coastline, many organizations felt that flying was the only option. The UN set up a parallel transport system including almost daily flights to and from certain coastal cities (Calang, Meulaboh). Other organizations, such as Oxfam, invested in their own helicopters (Musa et al. 2008). Still other organizations, such as CHF International, used Mission Aviation Fellowship (MAF), a Christian NGO specializing in flying light aircraft in remote locations. The effect was that international staff, many of them visiting experts, consultants and staff from headquarters, experienced the post-tsunami space in an extremely fluid, mobile manner. A construction manager for one of the largest housing implementers spent the first two months in Aceh "sleeping in five different places every week", flying between projects in Pidie (on the east coast), Meulaboh and Calang (on the west), Banda Aceh, and his home in Medan (on the east coast of Sumatra). As explored earlier, the experience of moving over or through a place in an enclosed vehicle will provide a very different awareness and experience of a place than other forms of transport, such as walking, or cycling, which force the person moving to interact with their immediate environment. In the case of Aceh, the differential experience of mobility contributed to the creation of a series of enclave projects that worked with micro-projects, or single communities, without approaching the reconstruction holistically.

The plans and approaches of the international community did, in principle, encourage a holistic and integrated approach to reconstruction, but such an approach proved impossible to achieve (Dercon 2009). I argue that the physical practices of the staff were a crucial explanatory variable in this failure. For example, the rapid, differential movement of the international community served to reinforce the divide between international aid workers, arriving to help, and their intended beneficiaries, the coastal Acehnese. One Acehnese interviewee felt that the constant arrival and departure of international staff was tantamount to tourism, commenting that this money would be better spent on concrete reconstruction work rather than on transport, salaries and per diems. According to a construction specialist for one of the major INGOs, the high number of people coming and going undermined any sense of continuity in the reconstruction. This sentiment was echoed by a BRR official, who complained that both the Canadian and British Federations of the Red Cross had to refer every little change back to their respective headquarters for approval, which dramatically slowed down the progress. For those NGOs without the money to spend on aid transport, their activities were concentrated in and around the provincial capital, Banda Aceh.

While international humanitarian actors have committed to international principles of coordination, harmonization and coordination via the 2005 Paris Declaration, the huge sums of money available for tsunami reconstruction meant that international actors (hereafter referred to collectively as NGOs) were competing for projects and beneficiaries. While, without constraints, such competition should have ideally distributed the actors and their projects evenly among beneficiaries, in the post-tsunami context it drew them closer together, further consolidating the auxiliary space. The tendency was for NGOs to concentrate their activities in and around the main towns owing to ease of access and because of the initial problems with getting permission to work outside of them. In areas such as Meuraxa and Lhongha, there was also physically room to work, as these areas, which lay close to the coast, had effectively been razed by the tsunami waves. But these areas were only a few square kilometres in size, and often surrounded by other built-up areas. With so many actors operating in such a small area, it became of paramount importance to brand one's project by rapidly erecting the requisite project sign or logo to demonstrate that money was being transformed into visible, 'concrete' results. The demonstration of measurable results was a key driver in the reconstruction: most notably in the prominence of the single-family home.

The single-family house

That the house would become a key issue is, on one level, completely understandable: a 600-kilometre coastline corridor was destroyed (UNORC/BRR 2009: 4) and up to 800 kilometres of coastline damaged. Within the corridor, varying in width from 1 to 4 kilometres, little was left standing (ibid.: 4). More than 120,000 families were left without shelter and up to 600,000 people were displaced (Dercon 2009: 10). Early estimates indicated that "the total number of modern, semi-modern and traditional houses that are totally or partially damaged ... have reached 252,223 houses" (Republic of Indonesia 2005: II-6), although the accuracy of these estimates was a source of constant deliberation.

It was not that the provision of shelter was itself an illogical or surprising aspect of a reconstruction strategy, but that it came to dominate the entire response strategy and came to be the key metric against which success was measured. Financially, housing was the highest-funded sector (or sub-sector, depending on the donor's designation) with $US1.424 billion or 25 per cent of all allocated post-tsunami reconstruction funds. Out of an estimated 841 NGOs, over one hundred were involved in housing reconstruction. This was in addition to the housing programmes which were being run by the BRR. Progress in housing became the key indicator of recovery both for donors, reporting back to headquarters, and for the BRR. However, that the provision of 120,000 stand-alone, single-family dwellings by an ad hoc consortium of international and national actors, almost none of whom had any experience in construction, came to be the preferred humanitarian response remains puzzling. For the international community, to physically rebuild permanent houses for an entire province is an unusual approach. Normally, reconstruction is either done through cash transfer (or an owner-driven model), as was predominantly the case after the 2006 Yogyakarta

4.1 IFRC transitional shelter, Banda Aceh

and Kashmir earthquakes, or the response concentrates on the temporary or transitional phases of an emergency (UN-HABITAT 2007b; Barakat 2003; Barenstein 2008; Dercon 2009).

In the case of the tsunami, the transitional response was restricted to barracks and IFRC transitional shelters, each bringing its own problems. The establishment of barracks both by the Indonesian Army (*Tentara Nasional Indonesia* or TNI) and select agencies such as the GTZ became the source of significant controversy and problems (Age 2005). The initial fears that the TNI were using the barracks for some underhanded purposes of population control proved unfounded. The barracks did, however, become a magnet for renters and homeless people, who proved extremely difficult to relocate, and would lead to the creation of an entire institutional response mechanism dedicated solely to their rehousing, according to one interviewee. While according to best practice guidelines on the provision of humanitarian shelter, transitional shelter is the next response phase after the emergency phase (Dercon 2009; Corsellis et al. 2006; UNDRO 1982), in the post-tsunami reconstruction, transitional shelter was largely ignored until it was too late.

When, in December 2005, the IFRC began to provide 9-metre-square, one-room aluminium and plywood shelters, people were no longer interested in living in what amounted to a plywood shed. This was even more the case as the shelters continued to be erected through 2006 and even 2007, as permanent reconstruction was gaining pace (Dercon 2009: 17). While the shelters were credited with taking the pressure off the permanent construction drive, large blocks of them remained empty. Others were used as storage sheds or barns.

From January 2005 to the establishment of the BRR by presidential decree five months later, the response strategy was, as stated, supply-driven by the NGOs and concentrated on the architectural form of the house. The house that was provided was generally between 36 and 45 metres square, single-storey, and rectangular in shape with a pitched roof made of aluminium. Most had a front and a back door, between two and four rooms, and were made of cement. The materials ranged from timber (initially), to bricks and mortar, to poured concrete over rebar.

In the original GoI (BAPPENAS) directives of January 2005, housing reconstruction occupied only eleven pages in a 190-plus-page document and focused more on process than design or architectural form. Based on what was considered to be international best practice in post-disaster recovery (Corsellis et al. 2006), it stressed the importance of an owner-driven approach. Recognizing the need for organizational flexibility, it also laid out five different alternatives for approaching the reconstruction of houses. When judged normatively against the rules of established humanitarian response, for example the Sphere Standards (Wilson 2004) or the Paris and Rome Declarations, which stress the importance of donors aligning behind government leadership at all levels, the plan was an international gold standard. But in the context of post-tsunami Aceh, the lack of organized government leadership in the first six months meant that this type of approach effectively translated into carte blanche for NGOs to pursue independent strategies.

4.2 Example of a post-tsunami house, Banda Aceh

With the exception of those organizations and agencies with a narrow relief mandate, the strength of the majority of NGOs that arrived in Aceh lay in community-based approaches such as facilitation and capacity-building. But in the case of the tsunami, the communities that they were supposed to assist had fled. According to one informant, an aid worker, "the NGOs were used to working with communities. After the tsunami there were no communities to work with. They built houses to get them back." In the absence of a clear government coordinating presence in Aceh, momentum was created whereby hundreds of NGOs made largely bilateral commitments to individual communities to provide between a handful and hundreds of houses. While sector groups had been set up to share information, these were denigrated as 'talking shops' and appear not to have been very useful in coordinating a response, at least in the first eighteen months. This is understandable given the size of the sector, and the fact that many actors failed to attend. Many of the agencies and organizations working in Aceh were not even registered with the government, and were either not aware of the existence of such meetings or lacked the capacity to attend. This led to many "hit and run" projects, as one interviewee called them. Among them, a wide range of modalities were deployed, including precast frames and reinforced concrete frames with brick infill, built according to a range of specifications and requirements (Da Silva and Zubkowski 2006: i). A review of the Aceh Housing Programme undertaken in April 2006 by architects from the London-based firm Ove ARUP stated,

> [t]he Building Code issued by the Ministry of Public Works in July 2005 is not comprehensive with respect to seismic design single storey residential houses. As a result several agencies have developed their own guidance. Whilst these all contain useful data, they have not been developed with reference to each other, and in some cases provide incorrect or conflicting information. (Ibid.: i)

By the time BRR was created and stepped in to coordinate the reconstruction, they found themselves chasing after housing developments (also known as starts) of varying types, location, quality and cost, trying to retroactively impose a building code that would provide some sort of consistency to the reconstruction.

Despite the initial focus by NGOs on community-driven reconstruction (Multi Donor Fund 2007: 2), and the lack of centralized coordination and directives, there was remarkable consistency in the type of houses that began to spring up, further supporting the hypothesis that the push for permanent housing was initially donor driven. According to Dercon (2009), the initial guidance given by the Consultative Group on a 36-square-metre house was based on minimum social housing standards in Indonesia, and was by these standards quite generous. Still, in contrast to many of the houses that had previously stood in Banda Aceh, they seemed tiny, almost doll-like (see Figure 4.1). According to one informant who had previously worked in the construction industry, during the initial period informal guidelines were put together by those individuals inside various agencies with experience or background in construction or engineering. These guidelines were often based on international standards, which could not be implemented even by qualified Acehnese or Indonesian builders, a group that was already in short supply. Australian building codes were advocated as a gold standard of earthquake-resilient construction and engineering, but the expertise required to implement them was lacking in the post-tsunami context. Further, as almost none of the NGOs had backgrounds in construction or engineering, they approached the reconstruction of houses in the same way that they approach other types of social challenges, by adopting a consultative approach. And although, according to the reports of the NGOs, they adopted a client-driven approach in which the communities would decide upon the type of houses that they wanted, according to the communities they were offered a narrow

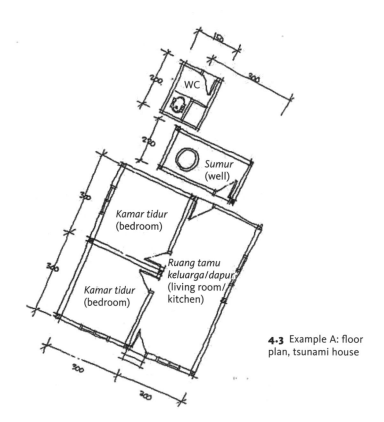

4.3 Example A: floor plan, tsunami house

Tampak depan (front elevation)

4.4 Example B: floor plan, tsunami house

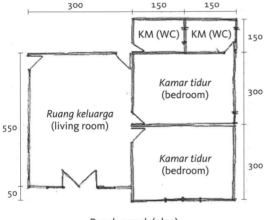

Denah rumah (plan)

range of slightly different patterns to choose from (see Figures 4.3 and 4.4). As examined further below, although the differences were small – for example, between 36 and 45 square metres of floor space, or the absence or presence of a front step – they proved to be a significant issue between communities.

Part of the reason for the dominance of the permanent house was financial. As we have already seen, there was an incredible amount of money available for reconstruction. Even the larger international multilateral and non-governmental agencies were not used to this level of financing. Rather than begging for funding,

they were begging for beneficiaries. This meant that beneficiaries had a larger amount of leverage than they normally had,
and could bargain for the type of assistance that they wanted.
When many asked for houses, this preference coincided with the
donors' need to spend large amounts of funding relatively quickly,
preferably in a way that was visually appealing to audiences 'back
home' and provided an ideal output indicator that they could
be counted and reported on. Houses had the added benefit that
they were seen to be relatively non-political: they were a basic
human need (Maslow 1943). However, in the context of Aceh, a
tropical country, there was no immediate danger of populations
freezing to death. As the disaster was a geographically narrow
one, affecting only a thin stretch of land adjacent to the coast, it
was easily accessible from inland and emergency provisions were
quickly being sent down from the hills. My research leads me to
suggest that the inordinate focus on houses offers insight into the
way in which the process of reconstruction works more generally,
and how beneficiaries specifically are thought of within what can
be called the humanitarian imaginary. In particular, the initial
approach adopted has demonstrated a Maussian understanding of
the relationship between the giver (the NGOs, broadly defined)
and the recipient (the tsunami-effected Acehnese): the house
was a gift.

The gift of the house

In his classic treatment of the topic, *The Gift*, Mauss (1969)
describes how primitive societies engage in the ritual of gift
exchange as a way of establishing and solidifying social bonds.
In this way, the gift object is no longer only an object, but both
a symbol for and an extension of human relationships. Carrier
(1991) identifies three key aspects of Mauss's theory of exchange.
The first is that the exchange involves three obligations of transference: the obligation to give presents, the obligation to receive
them, and the obligation to repay gifts received. The second
aspect is the inalienable quality of gifts as objects: "the thing

itself is a person or pertains to a person ... one gives away what is in reality a part of one's nature and substance, while to receive something is to receive a part of someone's spiritual essence" (Mauss 1969: 10). As inalienable objects, they are likewise unique, with "a name, a personality, a past, and even a legend attached to them" (ibid.: 22). This is distinct from a commodity, which is alienated, bearing no substantial relationship to the person who sold it (Carrier 1991: 125) and indistinguishable from others in its class. It follows that to reject a gift is not merely to reject an alienated object, but is to reject the giver as well as the gift. The third aspect is the related and mutually obligated nature of transactors. This means that "gift transactors are not individuals who are defined independently of their social relationships, but social persons defined in significant ways by their inalienable positions in a structure of social relations that encompasses them" (ibid.: 129). For Mauss, "it is not individuals ... but moral persons who carry on exchanges" (Parry 1986: 456). In contradistinction, people linked through commodity relations are also linked to one another, but through "their complementary positions in the system of production and distribution, which is to say the class system and the division of labour" (Carrier 1991: 129).

Within the context of reconstruction, all three of these elements repeatedly exhibited themselves in my interviews with the international community. First, the three obligations of transference were clearly shown. The first, the obligation of the giver (in this case the donor) to the recipient (the tsunami survivors), was one of the defining features of the response. The phenomenally high levels of personal donations from OECD countries have largely been attributed to three factors. First, the disaster occurred on Boxing Day, which is a holiday in the Commonwealth. This meant that the news coverage occurred on a day when a higher portion of the population than normal was watching television. Following the hypothesis of Maussian gift, it is also possible that after Christmas people felt generous, and under a certain degree of personal obligation to give. While such an observation might seem trite, it is easily supported by the funding profile, which saw religious organizations such as World Vision, the Mennonite Central Committee and Christian Children's Fund receive unprecedented levels of funding from individuals. It is reasonable to assume that the people who give to these organizations would also consider Christmas to be a spiritual time, and a time for sharing, and gift-giving in a more profound rather than strictly commercial way. Within Christian theology, there is also the imperative to help those less fortunate than oneself; an imperative that would be conceivably strengthened immediately following one of the most important holidays of the Christian calendar.

The perception of the beneficiaries' 'obligation to receive' the houses was seen in the way in which the NGOs initially distributed their services among beneficiaries. Communities were identified to be recipients of a particular NGO's donation and to work with that NGO. While communities did have a say in the content, the focus of the project – for example, housing or water and sanitation or education – would often be decided at a higher administrative level – not always in keeping with a particular NGO's area of functional expertise. In the case of Aceh, once a community was identified as in need of houses, there was an implicit obligation on the part of the community to receive those services. Reports of communities 'shopping around' for better deals (notably for better designs, different or better-quality materials or more floor space) raised the ire of NGOs. International informants expressed annoyance with this practice and complained of beneficiaries being ungrateful and demanding. That beneficiaries were in their words ungrateful violates the third aspect of obligation, that of the obligation to repay gifts.

In the context of humanitarian aid, a repayment in kind is obviously not intended by the donor. Here repayment is something more ephemeral. It is the feeling or knowledge that the gift is being used, and most importantly appreciated in the way that it was intended. People give gifts, and in particular charity, to fulfil their obligation as moral citizens (Rozario 2003), and the value of an act of giving is dramatically augmented when there is certainty that it is contributing to an equally moral outcome. When faced with a request for spare change by a beggar on the street, many potential givers want to be assured that their donation will not go towards drugs or drink, but towards a noble end such as food or shelter. Similarly, for the 'givers' of humanitarian aid, there is the need to know that their contribution is reaching its intended end. Here, the role of NGOs is both facilitating and complicating. On the one hand they provide a service that attempts to materially demonstrate that the money is reaching its intended end – for example, through the provision of pictures of, and handwritten letters from, the recipient. On the other hand, they introduce an added level of mistrust when their administrative costs or perceived bureaucratic waste detract from the total value of the gift. Post-tsunami, NGOs were conscious of the pressure to demonstrate that the obligation of repayment was being discharged: that people were not only receiving aid, but that it was tangibly contributing to the reconstruction of their post-tsunami lives.

In the context of housing reconstruction, it is here that demonstration of use and satisfaction on the part of the beneficiaries became crucial for NGOs. When NGOs perceived that the intended beneficiaries were abdicating their obligation to repay, they felt morally wronged and manipulated and expressed contempt for the moral character of the beneficiaries. Even at a more institutional level, there is the need to demonstrate that the funds are being appropriately used. This is typically done through the form of outcome indicators that document the number of items that have been provided. In the case of the tsunami, the houses provided a useful and easily calculated outcome indicator to report back to headquarters and donor governments.

The second key aspect of Mauss's gift is that it is not simply an abstract object but, through its designation as a gift, is elevated to a quasi-spiritual plane: it contains within it a part of the giver. The gift also, and necessarily, contains within it a part of how the giver perceives the recipient. To present someone with a gift is to go through a process by which the giver determines what the recipient needs and wants and, in doing so, must formulate an image or idea of what constitutes the 'other'. In the case of the tsunami, that image was crucial to the provision of the house as the dominant reconstruction strategy.

The simplicity with which the victims of the tsunami were initially regarded is in keeping with the construction of the native: a long-running theme in post-colonial literature. Work by Bhabha (2004) and Said (1995) discusses the orientalist dynamics inherent in the creation of a colonial subject. Such discussions resonate within the sphere of contemporary aid practice, where the humanitarian subject is constructed in a way that fits the overall occidental narrative of aid provision and the narrative of the gift. As recipients of aid, the Acehnese were constructed as beneficiaries, recipients and victims. For example, initially myriad websites, promotional tracts and reports displayed resilient Acehnese, bravely rebuilding their homes and their lives (UN-HABITAT 2007a). This was amplified by the lack of 'on the ground' knowledge of the disaster zone. In less favourable encounters, it may also have contributed to an idea of the Acehnese as lacking in capacity, as being impoverished, isolated and hyper-traditional. Instead of conceiving of Aceh as a rich and cosmopolitan place with a capital city that had resisted Dutch colonialism for many years and valued its independence, the province was seen as a poor and bounded place that should be grateful for what it received. Many aid workers were surprised at the high level of economic and social development in Banda Aceh (its capital) and focused on the visually remarkable but relatively uncommon architectural form of the traditional house.

As described by Nas (2003: 136), traditional Acehnese houses "are compact, enclosed wooden structures on posts. Often these posts are nothing to write home about, sometimes appearing far from sturdy. The roofs are covered with palm-leaf thatch or corrugated iron." Other features include gabled roofs, generally aligned east to west. "In most cases, doors are not situated in the gable sides, and face either the north or south" (ibid.: 136). The gables are decorated with triangular gable screens which "slant outwards and are ornamented with woodcarvings", as are other parts of the house, such as around "windows and boards" (ibid.: 137). The interior space of the houses is generally divided into three parts: a front gallery which runs along the front part of the house and is used to receive guests and is "the most public part and the male part of the house" (ibid.: 137); a back gallery, which runs along the back part of the house and is the domain of the women and children; and a raised middle section, where the bedrooms are located. Kitchens may be located either inside or outside of the house, and toilets would be outside. The space underneath the house would be used for storage.

Although this housing type is almost everywhere in retreat, it was initially the focus of elaborate discussions between donors and beneficiaries. Donors were at first very concerned that 'local knowledge' be used in the reconstruction, which arguably led to an overemphasis on the ornamental and stylistic aspects of building. As the raised timber house seemed to donors to be an exceptional example of local building techniques which had emerged out of local circumstances, this style was initially encouraged. And yet, recipients were not interested in discussions over whether their houses should have a balcony, what colour they should be painted, or whether the toilets should point away from Mecca. Ultimately, the majority of recipients were more concerned about the overall size of their house compared to their neighbours' and whether it was built of concrete or brick; brick being considered more prestigious.[2]

Arguably, the fact that donors were promoting the vernacular Acehnese form contributed to a resentment towards them

---

2 Although the general consensus was that the preference of brick over other materials was based upon social prestige, one Belgian UN worker felt that the preference was based, in the context of a long-running civil conflict, on the need for the physical security that brick provided.

4.5 Example of a 'traditionally inspired' tsunami house, Banda Aceh

on the part of the Acehnese. Within contemporary Acehnese society, "[p]eople living in traditional houses are often associated with backwardness and poverty, especially in the context of the big city", which is where the donors began their reconstruction programmes (ibid.: 133). One informant said, "[i]f you are poor, then you will have timber houses, if you are rich enough you will go to brick masonry house. That is the mind set over here." The form itself, the choice of the house, arguably also said more about the West. The concept of the home is held up as the archetype of stability and comfort, and people will often consider their home to be an integral part, or even extension, of their identity (Blunt and Dowling 2006; Forced Migration Review 2004). Within a globalizing concept in general, the idea of the home, or the neighbourhood, has come to acquire almost a sacred status (Beck and Ritter 1992). Particularly within the humanitarian aid community, the idea of home is a simultaneously omnipresent and elusive concept.

The third aspect of Mauss's theory, as identified by Carrier, is the mutually obligated relationship of the transactors. According to Carrier, the "inalienable identities and obligations" of the transactors is created and maintained through the process of gift-giving (Carrier 1991: 130). The failure of beneficiaries to act in ways appropriate to their role in the transaction could, from the perspective of the donors, have both undermined the logic of the entire transaction and threatened their own identity as givers. In particular three types of behaviour became particularly threatening to the stability of the mutual relationship.

First, there was the issue of corruption. When reports circulated of houses being allocated to ineligible persons, donors were initially shocked. Such people included those individuals who had not lost a house in the tsunami, ex-combatants, or people who had more than one house. In the case of transitional housing, the decision to provide houses to the residents of the temporary accommodation (i.e. barracks) resulted in people who were not tsunami victims moving into the barracks in order to be allocated a house. Such behaviour came to be held up by internationals as a prime example of the corrupt and dishonest nature of Acehnese society, and has subsequently been used as an explanation for slow project delivery and mismanagement. It has also been used as an excuse for the use of increasingly interventionist and non-participatory methods, as well as the termination of projects.

Secondly, there was the issue of social networks and transference, whereby houses, housing contracts or jobs in BRR were exchanged according to a logic which lay outside the parameters of the gift logic. According to Aspinall (2009), jobs within BRR were allocated to ex-combatants as a way of providing a financial cushion for the reintegration process. From the donors' perspective, however, the two processes, of post-tsunami reconstruction and post-conflict reintegration, needed to be kept programmatically, financially and functionally distinct (Barron 2007).

A third destabilizing factor was the reports of violent behaviour towards international NGOs and internationals in general, which began to surface as the communities grew increasingly dissatisfied with what the NGOs (and BRR) were providing. To counter such behaviour NGOs adopted various techniques, including exit, socialization and arm's-length contracting. The first is self-explanatory. During the first year, many NGOs simply packed their bags and left the province, leaving broken promises and half-built houses in their wake. In most cases, these were either individuals or very small-scale organizations, which did not have large commitments or international reputational concerns to contend with. The second, socialization, or teaching the Acehnese to behave correctly, was frequently cited by INGOs as being key to getting local communities to cooperate, to use the house appropriately, to understand the limitations of the NGOs' responsibilities as givers, and also to stress the responsibilities of the recipients (Rizal 2007). A commonly cited case was the forced introduction of underground septic tanks, which are not normally used along coastal Aceh. Bruno Dercon, head of UN-HABITAT in Aceh throughout the reconstruction process, describes the phenomenon in his excellent retrospective report.

> Early on, 'building back better' expectations had been fed
> by the many humanitarian INGOs who often are specialised
> in the provision of clean drinking water ... BRR published
> ambitious technical implementation guidelines, requiring a
> two-room septic tank and a filtration yard or a planted leach
> field. But the technical realities were cumbersome: tradition-
> ally, urban people used a simple soak pit while toilets were not
> common on the countryside. Making new water tight septic
> tanks required strict construction supervision, which was a rare
> expertise both before and after the Tsunami. In waterlogged
> areas, new lightweight fancy plastic septic tanks even floated
> up due to the upwards water pressure. The social realities
> were often even more cumbersome: except where high-quality
> contractors were paid to put in a small number of systems at

a high cost without asking people, or where social facilitators put in tremendous efforts to educate a small number of households, the change from very poor sanitation provisions to state-of-the-art amenities was perceived with incredulity or even rejected. Simple hygiene education had to come first, but by that time, tens of thousands of poorly built septic tanks had been put into the ground. Organisations like IOM and UN-HABITAT, with support of BRR, Red Cross organisations and ADB and in collaboration with the provincial Human Settlements Departments, have lately started to amend the problems, but this will be a long process. (Dercon 2009: 26–7)

More successful socialization methods were deployed by the British Red Cross, which, after initial difficulties, was able to ascertain who "the important people in the village were" and have coffee with them, as one informant described it. The key people included the *Keuchik* (village leader), the *Teuku* (prayer leader) and the GAM leader. "I got fat drinking 12 cups of coffee a day," laughed the Acehnese staff member in charge of forging these liaisons, as he patted his stomach through his T-shirt. Once established, these relations allowed the Red Cross to explain that standards on building materials needed to be met by local contractors, because "this is for your family; do you want the quality to be bad, do you want it to fall down in an earthquake on their heads?" Another method of socialization was the use of comic books. Plan International, an INGO that works to promote children's rights and lift them out of poverty in forty-eight developing countries, produced a comic work to help disseminate information and socialize beneficiaries with regard to the "sustainability of the program and benefits to stakeholders" (Plan Aceh 2007). However, while the stated aim is to clarify the goals and parameters of the intervention, the text itself seems more interested in establishing correct attribution for past mistakes. For example, it makes multiple references to Acehnese or Indonesian corruption or laziness as a contributing factor to slow delivery and related problems (ibid.).

But socialization worked only in areas where the NGOs had expertise, and even well-established NGOs were not experienced in the area of construction. The IFRC did not have a dedicated shelter department and little to no experience designing and implementing full-scale construction projects. One informant commented, "if you look at the agencies that had come here, almost none of them had built houses before ... Canadian Red Cross? Never run a housing project in their lives. This was twelve times the size of any project that they'd ever done before." In the area of housing reconstruction, some of the most influential and experienced staff drew on their own personal experiences from East Timor, Afghanistan and Kashmir. Others had previously worked in the construction industry in North Africa, Australia and the Middle East. These experiences contributed to the way in which the reconstruction was imagined. The work in active combat zones arguably contributed to a heightened focus on security in Aceh, while experiences as construction workers ultimately contributed to the donors' change in programming from a culture of the gift to one of the commodity.

Staff turnover in the first eighteen months was extremely high. Part of this was to be expected as a humanitarian response shifted towards longer-term recovery, rehabilitation and development concerns that required new types of expertise. But informants also expressed a sense of frustration and despondency that began to set in among the international community in Aceh as project targets proved to be unattainable, fraud and corruption were uncovered, and beneficiaries grew increasingly dissatisfied with the slow pace of results. NGOs began to bring in large-scale construction companies that were neither participatory nor particularly concerned with the impressions, needs and requests of the beneficiary. Many of these companies were overtly corrupt, adding to the negative impression that the international community had of the reconstruction experience. In turn, the low quality of the houses meant that the beneficiaries were unhappy: some complained openly to the media, government or directly to donors; others threatened particular agencies; and many others simply refused to live in the houses. This again reinforced the impression among the international community that the recipients were ungrateful, corrupt and potentially violent. The resulting level of disgust with Acehnese society was expressed by one aid worker in her analysis of Acehnese culture as based exclusively on the principle of exchange, completely lacking in such "Western emotions" as gratitude or love. While the first eighteen months were "a tough learning curve", they led to one of the most significant shifts in humanitarian thinking post-1992: the move from reconstruction as gift to reconstruction as commodity.

The house as commodity

Returning briefly to Carrier (1991), rather than being embedded within a network of social relations and tied to implied obligation, or future action, a commodity is completely removed both from the people and processes that have produced it, and from those who will use or own it. Its value lies in its fungibility. Within the context of humanitarian aid, the idea of an object as pure commodity is actively denied or ignored. For example, while the use of food aid as a commodity, rather than as a consumable (or gift), is widely acknowledged, various types of processes are put in place to discourage this type of behaviour. In the context of the tsunami, the form of the house as a commodity initially was resisted by NGOs, which saw the house as the fulcrum upon which hinged other, more traditional development approaches, such as improved sanitation and access to education and healthcare, as well as more ambiguous goals such as community empowerment and ownership. In some areas this has actually happened. For example, through the new land titling scheme, women are now legally allowed to have their name on the land certificate. However, more generally this was not the case, with NGOs actively distancing themselves from the provision of housing. According to one international adviser to BRR:

eventually they [the NGOs] figured out the construction model that for large-scale things like this, you pretty much have to use. That is, you hire an international consulting firm whose business is international contracting and they set up your tender process, they vet your potential contractors, they run the tenders. Then you award those tenders to local contractors.

Once the contracts are awarded:

these contractors behave just like contractors from Toronto and Sri Lanka. You make your money by winning the contract and then shaving off costs wherever you can, so you [the NGO] have to have a civil engineer out on the job site every day watching the contractors. So each construction site has an engineer ... so there are two or three other engineering companies who are monitors ... They bring in a fleet of engineers – Indian engineers, Canadian engineers, Indonesian engineers, engineers who are accustomed to how cement is poured and how much rebar goes in ... etc. and they make sure that these people [the contractors] build to spec ... what happened here, was a lot of people took a lot of time to figure this out.

I will return below to this transition from the house as gift to the house as commodity within the NGO community in Aceh. First, I will examine the way in which other parties to the reconstruction – beneficiary communities, GoI and BRR, and the GAM – understood the house as a commodity from very early on. In each case, I show how the tensions between the two paradigms help explain many of the problems that were experienced.

Communities By May 2006, eighteen months after the tsunami and nearing the end of the period of the gift, the main issue that representatives from NGOs wanted to discuss was corruption. There was a high level of frustration among NGO staff with regard to fraudulent claims, manipulation of the system, and demanding or even violent beneficiaries. By December 2007, the government agency responsible for investigating corruption in the reconstruction of houses had identified 1,000 cases of what was considered cheating. These involved from 5,000 to 10,000 houses and the collusion of as many as 50,000 individuals in multiple ownership schemes or "house banking" (Mate 2007). According to an informant with BRR's Housing Supplies for Internally Displaced Persons, corruption had become such an endemic part of the reconstruction process that entire villages colluded to gain extra houses. Part of the problem was bureaucratic, and part of it related to the culture of the gift. The bureaucratic part of the problem was the result of the specification that, in the area of housing reconstruction, there were only three possibilities for post-tsunami compensation: new house, partially built new house, repaired house. This led to a situation where even if the house that had been destroyed was large and housed multiple families, the beneficiaries were allowed only a single replacement house of 36 square metres. To ask for more houses was considered corruption, leaving people who fell outside of the categories of assistance to find ways around them.

That the problem was also a result of thinking about the house in terms of a gift can be seen in Oxfam's initial lack of understanding as to why communities would not value new houses in the traditional Acehnese style, nor why a single 36-square-metre house was not seen as sufficient in a culture in which: "[a] typical village consists of clusters of houses owned by sisters and aunts (mother's sisters) with the compounds often sharing a wall and a fence. The size of the clusters depends, of course, on the size of the families and the availability of land" (Siegel 2003: 52).

Generally, the Acehnese being assisted by the reconstruction were not poor. Because of the bureaucratic requirement to demonstrate ownership of the destroyed house, most recipients of the tsunami houses, as they came to be called, were middle- to upper-class. Many had either owned large, concrete houses with multiple storeys, or aspired to do so. Similarly, it is not uncommon for an extended family to live together in one house. In the case that the destroyed house was a large one, accommodating several generations, there was no provision available within the BRR guidelines for anything except the standard 36-square-metre house. While initially many NGOs tried to provide larger houses, inflation and other complicating factors meant that even the 36-square-metre houses were often built to a substandard quality. This created dissatisfaction among beneficiaries and led to attempts to circumvent the regulations, including obtaining more than one house to live in.

The idea of the house as a commodity meant that the link between using and living in the house, and caring for and owning it, was broken. Instead it was seen as a leverageable or fungible object that could be used as collateral on a bank loan, or rented out for income. Initially, another common way of making money from the house was not only to get the object, but to get the contract to build the object. According to one informant, who managed the process for one of the major NGOs,

> [a]n Acehnese person would go and register three or four different business names, and then all he would do is subcontract out the work to what they call 'labour leaders' so ... the contractor would supply the material and the labour leader would get the men to build it. So basically, at that time our houses were eighty million [rupia] and then the labour leader would give ten million of that to the labour leader to build the house and the rest would go for materials, and into their [the contractor's] pocket ... they made a lot of money on these houses.

He went on,

> what we were finding out was that we would advertise for bids, and we'd get all these bids in, and they would be on the same form, the numbers were almost identical, and just the name of the company was different, so they didn't try to hide it very well ... and so we'd laugh about it, but then you're kind of

stuck because we went through all the proper protocol that you're supposed to do and we would still have to use these guys ... we had some projects in Lamno where there were four or five different contracts and we found out that they were all one person between a man and his wife – together. Collectively, there were nine different companies but they were all still the same.

He concluded, "I use the word 'contractor', but all they were, were brokers and they weren't doing a good job."

Such brokering activities have a long history in the context of Aceh (Siegel 2003). While such conduct could be seen as entrepreneurial or adaptive, donors felt that they were examples of corruption. However, attributing the label of corruption to these activities, rather than using De Certeau's terminology of 'making do' or tactics, removes any agency on the part of the structures that permitted these behaviours (De Certeau 1988). It also implies that moral rather than simply bureaucratic contracts were violated. Returning to the moral contract that is implicit within the relationship of the gift, such behaviours were seen on the part of the international community as de facto abdication of the responsibilities of being a recipient.

The beneficiary communities, for their part, felt that poor construction quality, slow progress and lack of related amenities were a failure of provision in what amounted to a pure commodity relationship. One informant, a security adviser for the government, explained the reported violence against NGOs as just such a difference of perception. He recounted as example an incident that occurred between the Canadian Red Cross (RC) and a community along the west coast of Aceh. This story had become commonly cited among the international community as an example of the violent and ungrateful nature of certain Acehnese communities. The story was that a delegation from the headquarters of the Canadian RC wanted to visit some projects between Calang and Lamno, and went down the West Coast Road despite their (Acehnese) driver's advice that this was a bad idea as the beneficiaries were unhappy. The delegation insisted on going, and at around 4 p.m. they encountered a roadblock. They were forced to stop, at which point they found their SUVs had been surrounded by logs. The head of the Canadian RC in Aceh was called and the incident was reported as a kidnapping. Through back-channel, informal negotiation the security officer found the 'kidnapped' delegation a few hours later, in the local mosque, having tea and biscuits with members of the community. The community were very dissatisfied with the houses that the Canadian RC had built for them. They had initially been told that the houses were going to be a specific size, only to find out this was to be reduced. The community had been waiting for redress on this issue for two and a half years but none had come. On that day, the issue was resolved through a call to the *Bupati's* (local governor's) office; he told the community that all parties concerned would be invited to a meeting at his office in the near future. This was sufficient resolution of the issue for the community to let the delegation continue on their way.

From the perspective of the Canadian RC, this was recorded as an overtly aggressive act by the community. But in the opinion of my informant, it was an example of an 'enforced negotiation' that constituted a normal part of Acehnese business dealings. (The Canadian RC would not comment on these events.) It is also likely that the limited spatial and material experience of both the visiting delegation and the recently appointed head of mission exacerbated the situation. By immediately considering the situation to be a kidnapping it was labelled as an overtly aggressive act on the part of the community. Categorized as such, the act entails certain protocols, and under other circumstance could have led to an unwarranted escalation in violence between the Canadian RC and the community. Returning to the gift/commodity distinction, the perception of the houses as a commodity could imply an escalation of bargaining tactics if one side felt that the implicit contract was being ignored. However, the perception of the houses as gifts implies a high degree of flexibility on the part of the beneficiary community, which should, according to a 'gift mentality', be happy to receive anything at all. It would also explain why NGOs were so annoyed that their beneficiaries were reportedly 'shopping for houses' – that is, going from NGO to NGO to try to negotiate more favourable terms on housing provision.

Government of Indonesia and BRR While BAPPENAS initially tried to spearhead the recovery and reconstruction, the GoI quickly decided that an independent bureau was needed, and in March 2005, a presidential decree established BRR as the lead agency to oversee the rehabilitation and reconstruction phases of the response. Physically located in Aceh, BRR was to be the key coordinating body and would have ministerial-level authority over almost all areas of decision-making. The organization was mandated to uniquely manage and lead all aspects of reconstruction coordination and oversight. However, from the outset, the organization's mandate was shaped by the disproportionate focus put on housing by the NGOs that were already working in the province. Although, according to the GoI, the rehabilitation phase was to proceed from the emergency phase, it was already well under way by the time BRR had established itself in Aceh, most notably in the reconstruction of permanent houses. While many of the NGOs had, by May 2005, made only minimal progress on the houses, commitments had been made to both communities and donors. This forced BRR into the awkward (and untenable) position of trying to spearhead a process that had been unfolding apace for the past four months.

The establishment of a government-led response was, from the donors' perspective, an ideal strategy: ticking the boxes of international declarations supporting country ownership of a humanitarian response. But the weight of the intranational dynamics that emerged with BRR's establishment was perhaps not immediately apparent to the international community. The person chosen to head the organization was Dr Kuntoro Mangkusubroto: the "unimpeachable Minister of Mines", as one informant described him. With a doctorate in engineering, he was widely seen both inside and outside of government as incorruptible, and he proved to be the ideal candidate for the job. Along with Kuntoro came a range of hand-picked government employees, from directors to secretaries, straight from Jakarta. During interviews, several expressed a dislike for Aceh and the desire to return to Jakarta as soon as possible. Although it was never said explicitly in any interview, conversations with regular Acehnese gave the impression that BRR was popularly regarded as a Jakarta-led organization, drawing its manpower from the same elite networks as other forms of government.

Within the context of a newly peaceful Aceh, the presence of a Jakarta-led organization, in charge of the largest direct transfer of money ever seen by the province, was not lost on either the Acehnese leadership – the GAM – or on the GoI. With regard to the GoI, interviews indicate that the decision was taken early on to relinquish a degree of control and, inevitably, of quality in exchange for quick and visible results and a timely exit. Said one informant, "the decision [within government] was: fast-track it, accept that you're going to get a whole lot of foreigners in here, there will be limited vetting, and there will be quality issues". Another said,

> For our housing programme, in an environment where you can't test everyone's bona fides, we had a reasonably broad tolerance for failure. And we knew that we would have to pick up the pieces. But here's the point – are you better off building perfectly but taking ten years to do it, or building it fast, fixing up ten per cent of the problems, having communities in houses … we were under severe pressure. The political fall-out was our heads on the chopping board.

According to one informant, as early as September 2005 it had become clear to BRR that many of the housing pledges, made to communities by NGOs, would not materialize. In addition to implementation problems, the repeal of the nationwide fuel subsidy in November 2005 only amplified the already all too predictable reconstruction-driven inflation. This forced all NGOs to drastically reduce the number of promised houses owing to skyrocketing input costs. As it was the face of reconstruction in Aceh, people often complained to BRR when NGOs failed to deliver on their pledges: protesting vocally outside their offices or to the local press when they were unhappy.

There were also indications that the GoI was well aware of the more far-reaching implications of the trade-off between delivery and quality. Within BRR there was an awareness – shockingly lacking within the international community – that the nascent peace process could be easily destabilized if tsunami reconstruction were to go awry. If well managed, however, BRR and its funds could provide ballast to the peace process. The decision for BRR to go into housing reconstruction was regarded, by many informants, as a fundamental mistake. In their view it confused oversight with implementation and jeopardized BRR's claims to transparency and accountability. And while it is true that the conflation of the two roles within the same organization led to the construction of many houses of dubious quality, had the NGOs been left to their own devices the promised target of 120,000 houses (in just over three years) would not have been met.

The target number of 120,000 was itself somewhat arbitrary: based on initial assessments of damage and loss, without careful consideration of time frames. A common problem was that a house was built for a family where the only survivor was a young child. While it is true that the house could be kept in trust for the child, given the quality of the houses and where some of them were built, there could be no guarantee that the house would still be standing in ten years' time. However, BRR adopted the target of 120,000 as doctrine. They created and maintained a database (the RAN-D) of all housing contributions and doggedly made up the shortfall (Tsunami Global Lessons Learned Project Steering Committee 2009).

As of 16 April 2009, when BRR officially shut its doors, the target of building 120,000 homes for tsunami survivors had been achieved (and even slightly surpassed) and the humanitarian relief and reconstruction effort was branded a success by the GoI (Yudhoyono 2009). While difficulties with the process were acknowledged (Jakarta Post 2009), overall the reconstruction was represented as fulfilling its goals, judged primarily by the physical presence of the houses. Whether they were occupied, adequately built or had contributed to the funding base of various quasi-criminal networks (International Crisis Group 2008; Aspinall 2009) was downplayed. From the perspective of the GoI, the commodity value of the houses lay largely outside of Aceh, in the political capital it would provide. According to one informant, by leaving on schedule, the GoI closed the doors on the reconstruction, claimed it as a success, and left the newly elected GAM leadership to manage the fall-out.

Indonesian president S. B. Yudhoyono was able to leverage the reconstruction in two significant ways. First, domestically, he was able to use the successful tsunami reconstruction as a success story of his previous administration. Regionally, he drew upon the Aceh experience to position Indonesia as a credible alternative to Western humanitarian solutions. For example, following Cyclone Nargis, a key member of BRR was asked to spearhead the ASEAN response team, based on the perceived success of the post-tsunami reconstruction. Secondly, Indonesia could now be seen as a credible, accountable partner in the international sphere. However, should the housing reconstruction be seen as a failure over the next few years, the damage would be done primarily to the Acehnese leadership under the GAM.

There are indications that the reconstruction more generally, and the houses in particular, were viewed as commodities, not gifts, from very early on. From the beginning of the response in January 2005, the entire approach was conceptualized in business management terms, according to one informant. It is important also to acknowledge the impact of specific individuals and experiences on the overall outcome. Equally, the main vehicle for government response, BRR, was a new organization with the accompanying characteristics and pathologies of any new organization. However, as explanatory factors of the outcome, both factors – personalities and organizational birthing pains – were equally present within the sphere of the NGOs.

Corruption may appear to be the most obvious example of thinking in terms of commodities, particularly given that there were documented cases of corruption within BRR (Afrida 2006). According to informants at the highest levels of BRR:

> BRR has corruption in it. There's no question about that. But it is not systemic. It is contained. It is dealt with when we discover it. We've got very good systems – both internal and external. We will pursue prosecutions … what we can prosecute … but that doesn't mean that there aren't people who know their way around, that keep two sets of books … but it's never got its tentacles inside.

This is supported by a comprehensive external review conducted by UNORC, which stated that "corruption levels were kept remarkably low" despite the unprecedented levels of funding (Tsunami Global Lessons Learned Project Steering Committee 2009: 61). And yet, according to the World Bank, corruption was cited as the third-biggest source of anti-BRR protests by beneficiaries (World Bank/DSF 2008: 6).

It is also important to note that the construction industry is itself widely perceived to be extremely corrupt. Many of the considerations that enter into both formal and informal tendering processes could be seen as constituting corrupt behaviour, as certain groups or individuals benefit disproportionately. The involvement of large, Jakarta-based construction companies such as P. T. Wyjaya Karya in the reconstruction process only reinforced the perception that the process favoured the interests of certain Jakarta-based politicians. This perception was so widespread that even a children's cartoon on the tsunami reconstruction devoted an entire page to the presence of the infamous 'KKN' (*koruptsi, kolusi, dan nepotisme*

= corruption, collusion and nepotism) practices, implying that this was ongoing (Plan Aceh 2007: 16). However, the involvement of large construction firms was not the preferred option for either the NGOs or BRR. Initially, BRR was under a lot of pressure to hire Acehnese contractors, both from local government, which did not like BRR as they felt that they were overruling their power, and from Jakarta, which felt that the "modality of delivering through the 2000 local contractors was correct at a political level". It was only when these local 'contractors' failed to deliver that the big firms were brought in as the preferred solution.

In summary, while it is beyond the capacity of this study to establish, with certainty, whether personal enrichment through kickbacks and graft occurred within BRR, it is clear that within Indonesian society the expectation that this activity would take place was pervasive. This supports the argument that the house was seen primarily as a commodity, without decisively establishing the degree to which BRR's staff engaged in corrupt business practices.

GAM Perhaps no other group regarded the reconstruction of houses in such a commodified way as the GAM. Following the August 2005 Helsinki Accord between the GAM and the GoI, money and resources were allocated for the demobilization and reintegration processes, although nowhere near the amount that had been allocated for post-tsunami reconstruction. Initially, the two types of post-crisis assistance were, by and large, kept financially and programmatically apart (Barron 2007). Separate institutions were created to oversee the respective processes. The largest pooled fund of post-tsunami money, the Multi Donor Fund (MDF), worth $US673 million, although espousing a conflict-sensitive approach, could not be used on post-conflict projects.[3] Ignoring years of policy analysis on the need to adopt conflict-sensitive approaches to development (Burke and Afnan

---

3 It was originally named the 'Multi Donor Trust Fund', but 'Trust' was dropped from the title, according to one facetious interviewee, because there was no trust left.

2005), post-tsunami projects and programmes initially adopted a largely 'conflict blind' approach. It was considered to be relatively easy to distinguish between tsunami-affected areas and conflict-afflicted ones, and the two issues were seen to be programmatically separable.

However, as the reconstruction developed, it became increasingly clear that the two processes were not as separate as initially hoped. In some geographic areas, such as Bireuen and Aceh Utara, there was significant overlap between the two groups of beneficiaries, creating tension between individuals receiving different levels and quality of support (Armas et al. 2008; UNORC/BRR 2007). Even in areas where the two categories of beneficiaries were not overlapping or contiguous at the outset of the reconstruction, people would move. On the west coast, while the GAM was initially concentrated in the Calang area, as the reconstruction wore on, they "spread outward", according to interviewees. The search for beneficiaries on behalf of NGOs may have contributed to this movement, as did their demand for reconstruction materials and labour (International Crisis Group 2007). Also, the character of the conflict – long, entrenched, rural – meant that its reach was far greater than originally assumed or understood by the majority of the international community coming to assist.

The long-running, primarily rural conflict in Aceh meant that the GAM was deeply embedded within Acehnese social structures (Schulze 2003). As in other 'rural rebellions', the line between combatant, civilian and supporter was often blurred. GAM's refusal to directly identify former combatants meant, in turn, that the peace deal failed to include a comprehensive demobilization component (BBC 2005a). This resulted in the majority of combatants and many civilians retaining their weapons. Further, the financial compensation was neither sufficient, nor its disbursement sufficiently monitored, to provide a strong incentive for ex-combatants to make the already difficult shift from militia to civilian and to move away from the illegal activities that had previously provided their income, such as logging and marijuana

(International Crisis Group 2007). In 2007, Barron (2007) observed that the use of individual compensation approaches in the reintegration of ex-combatants might be (re)producing the very conditions that made conflict likely in the first place: decreases in social cohesion, the hardening of conflict-era group identities, the aforementioned development of an entitlement mentality, and the perpetuation of a lack of trust in the state on the part of communities. But the most important factor lay not within the peace agreement, or more specifically the MoU, itself, but alongside it: in the projects, contracts, tenders and supply chains surrounding the tsunami reconstruction.

Unlike the donors who tended to see housing reconstruction as a gift, delinked from surrounding processes and part of the humanitarian imaginary, or the GoI/BRR, which quite quickly perceived it in terms of political capital, the GAM saw the reconstruction as a resource stream that could be tapped into at all levels. At the highest level, the tsunami provided an opportunity to change the direction of the country – be it by intent or accident (Christian Science Monitor 2005; Renner 2006). Originally, the explanations of how the tsunami contributed to the resolution of the previously intractable conflict pointed to a coincidence of several causes. In Aceh, psychological causes were commonly cited within civic or religious tracts on the tsunami: claiming that its might and devastation made petty human rivalries pale in comparison. They often referred to the tsunami as God's wrath on an unfaithful Aceh (Sufi and Budi Wibowo 2004), and called for the tightening of Syari'at law in the province. Other commentators claimed that the intense media attention internationalized the conflict (Hyndman 2009; Waizenegger 2007), providing a window that allowed the parties to move away from entrenched negotiation positions and/or focused international attention on the conflict in a way not previously seen, forcing the parties to settle, and included reputational concerns on the part of the GoI and the possible overstretch of resources on the part of the TNI. At no point during my research did I encounter any discussion of whether the tsunami funding might have been contingent on a settlement. More recently, commentators have highlighted the role that the tsunami funds have played in the transformation from GAM as combatants to GAM as elected officials through the control or predation of key resources, be they natural or man made (Le Billon and Waizenegger 2007; Aspinall 2007, 2009). I believe that had it not been for the large resource streams of tsunami aid, the peace process could not have succeeded.

My evidence does not suggest that, in the first eighteen months after the tsunami, the GAM had any particular rent-seeking advantage over other groups or individuals. During this period, NGOs and BRR alike adopted an approach to reconstruction that concentrated on using local labour and resources. The problems with this were manifold. Beyond the problems with the traditional NGO model, the lack of both qualified labour and affordable materials proved insurmountable. The most frustrating aspect of contracting local tradesmen to build, design or supply housing projects, according to one informant, was that instead of admitting they did not have the requisite skills, individuals (or families) would bid for, and win, the contracts, only to turn around and sell the contracts on to someone else. Not only did this preclude any possibility of accountability, it introduced a way of making additional money from the tsunami funds: an activity at odds with the gift culture of the donors. With the MoU signed in August 2005, the GAM began the process of disarmament and transformation into a peaceful political movement (Aspinall 2009: 8). This included the organizational transformation of the *Tentara Negara Aceh* (Armed Forces of the State of Aceh or TNA) into the *Komite Peralihan Aceh* (Aceh Transitional Committee or KPA). For the newly peaceful GAM,

[t]he influx of reconstruction funds provided multiple sites for predation, both in the key institutions disbursing funds (such as the BRR), where politically connected and technically savvy players could skim off funds or direct projects to favoured

partners, as at the thousands of building sites scattered throughout Aceh, where less sophisticated local actors lacking such political access could still exert pressure directly on those carrying out reconstruction work. (Ibid.: 10)

The initial demand for local products and inputs into the construction process, such as timber, also benefited the GAM, which had traditionally used illegal logging as one of their revenue streams (International Crisis Group 2008). The realization that the tsunami reconstruction was contributing to deforestation led to donors shifting to other materials, and suppliers. During my last visit in May 2008, stories were widespread of KPA 'protection' fees for sites and the burning of construction materials. An informant working for one of the major multilateral organizations said that it had got to the point where he no longer wanted to post the cost of a tender in a public place, as he knew that he would be exploited for X per cent of the tender (consistent with Aspinall's findings (2009), informants cited this as about 10 per cent of the overall cost). Informants repeatedly voiced experiences with threats to staff and sites. Indeed, three months after my last visit, in September 2008, one of my informants, Adrien Morel, was kidnapped for a ransom, apparently by GAM-affiliated individuals, while undertaking field research (Reuters 2008). In his own research with the World Bank, Morel and his team had documented the increase in violent incidents post-MoU, including disputes related to post-tsunami reconstruction (World Bank/DSF 2007, 2008, 2009).

That the GAM are deeply involved with the various aspects of reconstruction is supported by Aspinall's research. Replicating the hierarchy and territorial allocations of the previous TNA, the

> scale of economic activities engaged in by former GAM combatants roughly follows their position in the movement's steeply pyramidal structure. At the apex are those for whom all of Aceh is their economic arena: people like Muzakkir Manaf, head of the KPA and former supreme commander of

the TNA, and Sofyan Dawood, former TNA commander in North Aceh and former KPA spokesperson. Both individuals are widely understood to be involved in winning high level contracts and in feverish lobbying and brokerage activities with major state-owned enterprises, politically connected private companies in Jakarta, and foreign (usually Chinese and Malaysian) investors in mining, ... and similar fields. Moving down through the structure, GAM and KPA leaders target progressively smaller-scale economic activities in the areas they control ... influential KPA members and ordinary toughs who try to extract resources from whatever government agencies or NGOs carry out reconstruction or development activities in their *gampong* [village]. (Aspinall 2009)

One of Aspinall's claims is that the GAM failed to capture a productive share of the (re)construction industry in Aceh. Rather, he claims that their activities did not go beyond rent-seeking activity or predation in an industry that is considered by many as already quasi-criminal (Stansbury 2005).

The last part of this chapter will explore the relationship between the donors and the construction model of housing reconstruction, demonstrating how the donors' gift culture was challenged by the rent-seeking activities of the GAM, the political objectives of the GoI/BRR, and the so-called corruption of the beneficiaries, all of whom operated primarily within a commodity culture. I claim that Aceh, rather than a humanitarian outlier, destined never to be repeated again in terms of the scale and volume of response, is a decisive moment in the evolution of post-disaster response. In the context of the spatial distribution of humanitarian knowledge, it has served to reinforce the distinction between the culture of the gift and that of the commodity.

From donors to contractors

In the first eighteen months of the reconstruction, donors faced complexities and barriers to the reconstruction of permanent housing. In response to these, donors adopted three strategies: exit, socialization or outsourcing of oversight. While outsourcing is a common practice in humanitarian work, here I am using it to describe the types of arrangements that arose to intentionally obscure practices that run counter to the stated or implied preferred development/humanitarian approach; in other words, practices that violated the culture of the gift. In general, the preferred approach in contemporary development and humanitarian practice relies on principles that enhance or establish those values oriented towards the sustainability of individuals, communities and projects, and which include such concepts as local ownership, downward accountability and participatory development (Pupavac 2005). These were the principles that framed, and informed, the original community-led housing reconstruction projects in Aceh and which dominated for the first eighteen months of the reconstruction.

The shift towards outsourcing began in earnest from June 2006 onwards. Donors were shocked by the lack of progress (Casey 2006) and demoralized by reports of corruption among beneficiaries, at BRR (Afrida 2006) and even among the international agencies themselves (Musa et al. 2008; Oxfam Inter-Agency Meeting 2008). They found themselves under extreme pressure to meet their housing commitments. In the largest humanitarian response of all time, eighteen months after the event, only 40,000 of the needed 120,000 houses had been built. According to a construction specialist at one of the major INGOs, "all the organizations who were involved in construction faced problems of quality. After one and a half years, there was a big problem with quality. Media news too. Big hubbub."

A construction manager from one of the large INGOs described the situation when he arrived in May 2006. His organization was behind in its housing targets and he was given two weeks to build twenty houses, or lose the contract. Up to that point, his organization, like the others, had been operating on a development-oriented model rather than the management approach that would be typically used for large-scale construction projects. The arrival of my informant was only one part of a sea-change in that organization which brought in people with engineering and construction backgrounds, not necessarily aid workers. In this way, they pioneered a new model of post-tsunami housing reconstruction. The construction experts quickly realized that the reason things weren't getting done was that the NGO "was not managing the contractor, they were allowing him to do whatever he wanted ... they were handling them with kid gloves". My informant and his colleagues instituted a system where warning letters were sent outlining the terms, and if the contractors did not like them, they were off the contract. Their efficiency permitted them not only to complete their own housing commitments to a high standard but to take over the housing commitments of other NGOs such as CARE, Oxfam and World Vision.

Explaining his NGO's success in the reconstruction business in Aceh, the head of the organization attributed it to a more "private sector approach" and compared their work to that of "enlightened contractors". Speaking in terms of commodities rather than gifts, he said that people are rational beings anywhere, and that the international community cannot subscribe to the idea of the noble savage any longer. He stressed the need to put in place accountable structures that cannot be manipulated. He considered his NGO's main competitors to be private sector contractors in the vein of Louis Berger, a multinational engineering firm that implements multimillion-dollar reconstruction contracts in Iraq and Afghanistan. While admitting that housing reconstruction is always politicized, he claims that his organization has managed to "offload the political aspects to BRR".

By 2008, the desire to "offload the political" was common among NGOs, which had begun to realize that the processes of post-MoU reintegration and transformation and the tsunami reconstruction could not be kept separate. For example, the second TRIP report began its analysis of the post-tsunami reconstruction with a section on "Areas Most Severely Affected by Tsunami *And/Or Conflict*" (emphasis added) (UNORC/BRR 2007). The 2008 Australian government's "Review of the Aceh Reconstruction Phase (2005–2008)" acknowledged that "over the next five years, assistance to Aceh needs to take into account the complicated and fragile context ... to ensure that aid makes a direct contribution to stability in Aceh while not doing harm to the complex peace building process" (Australian Government Development Cooperation in Indonesia 2008: 19). Echoing my previous informant's desire to keep aid and politics separate, the report also advises (in bold heading font) to "[a]void the most politically or socially controversial issues" (ibid.: 20). This contradiction epitomizes the tensions felt by many of the agencies involved in tsunami reconstruction. On one hand, agencies felt the need to check the 'do no harm' box of their cross-cutting conflict assessments; on the other, they were pressured to meet their agreed targets. The solution appeared in the form of outsourcing.

Sitting in the office of the same private-sector-oriented NGO, located on the building site of a new, $US8 million technical school they are building for Chevron, another informant described how the process of outsourcing is being operationalized. He admits that on this site the local GAM leadership have approached him to 'offer' their various services. While not entirely comfortable with the situation, my informant's NGO have had to use KPA as site security guards and felt that this was a necessary accommodation if the work was to be completed on time. In his opinion, most NGOs "got out of it" (out of politics) by "dealing with it": by incorporating KPA into building projects as a part of normal operating procedures. And while this NGO has been able to negotiate the various allegiances needed to complete their humanitarian work, it has been at the expense of forging new relationships and gaining a better understanding of the local dynamics, as in the case of the work of the British Red Cross. This NGO has decided that the end result of producing a product outweighs the risks of the practices: practices that directly fund certain parties in a context where the peace deal is still fragile.

The larger question that this raises is: if these implementation modalities or practices are going on at the local level as an open secret, why are the lessons learnt not incorporated back into the strategic frameworks at headquarters, back into the humanitarian imaginary? As with the experiences of the British Red Cross, there is much that could be gained from these truly local experiences and knowledge. By outsourcing these experiences, the international community maintains its idealized version of what constitutes aid, assistance and the gift. As expressed by one informant working for one of the more successful housing INGOs, "when you talk about 'building local capacity' it sounds a lot better than 'everybody's getting their cut'".

It is worth noting that I am not advocating the application of neoliberal approaches to development, but rather urging a re-examination of the underlying moral frameworks which inform and define the way in which international assistance is provided: "[t]he whole ideology of the gift, and conversely the whole idea of 'economic self-interest', are our invention" (Parry 1986: 458). But the way in which humanitarian and development practices are spatialized has, thus far, prevented these questions being addressed or even recognized. As a pioneering anthropologist, Mauss faced spatial constraints in his own fieldwork similar to those of contemporary aid workers and, indeed, Mauss has been criticized for falling prey to nativist assumptions of exoticism in his descriptions of the 'other'. His description of the tribal house, for example, can be indexed as contributing to the sublime regard in which the West holds vernacular dwellings: "[t]he houses and decorated beams are themselves beings. Everything speaks – roof, fire, carvings and paintings; for the magical house is built not only by the chief and his people ... but also by the gods and ancestors ..." (Mauss 1969: 43).

By recognizing the role that spatiality and materiality play in the construction of our larger developmental and humanitarian paradigms (or imaginaries) some of the basic categories, which form the building blocks of this schema, are destabilized. Issues of corruption on the part of the beneficiaries were, to a certain extent, attributable to the labyrinthine funding and implementation modalities, which made double reporting on houses easy to do, according to one informant. Is it not simpler to shift the blame for lack of progress on to corrupt and ungrateful beneficiaries than acknowledge mismanagement or corruption within one's own organization? This is not to discount the widespread predation and rent-seeking that did occur, and an initial survey of other reconstruction contexts suggests that this is a widespread phenomenon in post-disaster contexts. Instead of retreating into the sanitized imaginary and auxiliary spaces of the international, it is necessary to understand how the tactics, the 'making do' and the commodification of aid, are an inextricable part of the process. Ironically, this idea is well understood by other groups, such as Hezbollah in southern Lebanon or the Taliban in Afghanistan. And indeed, an emerging area of scholarship suggests that nothing 'wins hearts and minds' as much as contracts and kickbacks. According to one high-level informant,

> [t]here is utopian planning [among the international community] that we can turn a Timbuktu into New York if we have the resources. No we can't because New York is New York not because of the buildings, the structures, but because of the economy that goes with it.

But it is worth adding to this observation the comment of another senior adviser to BRR: "we need to consider that the cities of New York and Toronto were built by what we would consider today as mafia". Although the international humanitarian frameworks may not yet accept such observations, they need to be able to accommodate them, and engage with them, not outsource them and retreat – which takes us to the next disaster, where it's (imaginary) business as usual.

5 | PLAYING HOUSE: REBUILDING THE GULF COAST AFTER KATRINA

All of the great challenges that confront the 21st-century city – from class, race and environmental issues to the continuing duel between history and modernity – are crystallized in New Orleans. (Ouroussoff 2008) (Inside, outside, upside down – Stan and Jan Berenstein)

The previous chapter considered how, within the context of international humanitarian assistance, different epistemologies operated in the different spheres of donors and recipients. The discussion focused on the form of the single-family dwelling and concluded that the tsunami had opened up new directions for thinking about disaster assistance, primarily through the recognition that the built environment is everywhere and always political and politicized. One of the themes that emerged was the primacy of the built environment and, more specifically, the importance of the single-family home in shaping how donors conceptualize post-crisis reconstruction. The research also pointed to the sociological role that designers and engineers have played in the overall trajectory of planning, design, construction and oversight.

This chapter will further investigate the role that engineers and architects play and have played in reconstruction and, conversely, the role that disaster zones play in architectural agendas. By focusing on the post-Katrina reconstruction of the Mississippi Gulf Coast and New Orleans, Louisiana (NOLA), it also demonstrates that the spatial tensions identified in the Aceh example were not, as might be thought, of a North/South nature, but rather the outcome of the spatial imbalances that occur in any situation where categories of victims and donors emerge. The first section will look at the involvement of architects and urban planners in contemporary humanitarian assistance and provide some historical background. The second section will look at the case of green architectural reconstruction in New Orleans, focusing on the actor Brad Pitt's "Make it Right" project. The third section will examine the New Urbanist involvement in Mississippi's Gulf Coast reconstruction. The final section will consider the ethics involved in designing for someone else and how, ultimately, what is designed seems to be more about the designer (donor) than the recipient (victim).

The appeal of the blank slate

The post-crisis landscape has long held allure for architects and designers. Historically, a wide range of superstar architects have put forward their proposals for post-disaster housing. Corbusier's iconic Maison Dom-ino (1914–15) was originally intended as a "solution for the rapid reconstruction of regions such as Flanders, which had been heavily damaged during WWI" (Stohr 2006: 36). Between 1939 and 1945, Finnish architect Alvar Aalto designed a movable temporary emergency shelter designed to house war refugees, which "could be trucked to the site and house four families with a shared central heating unit" (ibid.: 37). And while not strictly designed for post-disaster response, during the 1940s Buckminster Fuller designed the Dymaxion Deployment Unit – a form of "emergency accommodation for troops in various locations during WW2" (ibid.: 38; Hays et al. 2008; Crain 2008). More recently, Studio Libeskind was involved in the design of a Master Plan for Unawatuna, a beachside community in Sri Lanka, devastated by the tsunami (although at the time of writing, the plans for this were stalled at the design stage). According to Rybczynski (2005), in response to post-crisis needs, architects have "proposed a variety of ingenious shelters, including prefabs, inflatables, geodesic dome kits, sprayed polyurethane igloos, and temporary housing made of cardboard tubes and plastic beer crates". Paraphrasing British architect Ian Davis, "not only are these often untested 'universal' solutions generally prohibitively expensive, their exotic forms are usually ill-suited to local conditions" (ibid.).

Throughout the 2000s, groups such as Engineers without Borders, Architecture for Humanity and Architecture without Borders (ASF) have all developed projects in response to various humanitarian disasters and have grown in membership and geographic and functional reach. According to the head of the US branch of ASF, post-crisis work attracts a certain type of person: a person who relishes operating within constantly changing circumstances, in a "climate of chaos". The volunteer model of these organizations also means that the members who come to help in a post-crisis situation will generally not stay for more than a few weeks or a couple of months, and tend to be students or young professionals with limited experience. These volunteers will be familiar with the failures of grand planning or utopian design schemes and will be aware of the need to consult with end users. But they will also be aware of the aspiration within architecture and urban design to build the iconic building or create the master plan. As constraints to planning within a typical project brief will preclude grand or utopian design experiments, the freedom of the post-disaster canvas is very attractive indeed (Ball 2008).

From a planning perspective the aftermath of a disaster is often seen to present a *tabula rasa*: an opportunity to build from the ground up rather than supplement existing developments (Schaper 2005). But the reconstructive or greenfield potential of a post-disaster site may be drastically overestimated. While in some cases, such as the Asian tsunami, a disaster may offer completely new cartographies to be mapped, they also will throw up entirely new sets of development challenges, such as environmental contamination and the need for large-scale repairs to basic infrastructure, as well as the emotional and psychological damage to the population. Perhaps more important than the physical greenfield potential of a post-disaster site is the regulatory vacuum that often occurs. Even where authorities are highly competent, organized and present, the multitude of humanitarian actors who arrive in a disaster site, the often overlapping and unclear channels of responsibility, and the overwhelming need of local populations provide a window where reconstruction standards and norms may be lowered, unfamiliar or unenforceable. Communities will be panicked and ready to listen if someone with resources and skills presents them with a solution. All these conditions make a post-disaster context fertile territory for amateurs, students or ad hoc organizations that are mobile, have low overheads and have a revolutionary or extreme vision that may not be easily implemented within the context of regular planning practice (Klein 2007).

These problems are widely recognized and institutional endeavours are moving towards establishing aid-industry-wide standards – for example, the SPHERE Project or the Humanitarian Accountability Partnership (Wilson 2004; Dufour et al. 2004). With no enforcement mechanisms, participation in these standards remains voluntary and unlikely to reach those actors who need it most. This includes the very small, the occasional and ad hoc actors and agencies that will not be aware of them, as well as the largest and most well established, who have no incentive to participate. Even where regulatory frameworks and consultative approaches are prioritized, the planning phase may overlook the spatial reality of the post-disaster context; a context that makes such an idealized and sanitized process difficult to realize. In the first instance, not all disasters are the same and will vary with regard to type, severity, scale and location, making it extremely difficult to provide guidance for all eventualities. Even when groups are aware of the guidelines and are trying to adhere to them, it may not be easy to correctly identify the affected community as populations may have moved or died. Property ownership may be difficult to ascertain as records may be absent or destroyed, property may have been destroyed, or pre-disaster community boundaries shifted. Further, the affected community may have a diminished capacity to participate in the reconstruction process. Emotionally, post-disaster trauma and stress may mean that they are less likely to be able to meaning-fully contribute to decisions and deliberations, or be able to understand the long-term implications of their decisions. Another common complaint is consultation fatigue, where key people such as local planning officials and local government representatives are rendered ineffective owing to the constant demands upon their time from a never-ending parade of well-meaning groups wanting to solicit their opinions or obtain their blessing. All these factors contribute to the dominance of a particular spatial epistemology that gravitates towards abstract, model-based solutions, which tend to reflect the desires of the donor, not the recipient.

Make it right or making it wrong: the solution of green architecture in New Orleans' Lower Ninth

The push to reconstruct New Orleans in an eco-friendly man-ner has been remarkable. Dozens of groups have been focused on ways to ensure that the reconstruction of New Orleans will be 'green', although the precise way in which this concept has been interpreted has varied. In March 2009, the Historic Green organization brought together "architects, engineers, planners, landscape architects, interior designers and contractors" to "work hand in hand with neighborhood residents on their historic houses, parks, playgrounds, and community centers" (Historic Green n.d.). Its goal was to capture and catalyse the many green build-ing projects that are going on in New Orleans post-Katrina, including a push for the Holy Cross neighbourhood to be carbon neutral by the year 2010 and climate neutral by 2030. Accord-ing to their website, "[n]owhere else in the world, perhaps, is this more possible than the Lower Ninth Ward" (ibid.). Other environmental non-profits feel the same way. Global Green, a non-profit organization based in Santa Monica, is building an "ultra-modern, low-income mini-neighborhood of five houses, 18 apartments and a community center" (Los Angeles Times 2007). According to the spokesperson for the organization, the intention is to "demonstrate to the residents of New Orleans and the South that these kinds of buildings can be built" (ibid.). Perhaps the highest profile of the green reconstruction projects is the one being undertaken by the Hollywood actor Brad Pitt, under the auspices of his foundation: Make it Right (MIR).

MIR was Pitt's response to what he saw as the lack of progress on rehousing displaced populations in New Orleans, Louisiana, following Hurricane Katrina, in particular the population of the Lower Ninth Ward. Historically one of the poorest residential areas of New Orleans, the Lower Ninth was decimated by the break in the levees caused by the storm surge following the hurricane. To address this damage, in June 2007 Pitt invited fourteen architecture firms to tour the Lower Ninth and to develop plans for single-family homes. No home could cost more than US$150,000 or be more than 40 feet wide to conform with the lot sizes. Since the Lower Ninth is in a zone which is in danger of flooding, all the houses had to be raised at least eight feet off the ground (Clarke 2009). The project emphasized the use of environmentally sustainable building technology. Geothermal energy and solar roof panels were expected to provide each house with at least 75 per cent of its energy (ibid.). MIR drew on the expertise of internationally recognized environmental experts, including William McDonough and Partners. While it was far from the only green rebuilding project in New Orleans, it was by far the most prominent, with coverage across major media outlets. The aim was to build 150 new single-family homes which would serve as a catalyst for redevelopment in the Lower Ninth Ward and possibly beyond (ibid.). As of 21 September 2009, four years after the disaster, thirteen houses had been built.

Of the fourteen firms involved, five were from New Orleans (including the lead firm), four from across the USA, and five others international. In general, all the firms used the form of the traditional shotgun house as inspiration in keeping with the MIR mandate to remain "true to the culture of New Orleans" (MIR n.d.). In response to initial complaints that the houses did not have front porches – an integral aspect of New Orleans urban culture – the designs were appropriately modified (Clarke 2009). Of the architects involved, Shigero Ban Architecture was the firm with the most previous experience in designing post-disaster housing. It had worked with the UNHCR in Kobe after the 1995 earthquake, in Gujarat after the 2001 earthquake, in Sri Lanka after the 2004 tsunami, and in China after the 2008 earthquake (Pollock n.d.). Shigeru Ban himself was perhaps best known for his experiments with temporary architecture, such as the use of paper tubing to create temporary spaces and shelters.

The idea of temporariness is typical of post-disaster reconstruction. Within the humanitarian imaginary, the idea of emergency and the corresponding idea of response are repeatedly romanticized (Calhoun 2004). A significant part of this romanticization revolves around the ideal of the temporary, the mobile and the ephemeral, and can be seen in the plethora of design competitions for temporary or mobile dwellings. Examples include the 2008 Architecture Biennale held in New Orleans (Smith 2008), the exhibit at the New York Museum of Modern Art on prefabricated houses, and work by Architects for Humanity on temporary and mobile post-disaster housing. In architectural theory there is a long-standing romantic interest in the concept and manifestations of temporary shelter, from the Mongolian yurt to the bivouac.

The temporariness was explicitly and ironically highlighted within some of the MIR designs. For example, the Dutch firm MVRDV prominently highlighted the inevitability of future catastrophe through their brief for Concept Bent (Figure 5.1).

Designing a house which was, by the designer's own admission, built to flood, highlights a key aspect of rebuilding in the Lower Ninth: that the original cause of the flooding, the inability of the levees to withstand the storm surge, has still not been adequately addressed (A. Liu 2008). MVRDV's design proposed five variations on the typology of the classic shotgun house and all were designed to stand completely or partially above the waterline in the case of a future flood. The descriptively named Floating House, Tilted House, House on a Ramp, House on a Lift and

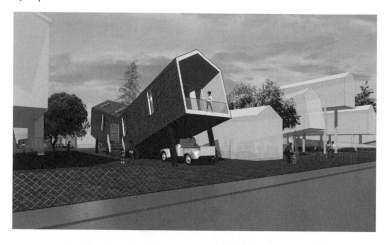

5.1 MVRDV's Concept Bent

Bent House all envisage the ability for life to continue in the midst of flooding. In the Bent House:

> [t]he centre of the house contains the kitchen and bath – it is the lowest level. Stairs lead to a living room on the one side, and bedrooms on the other. The bedrooms and living room are above floodwater level. This means that escape would be possible to both the front porch and the rear porch. (MVRDV n.d.)

Indeed, all the designs were required to include, as a safety feature, an emergency escape hatch that would permit residents to move up on to their roofs should they find themselves trapped by rapidly rising waters, as was the case in 2005 (Clarke 2009). In the case of MVRDV, the design was chosen to explicitly show the contradiction of rebuilding on a known flood plain. Similarly, the architecture firm Morphosis designed a "lightweight concrete foundation anchored by two pylons, like a pier, which would buoy the house if floodwaters rise", like a boat (Pogrebin 2007).

The MVRDV design has been criticized for mocking the very people that it has been commissioned to assist (Stamp 2008). However, Winy Maas, one of the designers involved in the MIR proposal, insists that the consciously ironic design is meant to convey empathy with the ongoing plight of the Ninth Ward residents (Frey 2008). But empathy implies shared understanding. To what degree do such international architects, or 'starchitects' as they are sometimes called, empathize with the concerns of evacuees (A. Lange 2007)? While MIR insisted that all residents would have the opportunity to both choose their specific design and to personalize it with options, the question arises of who exactly was the client in this type of project? Was it the former citizens of the Lower Ninth Ward, the 150 families who were lucky enough to be chosen to get one of the first round of model homes? Was it Make it Right and Pitt? Was it the government, the ward, the larger community that is New Orleans? These questions about the MIR project are also the questions that must be asked about the reconstruction of New Orleans, and of reconstruction in general.

By now, it should be becoming clear that the overriding concern expressed about the MIR project was the choice to rebuild in the Lower Ninth at all. While they were not alone in their decision to do so, many government reports, prominent firms and politicians have put forward the argument that the Lower Ninth (and other low-lying areas of New Orleans) were simply not safe places to build for residential communities. The 'why' of this is sometimes framed in terms of class or race (Giroux 2006; Dyson 2006), but the fact that the area consists of reclaimed land that is in danger of repeat flooding is widely accepted.

Pitt's own decision to build back in the Ninth Ward resulted from the requests of the people that he spoke with on his visit to the area in early 2006 to 'make it right': to help them build back on the sites of their former houses. However, the *tabula rasa* quality of the Ninth Ward did not go unremarked by the actor turned architect. As quoted in the *New York Times*, "If you have this blank slate and this great technology out there, what better test than low-income housing?" (Pogrebin 2007).

The great technology in question refers, in part, to the Cradle-to-Cradle technology pioneered by William McDonough and

Partners (McDonough and Braungart 2002). While the technology itself has garnered significant international kudos, McDonough's attempted implementation has received some unfavourable attention. In a PBS documentary, Lesle (2008) describes the results of McDonough's attempt to build an entirely green village in Huangbaiyu, China. Using exclusively Cradle-to-Cradle technology, William McDonough and Partners, in conjunction with the Portland-based China US Center for Sustainable Development (CUCSD), Tongji University and the local Benxi Architectural and Design Institute, attempted to build a model eco-village. As McDonough's firm admits, the "outcome has been a disappointment" (McDonough n.d.). As of January 2008, only two of the forty-two model homes were occupied (Lesle 2008). While McDonough blames overly high expectations, the local and national context and general management issues, others have pointed to a lack of understanding of the needs and wants of the intended beneficiaries as the major flaw. The intent was to raise the living standards of 400 families by moving them to the new bungalows. But once the bungalows were built villagers were reluctant to move in. The reasons for this are still not clear, but anthropologist Shannon May has suggested that part of the problem may lie in the quality of consultation that was undertaken. While villagers were ostensibly consulted, it is not clear whether they truly understood what they were consenting to, or whether the appropriate people were involved. May cites the desire of the intended residents to be 'polite' to the visiting contractors as one possible flaw in the process (Streeter 2006).

It is possible that the lessons from Huangbaiyu could be drawn upon in the MIR process; however, the spatial bias is such that problems with previous projects are often not adequately analysed, or, at least, not by the same people or institutions that undertook them in the first place. This may partly explain the tendency to repeat or recycle previous design schemes. Returning momentarily to the idea of the Katrina Cottages, according to Witold Rybczynski (2005), after the 1906 San Francisco earthquake the city of San Francisco built 6,000 two-room temporary wooden huts, which he refers to as cottages, some of which are still in existence today. Part of this repetition of humanitarian solutions is no doubt need-based. In the wake of a natural disaster people have lost their homes and need new ones. It is still intriguing that despite repeated negative experiences with certain design solutions, these very solutions are repeatedly advocated, implemented and often discarded. And each time, these solutions are presented as new, progressive and problem-based. For within the humanitarian imaginary the solutions represent, as material metaphors, ideal elements of society, which have yet to be implemented and yet to exist.

As a shared social imaginary, humanitarianism increasingly includes environmental or ecological considerations. International bodies lobbying for improved environmental standards, conduct and accountability are myriad, and international conferences and institutions are a prominent part of the international imagination. According to Hedren and Linner (2009), utopian thought is a necessary condition for the politics of sustainable development. They define modernist utopia as including notions of fixed truth, fixed territoriality and fixed final goals for politics. And within dreams of a 'green utopia', the development of a green house looms large in the minds of architects and planners.

Human settlements – buildings – are one of the largest consumers of energy and the largest emitters of carbon dioxide and waste. As one of the largest sources of carbon emission, the individual house is being targeted by architects and urban planners as the site where significant gains could be made in the area of the environment. The term green house refers to a residence that minimizes negative impact on its environment while maximizing energy efficiency throughout the building's life cycle. This implies improved living quality for its residents and neighbours and often includes such elements as harmonizing building style with local context and use of local materials. Were green building standards to be adopted on all new buildings, and retrofitted on existing

5.2 Computer-generated screen shots – design by Atelier Hitoshi Abe

ones, even only in OECD countries, the world would be well on its way to meeting its environmental targets. The reasons why this is not already done are attributable largely to cost (or perceptions of cost), cultural factors and manufacturing path dependence. However, most OECD governments have established green building codes that specify standards for energy efficiency for buildings (Lausten 2008). For those who can afford it, green building holds both a philosophical (i.e. socially conscious) and an aesthetic appeal.

Picking up on both realized and anticipated increases for green buildings, architecture firms in the USA, Canada, the UK and continental Europe are positioning themselves in a 'green light'. Graft, one of the firms involved in the MIR project, describes one of its recent domestic projects as a "genetic bastard", melding (or grafting) together different cultural approaches to space, building, light, aesthetics and, by implication ... common ecological concerns (Graft 2003). However, as green houses are often relatively expensive to build or retrofit, they have not seen the uptake that their advocates desire. Accordingly, the space of a post-disaster zone presents an attractive opportunity to implement innovative solutions in a context of relatively low levels of resistance and restriction. As late as August 2008, 85 per cent of addresses in the Lower Ninth remained vacant or unoccupied (Liu and Plyer 2008). It remains largely a blank slate in which to experiment with new technologies. And while the intention is to implement affordable green technologies, the question remains whether the proposed MIR designs would be affordable enough for former residents. For example, the most recent plans (these for duplexes) include interior shots filled with exquisite design pieces such as Eames chairs and rockers, wall-mounted plasma-screen TVs and tasteful modern art on the walls (Figure 5.2).

Computer drawings of projected schemes provoked one blogger to comment, "and what car is that in the picture ... a Corolla ... are you kidding me?" (Eco Dude, in Destries 2009). The decision to introduce duplexes into the project is an interesting one insofar as it expands out of the single-family home model, typically seen in post-crisis assistance. However, the fundamental principles of iconic architecture, cutting-edge environmental technology and pioneering design remain in all the renderings and plans. And while it is unlikely that the architects intended the residents of the MIR duplexes to be furnishing their new residences with US$3,299 sofas, I suggest that it belies one of several things. At first glance, it merely demonstrates a lack of imagination on behalf of the architects.[1] However, it also implies a fundamental lack of understanding of the means and aesthetic preferences of the end users of the houses. In turn, this suggests that the residents

---

1 Thanks to Henriette Steiner for raising this point.

of the Lower Ninth Ward were not the true target audience: a suggestion supported by the stated hope of MIR for the catalytic potential of this pilot project to inspire the adoption of green housing technologies farther afield. But the use of a primarily black, impoverished parish to test technologies to be marketed to middle- to high-income homeowners, located elsewhere, and contractors interested in green technologies, raises difficult ethical questions about the use of disaster victims as de facto volunteers for pilot projects in sustainable living. The degree to which this raises ethical dilemmas hinges on the degree of real choice that the target beneficiaries received.

Best practice in contemporary humanitarian reconstruction is very clear on the need to integrate the end user or beneficiary into the process of rebuilding their community (Humanitarian Accountability Partnership 2007). What is envisaged is a co-ordinated, well-regulated planning process wherein survivors meaningfully contribute to not only building back their community, but building it back better. What is enacted is often quite different, reflecting the way in which external humanitarian actors think about disaster and recovery rather than the particular circumstances or needs of the affected populations (Wall 2006). For example, while the MIR promotional material emphasized that consultations were carried out with the residents, it is difficult to imagine a scenario devoid of power imbalances. Even in the more carefully designed participatory models, subtle difficulties hamper their implementation, such as cross-cultural communication difficulties, post-traumatic stress and the personal biases of the individuals involved. In the context of the Lower Ninth Ward, the overall uncertainty of housing options and the general lack of visible progress probably meant that if residents were offered anything, novel or not, they would have been likely to take it. These imbalances of consultation run throughout the post-crisis process. The level of expertise, the foreign or celebrity status of the philanthropists, the timing and language gaps involved in the consultation, the over-demand for shelter solutions versus the perceived under- or slow supply on offer all contribute to a process which is arguably biased in the direction of the external actors. As discussed, in the case of the Ninth Ward the return of former residents was and remains controversial. Much of the debate was couched in terms of distrust and fear that the government or authorities were unable or unwilling to protect the rights of those who would be moved: either rehoused or compensated. By initiating the building process, Pitt effectively forced local and civic government to accept that the rebuilding would take place. A second case looks at the opposite scenario: where the external actors were invited by the government to assist the reconstruction and where, rather than operating with principles of individualism and innovation, they sought to return to tried and tested design principles. Yet they still encountered the same problems.

Imagined communities: New Urbanism and the post-Katrina Gulf Coast

Post-Katrina, Republican governor of Mississippi Haley Barbour was looking for ways to put together a reconstruction plan that would allow him to "get ahead of the line" for Federal Hurricane Assistance, so as to avoid the mistakes he made after Hurricane Camille. According to my informant, Barbour was advised by Leland Speed, a prominent Mississippi businessman, that a New Urbanist approach would ensure a quick and coherent planning process for the coast. Speed extended the invitation to architect Andrés Duany and the Congress for New Urbanism (CNU) – the main New Urbanist organization – to facilitate the planning process for the Mississippi Gulf Coast. Duany accepted and "put the call out" to anyone who wanted to be involved, warning them in advance that it would be low paid. The call was responded to with enthusiasm, and from 12 to 17 October 2005 a six-day mega-*charrette* of approximately two hundred architects, designers and urban planners was held in Biloxi, Mississippi.

Dubbed the Mississippi Renewal Forum, it was a planning

meeting, where many of Mississippi's coastal communities damaged by Katrina were introduced to the tenets of New Urbanist planning approaches and designs (Snyder 2007). While recognizing that they were not operating with a clean slate (Mississippi Renewal Forum 2005b: 5), New Urbanists considered it to be an opportunity to redress, from a macro level, not only the devastation wrought by the hurricane, but also, in words of a prominent New Urbanist who participated in the reconstruction, the "disaster of the pre-Katrina sprawl". Representatives were invited from all the affected communities along the coast, including: Waveland, Bay St Louis, Pass Christian, Long Beach, Gulfport, Biloxi, D'Iberville, Ocean Springs, Gautier, Moss Point and Pascagoula. Guided by some of the most prominent New Urbanists in the USA, participants were shepherded through a planning process that saw the development of New Urbanist master plans for all the participating communities. But what does a New Urbanist approach entail?

The architectural movement called New Urbanism (NU) originated in the USA, in the 1980s, in response to the problems identified with suburban sprawl. NU is best known for its model towns: planned neighbourhoods based on strict urban planning principles such as densely backed, walkable neighbourhoods with mixed use and mixed-age buildings. NU promotes architectural and planning decisions that take into account, and respect, the essential qualities and traditions of a place. Two of the best known New Urbanist developments are the towns of Seaside, California, and Celebration, Florida. Both Seaside (used as the backdrop for the 1998 movie *The Truman Show*) and Celebration, commissioned by the Walt Disney Corporation, perpetuate through their urban layout and architectural choices a neo-traditional aesthetic of small-town America, where "women call in their kids to do homework and old men sit outside the general store" (New Urban Guild n.d.). Through a call for a return to so-called traditional social relations by way of urban and architectural design, New Urbanists have been accused of perpetuating an imaginary idea of the USA, and their critics have seized upon what they perceive to be an exploitation of "a yearning for an imaginary small-town America" (Hales 2005; Risen 2005).

Within mainstream architectural and urban design practice, NU has historically been regarded with a large degree of distrust. Although the principles of walkability, sustainability, beauty and tradition are, on the surface, positive principles, when embedded within the larger economic and social realities of late-capitalist societies, less positive dynamics emerge. As identified by MacLeod and Ward (2002), without proper transport links, they can become enclave communities which reinforce class and race divisions rather than alleviate them. There is also the danger that, rather than reversing sprawl, NU could become a proponent of the very trends it seeks to avoid: merely replacing the grid-like suburbia of 1940s and 1950s America with the twenty-first-century version of the picturesque enclave (Hayden 2003). There are also considerations of whose tradition is being promoted, and whose version of beauty or nature triumphs. But while it was often derided within architecture departments as lacking in architectural merit, as a building method it proved to be remarkably resilient, attractive to developers and homeowners alike – the numbers of New Urbanist communities grew throughout the 1990s and 2000s, across the USA.

Unlike the iconic approach to architecture, which stressed the form, aesthetic and predominance of the building *qua* building, NU saw the form of the building as part of the larger urban and surrounding space (Talen 2005). Accordingly, there has been a stress on harmony of form and landscape. Most importantly, from a reconstruction perspective, by labelling oneself a New Urbanist, an architect or planner is effectively signalling to other architects and planners that s/he agrees with the basic principles of Smart Code planning, the idea of the "transect" and place-appropriate design. For planning purposes New Urbanists advocate the use of Smart Code, a concept developed by the foremost and best-known New Urbanist architecture firm: Duany, Plater-Zyberk and Company:

the SmartCode [sic] is a tool that guides the form of the
built environment in order to create and protect development
patterns that are compact, walkable, and mixed use. These
traditional neighbourhood patterns tend to be stimulating, safe,
and ecologically sustainable. The SmartCode requires a mix of
uses within walking distance of dwellings, so residents aren't
forced to drive everywhere. It supports a connected network to
relieve traffic congestion. At the same time, it preserves open
lands, as it operates at the scale of the region as well as the
community. (Duany, Plater-Zyberk and Company 2009: v)

This is based upon the idea of the transect: a planning tool
which takes as its assumption that different ecological habitats
(ranging from urban to peri-urban to rural) imply different types
of built environments. It proposes that generally the most resilient
or, in their terminology, 'most-loved' settlements result from careful planning or "evolved as compact, mixed use places because of
their geography and the limits of the transportation and economics
of their time" (ibid.: v). An analysis of the tenets of NU cannot
be tackled within the context of this book (for an overview, see
Talen 2005). Instead, the discussion will be limited to understanding what it was about NU that initially made it appealing as a
reconstructive approach and how the constraints of the process of
reconstruction dramatically transformed its original vision.

The New Urbanists are insistent that Smart Code is not
"persuasive or instructive like a guideline, nor is it intentionally
general like a vision statement. It is meant to be law, precise and
technical ..." (Duany, Plater-Zyberk and Company 2009: iv). The
implicit environmental determinism, which envisions and requires
particular physical outcomes in particular areas (ibid.: v), may
often feel, to those outside of the New Urbanist camp, as closer
to religion than law. According to one interviewee, this uniform
conviction of process and purpose was part of the appeal of
bringing in the New Urbanists to devise a plan for Mississippi
in the first place. According to him, unlike most architects, who

are trained to be competitive, New Urbanists all agree on core principles, are "on the same page", and are therefore very efficient immediately.

Other aspects of the New Urbanist approach that are appealing in a reconstruction context is that they think on a wildly ambitious scale but are simultaneously meticulous in their attention to detail. One aspect of this fastidiousness can be seen in their development of pattern books. These books, such as *Louisiana Speaks: Pattern Book* (Urban Design Associates n.d.) and *Gulf Coast Emergency House Plans: The First Book of Katrina Cottages* (Mouzon 2006), meticulously document the community, architectural and landscape patterns recommended by the New Urbanist approach and are examples of what New Urbanists consider to be place-appropriate design. Within the context of the initial Renewal Forum in October 2005, specific architectural forms do not appear to have been of central importance. Design teams concentrated their efforts at the broad civic level on such issues as economic renewal and improved transport links (Mississippi Renewal Forum 2005b). It is strange, then, that by September 2009, the point of submission of this manuscript, the most lasting impact of the New Urbanist input into the Mississippi reconstruction had largely been reduced to the form of the single-family dwelling: the Katrina Cottage.

The Katrina Cottage: emblem of the reconstruction

The Katrina Cottage is a small cottage-like permanent structure that is intended to provide affordable, dignified shelter for victims of Hurricane Katrina, specifically to replace the ubiquitous Federal Emergency Management Agency (FEMA) trailer that has been the government standard in emergency shelter. Originally designed by New York architect Marianne Cusato, the structure is a one-floor, downsized "Mississippi-style coastal cottage, complete with an inviting porch" (Brown 2006). To ensure elements of local vernacular Coastal style, inputs were solicited from the affected communities and 'fine tuned' by local architects. It has

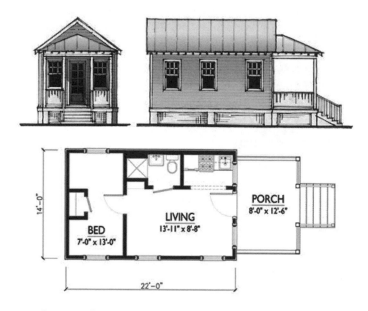

5.3 The KC 308 floor plan

since been upgraded to the status of a movement with different spin-off cottages being built, promoted and championed.

The original KC 308 (Figure 5.3) is a 308-square-foot (420-square-foot including porch) house composed of two main rooms arranged in a row: the living room (13 ft 11 ins by 8 ft 8 ins) and, behind it, across the rear of the house, the bedroom (7 ft by 13 ft 3 ins). A small kitchen, lavatory and storage space occupy one side of the house and can be accessed from the living room. According to its website, it can be built with wood or steel framing and is "finished with fiber cement siding and a metal roof" (Cusato Cottages n.d.). It is engineered to withstand hurricane-force winds. Key principles of the design include that it is based on local vernacular, that it is easily and quickly erected (estimates of building time range between seven days and six weeks), affordable, and can be easily modified. Certain elements, such as prefabrication and purported ease of construction, do make it a potentially good choice for post-disaster housing. Other purported benefits such as its affordability and adaptability are relative virtues: dependent upon the ability of the potential occupant to secure land tenure and access credit. (Costed at between US$30,000 and US$100,000 plus building costs, it is not cheap.) Following the unveiling of Katrina Cottage II – a roomier version of the KC 308 – in the Walmart parking lot in Chalmette, Louisiana, other models have been developed, including the Tiny House, the Thin House and the Double House. They vary in terms of floor space, number of floors, different layouts and cost. They are intended to fit a range of budgets and locations. An important part of the promotional material for the cottage is its growth potential.

The initial cottage is considered to be a Kernel House – which can either be expanded upon, through architectural additions, or converted into a garden shed or guest cottage at the back of the lot once the real house is built. Images on the Lowe's website have included time-lapse animation of the cottage being transformed from an isolated structure on the corner of an expansive, leafy yard into a new, expansive structure, many times larger than the original cottage. In the same way, the advice for "Using the Cottage: Building for the Future", previously found on the CusatoCottages.com website, implied limitless room for expansion, in the new borderland of the post-disaster setting.

However, what is omitted from these sketches is one of the most pressing problems associated with reconstructive work: that of property rights and ownership. In many cases, those people who lost their homes cannot return easily to their original place of residence: either it has been destroyed or it is being re-zoned within the larger scheme of redevelopment. While in the minds of architects and planners the transition between temporary and permanent is seamless, in reality this is rarely the case. In the wake of the FEMA trailer scandals (Keteylan 2008), the Mississippi Emergency Management Agency (MEMA) managed to find a way to use federal grant money for the production of Mississippi Cottages under their Alternative Housing Pilot Program.

However, the time lag in disbursements and production meant that by the time the cottages were ready to go out, MEMA had almost come to the end of the three-year window provided for the use of federal disaster funds. Even for those people who had already been lucky enough to receive a cottage, there was the very real risk that the cottage would have to be returned to MEMA because it did not meet the civic zoning requirements, which had classified the cottages as mobile homes. In Waveland and Gulfport, residents launched civic lawsuits and won the right to keep their cottages as permanent shelters. However, this has failed to mitigate the 'not in my backyard' syndrome which dominated the cottage debate, with nearby residents fearing that the presence of the cottages would drag down their own property value (Swope 2009).

It is common for intra-community conflict to arise in the wake of new urban development schemes. That it should arise from an urban planning movement that is defined by its contribution to community creation points to constraints and possible contradictions in the way in which community can be imagined following a disaster. Take, for instance, Cottage Square: the model town square which is being built in the City of Ocean Springs as a "living museum to the Katrina Cottage movement" (ibid.). It is meant to lead by example by demonstrating what a walkable, scalable, infill site would look like as an alternative to the sprawl that has dominated building trends along the Gulf Coast since the Second World War. But while the development is meant as a model for a reconfiguration of the entire urban fabric along the Gulf Coast, using it first in the context of post-hurricane reconstruction raises certain ethical issues, the most obvious being the potential creation of ghettos of post-disaster homes. As of September 2009, Cottage Square was occupied only by a few commercial properties associated with the Katrina Cottage movement, but as envisaged, it was supposed to be an 'old-fashioned' community. Take away the pitched roofs and the picket fences and it was not clear how this development was any different from a trailer park. If residents were opposed to isolated cottages of survivors being inserted into their neighbourhood, how would an entire cluster fare? If the people who were disproportionately in need of new, donated residences were the same people who were too poor to buy the insurance that would have replaced their homes, then the development of Cottage Squares filled with the poorest hurricane survivors will be tantamount to creating council estates without formal state support. Similarly, although the ideas behind NU are laudable, when judged against environmental criteria, the formalism of walkable neighbourhoods ignores the realities that require many people to commute, in cars, to and from their jobs.

It is easy, but perhaps slightly unfair, to critique the isolated development of a single Cottage Square as it was meant quite literally, as a model village for the redevelopment of the Gulf Coast at large. The eleven Master Plans that were developed within the context of the Mississippi Renewal Forum (MRF) redrew the entire coastline and envisaged the full-blown application of Smart Code and transect planning along the coast. They also identified the region's key economic drivers and put forward plans that would bring the previously offshore floating casinos inland and convert much of the beachfront property into tourist-friendly promenades, condominiums and golf courses (McKee 2005). These changes roiled residents, who felt that their entire way of life was being altered through changes to their built environment. As quoted in the *New York Times*, one Biloxi resident said, "are you trying to turn this into a Sin City, or what?" (ibid.).

New Urbanists strongly denounce such claims, pointing to the strict planning and building codes which may go so far as to specify the pitch of a roof or the shape of a window (Lewis 2006). And while these codes can be seen as necessary to ensure a particular aesthetically and socially desirable environment, they were also perceived by some as a cynical attempt to increase profit margins by allowing a new, higher density of building to take place. According to one interviewee, "[t]he idea of Smart Codes was readily accepted by folks whose lives and property had been destroyed as well as by some rather unscrupulous developers who saw a way around the zoning laws that limited density, therefore limiting profit".

Why the Smart Code and NU were initially so attractive to the people of Mississippi brings us back to the architectural form, and ultimately the idea of the Katrina Cottage. Over and over, in the promotional material for the KCs, the image of small-town America is presented as the future of any city that adopts their approach. The return to a time, as phrased by one interviewee, when "we had storefronts in primarily residential neighborhoods, when business owners lived above their shops. We walked and rode bikes everywhere. We were never more than a few blocks from a little store where we could get an RC cola and a moon pie." He goes on to say that "I would love to see us move back in that direction, but it is not going to come easily."

This return to a Golden Age America is something that the New Urbanists are repeatedly criticized for. The critique generally has three tracks. First, there is the argument that the period in question, of small-town America, never really existed, not as such. Instead, what is remembered is both a nostalgic amalgam of small-town sensibility and post-Second World War economic prosperity. Such a pastiche picks the pieces that are comforting and familiar (e.g. moon pies) and whitewashes those aspects of small-town America which are less palatable to a twenty-first-century social sensibility, such as racism and restrictive gender roles.

The second argument is that NU fails to address the underlying economic issues that led to sprawl in the first place, such as the demand for affordable housing and the incentives for construction and manufacturing companies to mass-produce prefab homes. This argument has been deployed with regard to the original Seaside development, which has seen the original, popular cottage development replicated along the Florida coast. It is also worth noting that although New Urbanists cite Jane Jacobs and her idea of promoting an organic and vibrant street culture as a key inspiration, the presence of local street life is directly related to the availability of time for its residents, which is at least partially economically dependent (Jacobs 2000). In the current system of socio-economic organization, for the vast majority of the population, the car remains a key instrument for living, required to get to and from work; the commute and other daily demands allowing little time to wander down to the corner shop to buy an ice cream. It is the economic organization of everyday life which structures our space, not the other way around. New Urbanists will counter that spatial organization can influence behaviour and encourage physical engagement with local environments. However, the vast majority of their developments have been in mid- to high-income areas.

Thirdly, developments like Seaside and the revisioned Biloxi waterfront are primarily for seasonal residents, tourists or temporary visitors. The ironic outcome is that the people who will occupy Biloxi, Seaside, Celebration or Niagara-on-the-Lake and other New Urbanist developments are merely passing *through* an old-town setting, using their vacation to immerse themselves in the childhood they never had. What is for sale is a façade of community, which appeals to the aesthetic and affective needs of its users to feel at home while meshing with the underlying capitalist processes which seek higher profit through higher density and urban infill and the chance to re-zone residential areas for mixed-use purposes.

Since the initial flush of excitement and support for a New Urbanist approach along the Mississippi Gulf Coast, the process has been quietly downgraded from large-scale, civic Master Plans to a few small developments under negotiation at the time of writing this book. However, this has not stopped the recipients of the Mississippi Cottages from fighting, as mentioned earlier, to keep their cottages as permanent homes. Nor has it stopped the Lowe's company continuing to promote the Katrina Cottage on its website and Marianne Cusato adapting her marketing approach from one aimed at Hurricane survivors towards survivors of the economic crisis. Marketed as "the new economy home: adaptable, sustainable, beautiful ... within your means" (Cusato n.d.), it markets the same dream that was being sold to Hurricane Katrina survivors: that, despite catastrophe, the pastoral American dream is within your grasp. From a profit perspective, the *opportunity* of Hurricane Katrina provided a testing ground to set up the production of the Cottage on a much larger scale. And although it was surely not Cusato's intention to use the post-Katrina space to experiment with housing solutions for the nation, this has proved to be the outcome. But doing so has not only lent more credibility to the paradigm of the single-family home and social ideal, but has provided NU with the opportunity to gain knowledge and experience within an initially uncontested space. Nor is there any formal follow-up mechanism or process by which the original designers of the cottages or the plans can nurture or support the Smart Codes or Master Plans they initiated.

Possibly the answer to why this occurred lies, at least partially, in the initial space of the planning *charrette* itself. The definition of a *charrette* that was used within the context of Mississippi Renewal Forum was a "planning session that usually takes anywhere from several days to a week and incorporates the expertise of a variety of individuals ... The *charrette* is held on or near the project site and in the presence of those affecting and affected by the outcome" (Mississippi Renewal Forum 2005a: 3).

While effort was made to try to achieve these principles, the nature of the post-disaster context made them difficult to realize. As described by one participant, the *charrette* was held about one month after the hurricane. The National Guard was still in the disaster zone. It was not possible to get as many people to attend the MRF as government and the planners would have wished, as most of the people that had been affected by the hurricane were not in the "head space" to sit in a conference centre and plan. This led to the *charrette* being dominated by designers, and out of the approximately two hundred people in attendance, about a hundred were international and national and a hundred were from Mississippi. Although "[u]ltimately, the purpose of the *charrette* is to give those concerned enough information to make rational decisions" (ibid.: 3), the New Urbanists saw the urban sprawl as itself a type of natural disaster, so when communities like Biloxi were reluctant to adopt their approach, choosing instead the "man-made disaster" (as described by one informant) of casinos and sprawl, the New Urbanists found it difficult to understand or accept. According to one interviewee, the New Urbanist architect assigned to work with the Biloxi team left the process in frustration at the narrow-mindedness of the officials he was working with.

The space of the *charrette* is remarkably similar to the auxiliary space of international humanitarianism that has been examined in previous chapters. For example, within the space of the *charrette*, removed from the communities that were being assisted, the architects effectively spoke their own language and had uniform ideas about what the victims of the disasters needed and, ultimately, should want. While both the New Urbanists and the MIR representatives go to great lengths in their promotional material to emphasize that their approach is led by the needs and demands of the victims of the disaster, I argue that this is not the case. In the final section, I examine how the choice of one particular form – that of the shotgun house – belies a biased epistemology regarding the victim and demonstrates the underlying power asymmetry inherent in the process of humanitarian assistance.

A shotgun reconstruction

It is not surprising that the most lasting aspect, at least at present, of the New Urbanist post-Katrina push has been the production of a revamped FEMA trailer. The focus on architectural form in the reconstruction of place is a common feature of post-crisis reconstruction as envisaged by external humanitarian forces. Place, as famously defined by Agnew (1987), can have at least three basic meanings: as a location, as a locale, and as a sense of place. By location, Agnew means the physical, geographic coordinates of a place. By locale, he is referring to the "material setting for social relations" (Cresswell 2004: 7). Within the context of reconstruction, as it applies to already established human settlements, the first two are incredibly contentious and generally beyond either the ability or time frame of external humanitarian actors to engage with.[2] This leaves the third – a sense of place – as the primary focus for reconstructive efforts. As we have seen with the New Urbanist rebuilding, a recurrent theme in the re-creation of a 'sense of place' has been the creation of styles and forms that evoke a particular aesthetic experience. More narrowly, the focus in the context of post-Katrina reconstruction, both within the New Urbanists' work in Mississippi and within the reconstruction of Louisiana (broadly), and New Orleans (in particular), has been on one form in particular: that of the shotgun house.

As described by Fred B. Kniffen in his paper "Louisiana housing types", the shotgun house is composed of "one room in width and from one to three or more rooms deep, with frontward-facing gable" (as quoted in Upton and Vlach 1986: 59). The number of rooms varies, but is usually two or three, with the entrance on the gable end, leading to a front porch. The roof is pitched, and the construction tends to be of timber frame with a façade of horizontal siding. While the doors tend to form a straight line, this is not always the case, and examples of the type with one of the doorways offset have been

---

2 It is well established that natural disasters disproportionately affect the residents of those areas which are more hazard-prone and therefore less insurable. Most major disasters eventually raise the question of whether the place that was devastated by a disaster *should* be rebuilt in the same location, or whether new restrictions should be put in place that limit future settlement. Inevitably, in the absence of an autocratic and omnipotent state, the ability to change legislation and regulation to alter future building codes, enforce this legislation and afford the social cost of widespread social change means that a more common post-disaster outcome is that people tend to rebuild in the same areas that they occupied prior to the disaster. For more on these issues, see Vale and Campanella (2005); Birch and Wachter (2006).

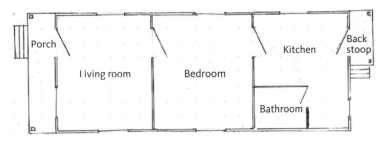

5.4 *Maison basse* floor plan

documented (ibid.). While currently occupied by all classes of society along the Gulf Coast, the shotgun house has historically been associated with poor, black communities. The traditional shotgun house resulted from the size of the long, narrow lots upon which they were built. In order to save on building costs and to maximize space, no hallway was built. Instead, the rooms followed on, one from another, so that if you shot a gun from the front of the house, you could shoot a dog out the back. Vlach traces this history to the presence of free Haitian slaves in New Orleans at the turn of the nineteenth century, and their use of *maison basse* building techniques. He shows the similarity between the floor plans of traditional Haitian homes and the shotgun house of New Orleans (Figure 5.4).

But Vlach's inquiry does not end in Port-au-Prince. He is interested in demonstrating that the Haitian *maison basse* has an even older architectural genealogy, based simultaneously in West Africa, and with Caribbean Amerindian populations and their *bohio* house type – a type strongly resembling a shotgun house (see Figure 8 in ibid.: 73). According to Vlach, the shotgun house represents an architectural response to slavery whereby African slaves from the Awarak sugar plantations "maintained their own African house form by making one morphological change (shifting a doorway [from the long end to the garret end of the house]), adapting one secondary feature (a front porch), and learning a new technology" (ibid.: 76).

He goes on to say that "Africans in Haiti did not drift aimlessly in a sea of alien experiences. Their response was to make sense of their new environment by transforming it so that it resembled a familiar pattern" (ibid.: 76).

Likewise, within the New Urbanist project, the search for patterns is a recurrent theme (Alexander et al. 1977). And in the reconstruction of the Gulf Coast, the use of the aforementioned pattern books, which detailed place-appropriate, vernacular styles and approaches, has been an important element of the process. The *Louisiana Speaks: Pattern Book*, put together under the direction of the CNU-affiliated architecture firm Urban Design Associates, fastidiously documents the stylistic and ornamental requirements for the five Louisiana Architectural Styles: the Louisiana Vernacular, the Louisiana Victorian, the Louisiana Classical, Louisiana Arts and Crafts and Modern (Urban Design Associates n.d.). It is worth considering that within the *Louisiana Speaks* pattern book, the shotgun house is not even given its own description; it is considered simply to be a subset of 'Creole-influenced' Louisiana Vernacular. So why is it that the idea of the shotgun house has become almost interchangeable with the idea of post-Katrina reconstruction?

In addition to the Katrina Cottage movement, other prominent philanthropists have independently adopted the shotgun houses as inspiration. Work done by the Massachusetts Institute of Technology professor Lawrence Sass used the shotgun as a model for digitally prefabricated houses or, as they became known, Instant Houses (Bergdoll et al. 2008). The objective of the project, commissioned as an art installation by the Museum of Modern Art, New York, was to create a low-tech, low-cost, easily reproducible and buildable shelter that could also be adapted to its local vernacular surroundings. Drawing his inspiration from Venturi and Scott Brown's distinction between buildings as "structures which articulate their programmatic content in sculptural form" (or ducks) and "mundane structures dressed up in decoration that articulates their programmatic content" (or sheds), Sass and his team chose to build sheds (ibid.: 198; Venturi et al. 2007).

This means that the basic form of the house is a prefabricated 196-square-foot one-room shotgun house that can be put together in a matter of days using minimal tools and at a relatively low cost (Bergdoll et al. 2008: 196). Only, given that the main form of the house is a standardized monocoque shell (effectively a one-room box with a pitched roof), the shotgun effect comes exclusively from the addition of a prefabricated façade that replicates one of four vernacular architectural styles identified by Sass and his students, in four areas of New Orleans. One house was chosen near the Garden District, another in the French Quarter, and two others in the Marigny.

There are several potential interconnected answers to the pre-dominance of the post-Katrina focus on shotgun housing. The first is admittedly that the shotgun house is, next to Mardi Gras beads or a jazz band, one of the most iconic, emblematic visual images associated with New Orleans. And in the post-Katrina reconstruction, New Orleans dominated media and humanitarian agendas, owing largely to the high-profile atrocities that occurred when the levees broke. However, the elevation of the shotgun house to the status of the icon of the reconstruction ignores major aspects associated with its form.

In addition to the history of poverty and racial inequality associated with shotgun houses, in New Orleans the best-preserved and -maintained examples of the type are also those that can be found within those areas aimed at tourists. When previous visitors to New Orleans recall their time there, they may think of the Creole cottages of the Faubourg and the French Quarter. They remember the bed-and-breakfast that they stayed in or the architectural walking tour that they took – the places that are occupied by the same class of people who have come to help rebuild: touristic and temporary.

The focus on the architectural form of the shotgun house, and in the case of Sass of the mere façade, emphasizes the inability of these external humanitarian actors to tackle the underlying structural causes of the disaster. Rather than seeing the disaster as part of the ongoing existential condition of a particular place, they see it as a one-off and potentially all-transformative occurrence. They see it as a discrete event, as a moment, when for the people who live there it is a lifetime. Indeed, even prior to Katrina, blighted houses were a major problem in New Orleans. The vacant, decrepit houses were both a contributing factor to, and a symptom of, urban decay. And while the String of Pearls, the cities along the Mississippi Gulf Coast, had more peaceful pre-Katrina profiles, their socio-economic situation was also difficult, with unemployment at over 7 per cent, significant immigrant populations, and disproportionate economic dependence on the gaming and casino industries accompanied by associated social ills. As described by one of the key players in the MRF, the Katrina Cottages were "camels' noses under the tent of neighbourhood, district, and regional (re)design according to New Urbanist principles", a redesign that would tackle the pre-Katrina Mississippi sprawl in a way that would be affordable to communities but also attractive to investors and gaming tourists.

A second, and related, explanation for the overwhelming focus on this form of house as a key plank in the reconstruction was demand. When people have nowhere to live, it becomes their overwhelming priority. However, the appeal and popularity of the specific forms of the Katrina Cottage and other neo-shotgun designs need further explanation. As discussed, in Mississippi the presentation of the cottages as a dignified and safe alternative to the FEMA trailers caught the public's imagination, and residents of a number of coastal cities have been suing the cities to keep them. This raises the question of what is more dignified about the cottages than the trailers. The cottages are not necessarily architecturally coherent within the context of Mississippi coastal architecture, past or present. Their new residents will not have lived in something like this before. Yet the architectural form of the house and its presentation on the Lowe's online model cottage gallery, accompanied by white picket fencing, rocking chairs and bushes, appeal to iconic dreams of home (Lowe's n.d.). But the focus on ornament and façade conveys both the possibility of a new life(style) for its inhabitants, and obscures, or downplays, the class and racial divides that tend to affect the groups most in need of the cottages. This observation was supported through an interview with Marianne Cusato, the originator of the cottages. She claims as inspiration for the cottages the work of Sarah Susanka, originator of the Not So Big franchise. Through her books, Susanka advocates a return to Not So Big houses, spaces, lives. But aimed at the middle to upper classes, rather than merely "living small" it emphasizes quality over quantity, and presents a highly bourgeois, middle-class aesthetic (Susanka and Obolensky 1998). Similarly, within the Katrina Cottages, the aesthetic and heritage that are being preserved are not the residents' own, but the simulacrum developed within an asymmetric planning process. There was room for consultation, because in the end it is focused at a level that will not address the underlying issues of who is most affected in the event of a disaster.

It is well established that natural disasters are anything but natural, disproportionately affecting the uninsured, renters and those on social benefits (Oliver-Smith 1996; Davis 1978). This is supported by work documenting the uneven swathe of damage caused by Katrina: those who lost the most were exactly those people who could least afford to do so (Giroux 2006; Smith 2006; McFarlane 2004). With persistent ambiguity over insurance claims, property rights and ownership, the dream of re-establishing oneself on a clean lot remains, for many, exactly that. The post-Katrina introduction of even more stringent zoning requirements by FEMA has meant that the cost of building has increased still more (Moule 2005). The New Urbanists opposed FEMA's regulations both on cost but also on design and aesthetic grounds. This aligned the New Urbanists, in places like Waveland, with residents who could not afford to make more changes to their houses. This alignment is crucial in that it brought together the external New Urbanists with local residents by unifying them against the federal state body that so many residents felt had abandoned them in the immediate aftermath of Katrina. But it is important to recognize that, although external to the area, the New Urbanists were in Mississippi at the behest of Governor Haley Barbour, a politician who is, according to Woods (1998: 275), strongly aligned with the Plantation Bloc ideology, which is "based upon the relentless expansion of social inequality" (ibid.: 1). By focusing on the form of the single-family home and on the idea of 'timeless spaces' where citizens ostensibly would live in complete harmony with one another, the underlying structural socio-economic conditions which contribute to the systematic oppressions of certain social groupings were obscured (Lipsitz 2007).

Lipsitz (ibid.) discusses this process in the context of the spatialization of race. He claims that "the contemporary ideal of the properly-ordered prosperous private home" is a 'spatial imaginary' that excludes those structurally disadvantaged social or racial groupings which, through necessity, rely on a spatial imaginary that "revolves around solidarities within, between, and across spaces" (ibid.: 1). In the context of the Katrina Cottage debate, the focus on the house has potentially undermined these spatial networks by inserting lone-family units into unwelcoming neighbourhoods. For people who need to recover from a disaster, the form of a house is not sufficient when your neighbours are petitioning to have you evicted, or the zoning regulations have been bent so that they do not meet the basic FEMA disaster risk levels. Within the context of the Mississippi Gulf Coast, the KC movement has also paved the way for increased profit margins for developers through appeals for higher densities, inland casinos and seafront shopping arcades, all under the guise of community affordability. It may be that community becomes community only for those who can afford it.

For the originator of the KC, Marianne Cusato, the reconstruction has also provided the opportunity to pioneer a prototype that was rolled out by Lowe's across America as an affordable solution to the 'credit crunch' that followed the 2008 financial crisis. For other New Urbanists, the involvement in the reconstruction of Louisiana and Mississippi has provided an opportunity to observe and understand what makes a community tick. For example, one of the key figures in the New Urbanist movement, Andrés Duany, set himself up an office in New Orleans to try to get a sense of what contributes to the street culture and spirit that make New Orleans so special. How he will replicate, commodify and distribute this sense of community remains (at the time of writing) to be seen, but it seems inevitable that what is sold will need to be a sanitized version, since the same vibrant street culture that makes New Orleans so exciting also contributes to one of the highest urban crime rates in the USA: an aspect of urbanity that is less marketable to the target consumers of New Urbanist communities.

A third explanation for the overwhelming focus on the house was the way that it was portrayed in the wake of the disaster. The infamous aerial photographs of post-Katrina New Orleans showed only the roofs of the houses peaking out like islands from the waters that surrounded them. Historic Green, an environmentally oriented reconstruction coalition, directly equates the destruction of architectural heritage and history with the destruction of people and family (Historic Green n.d.). Similarly, the now famous post-Katrina photographs by Robert Polidori presented the house as a victim, damaged, destroyed, lifeless, with the focus on the destruction of the built environment rather than people (Figure 5.5).

As has been well documented, while the violence that occurred in New Orleans was of an undeniably racial nature, the house provided a neutral, deracialized object that could be addressed and repaired – unlike the underlying social and race relations. While New Orleans has a rich and multiracial history, it has also been affected by deep divisions in wealth and privilege that the disaster brought to the fore. The focus on the architectural form of the house brought the debate back into the comfortable common ground of home, place and security while overlooking the fact that for many people affected by the disaster this imaginary is indeed a dream.

5.5 2732 Orleans Avenue (Polidori photograph)

Where, for residents of the reconstruction sites, the disaster and the consequent reconstruction are part of the continuum of their lifetime, for external actors the disaster and the reconstruction represent an event that is temporally disengaged from the longer existence of the place. The disaster is privileged as a unique occurrence, and the response as an exception, obscuring the more permanent or entrenched dynamics which make the event into a way of life for certain sectors of the population (Hughes 2007; Rubenstein 2007). It is worth noting that following Katrina the concern of many people was not necessarily that they had 'lost their place'. Rather, as shown by Polidori's photographs (2005), the unsettling aspect was the damage to and destruction of the accoutrements and instruments of living: photographs, family records, clothes and toys (see also Piazza 2008; Brinkley 2006). And by focusing, as all three examples do, on the form of the house as a technological solution, the deeper, structural inequalities were missed.

Consider, once again, the form of the shotgun which has been so inspirational in the revisioning of the Gulf Coast. While the language and imagery used to market both the MIR and the Katrina Cottages has been one of Rockwellian Americana, do-it-yourself attitude and a narrative of progress, the architectural form of the shotgun house alludes to a less publicized historical narrative of the USA: that of slavery and its legacy of racial inequality. In the context of New Orleans, the spatial dimensions of this legacy were shown by the unequal impact that the hurricane had on its inhabitants, with inner-city, black populations being disproportionately affected both by the hurricane itself and by their lack of financial insurance against such an eventuality. Katrina revealed how topographical gradients were proxies for race and class gradients in New Orleans, with largely white neighbourhoods situated on higher, drier ground. Simply put, white privilege underlay the spatial location and racial composition of communities most vulnerable to flooding (Bakker 2005: 797; also Smith 2006; Cutter 2006).

It is ironic, then, that the solutions offered not only draw upon a local, vernacular architectural form but subsume a subaltern architecture beneath a veneer of archetypal middle-class America. The provision of an architectural form, which arguably embodies a legacy of subjugation, as the solution for the structurally disadvantaged groups hit by the hurricane contains within it a double message. Superficially, the ornamentation and presentation of the houses – be it the picket fences of the Katrina Cottages or the plasma-screen televisions of the MIR duplexes – offer the promise of a better life. The plans show the growth potential of the structures and emphasize the need of the new owner to work towards embedding it within a larger landscape of success; of using the cottage as the stepping stone to a larger house, and a permanent, grounded home. The promise of the ornament is counterpoised to the threat of the form – the shotgun house – which evokes the memory of slavery, of structural poverty and entrenched discrimination. This tension suggests that unless the necessary actions are taken to improve the basic house, the fate of previous generations of shotgun owners is likely to be experienced again.

CONCLUSION

This book has demonstrated how material and spatial factors are essential to understanding contemporary humanitarianism. It has examined how the built environment of the field shapes the spatial experience of aid workers and how, in turn, this contributes to the way in which humanitarianism at large is conceptualized. The resulting imaginings are then delivered back to the beneficiaries as humanitarian assistance. The objects and assistance that are given represent the needs, wants and understandings of the humanitarian community, rather than those of the beneficiary. If, and when, the beneficiary adapts the aid to better accommodate their own needs, these modifications rarely match the expectations of the humanitarians involved. This mismatch does not result in the donor undertaking a re-evaluation of the approaches and techniques that have been used or why they haven't worked. Instead, the material and spatial constraints of humanitarianism mean that any anomalies are written out of the official transcript of a given response.

This is not to say that humanitarian interventions do not result in reflective assessment exercises, either by the agencies themselves or by external bodies. They do. However, the assessments and exercises face the same constraints as the original projects. First, as products of auxiliary space, the observations and recommendations of aid workers and of visiting consultants and experts are framed by the material and spatial circumstances of the field (Goffman et al. 1997). Secondly, even when the analyses are the outcome of less constrained research – for example, of in-depth academic research or locally produced studies – the material and spatial characteristics of humanitarianism effectively neutralize any potential for change that these inputs may contain. Because the material and spatial aspects of humanitarian intervention are an almost completely overlooked aspect of any intervention, they tend to undermine proposals for significant change and perpetuate the dominant modality of antagonistic assistance.

The concluding section of the book will synthesize these findings into a spatial model that illustrates the dynamic which occurs between the field and headquarters. The model is tripartite, inspired by Lefebvre's trilectic model outlined in Chapter 3 (Lefebvre 1991). It has three components: auxiliary space; the space of the humanitarian imaginary; and the space of tactics.

A tripartite model of space

In the first part of the book, I identified the concept of auxiliary space. This refers to the physical, material and spatial environments resulting from the everyday practices of the international community when performing an intervention. These include the logistical aspects of working in the field but also include the spaces that are created through institutional factors. For example, high staff turnover and heavy reliance on short-term experts mean that most employees will only minimally engage with local culture, place or language. Further, field missions operate on a different timescale to their surroundings: working according to the budget cycles of their domestic governments and defining their own holidays and working hours. Safety and security requirements mean that field staff may live and work in enclosed areas, creating path dependency whereby expat employees frequent the same bars and restaurants. This all contributes to a unique auxiliary space, which is effectively delinked from local circumstances. Within this auxiliary space, the material trope of the compound is prominent and can be considered as a metaphor for the current practices of securitization of field missions.

What I have referred to as the humanitarian imaginary is the second aspect of my proposed model. It is the abstract, conceptual yet programmatic way the international community thinks about the so-called problem of underdevelopment (Easterly 2006; Ferguson 1990). The imaginary refers to the shared norms, institutions and legal frameworks that shape and constitute international discourse on humanitarian assistance. It also includes the associated policies, technologies and expertise. Examples here are needs assessments, logical frameworks or conflict assessment matrices. The imaginary is sustained through the development and promotion of campaigns, targets and slogans such as the MDGs or, in the context of reconstruction, building back better. It includes the "sanitized worlds of civil society and good governance" (Corbridge 2007: 194). This humanitarian imaginary is based largely upon inputs from auxiliary space: on the feedback, evaluations and pictures that are reported back from the field. And because these inputs are developed primarily from within the auxiliary space, which is delinked from local environments, a dynamic is created whereby the 'real' local circumstances are always kept at bay, always outside the process. This, in turn, creates the tendency to seek out or create the spectacle of the development problem or need. Any solution is biased towards the needs and expectations of the donors, rather than the beneficiaries. Even when the solution is more nuanced and originates from beyond auxiliary space, the material and spatial processes will eviscerate its critical potential by transforming it into the sanitized language and mechanisms of the humanitarian imaginary.

The third aspect of the model refers to the way in which the projects that are built are experienced and adapted by their intended (or unintended) user. It can be considered as lived project space and used to understand how the beneficiaries respond and adapt to what the aid workers build and provide. De Certeau refers to these practices as 'making do' (De Certeau 1988). In the book, this process of 'making do' has been explored in the context of the post-tsunami solution of the single-family house in Aceh. Instead of using the houses to live in, as the donors anticipated, the beneficiaries and other stakeholders, such as the GAM and BRR, used the process of housebuilding as a revenue stream and the house as a fungible commodity. Such tactics stood in contradistinction to donors' perception of the house as a sacred gift and challenged their idealized conception of what a humanitarian response is supposed to look like and how a beneficiary should act. But the space of the humanitarian imaginary is an abstract space that relies on conceptual, reified models and templates. There is no room in this space for any feedback that destabilizes the fundamental principles of humanitarianism as they are understood within the imaginary. It pushes out these dissonances, privileging the spectacle of humanitarian as represented within auxiliary space.

This framework is also not necessarily limited to North/South relations. In the context of the post-Katrina reconstruction of the Lower Ninth Ward in New Orleans, Brad Pitt's version of 'building back better' uses techniques derived from international best practice in so-called green architecture. However, the houses are being built back on the original land, despite the fact that the area is still considered at risk of future levee breaks. While the residents of the Lower Ninth Ward were not unhappy to have solar panels and carbon-neutral cladding, their real needs and desires were downplayed in the humanitarian imaginary. In the space of the imaginary, the global ideal of green housing developments and innovative architecture superseded the residents' immediate and basic need to have their neighbourhood made safe from future hurricanes. Similarly, New Urbanist planning principles of community-centred development are to be commended for their socially and environmentally responsible tenets. However, the New Urbanist aspiration of a full-scale revisioning of the Mississippi Gulf Coast failed to account for the conservative predilections of their clientele (or beneficiaries), who preferred McMansions and SUVs to 'small homes' and public transport. Examining issues of donorship in an American (or North/North) context also highlights the ethical issues involved in designing for another group or even person. Here, approaches used in the architectural profession, such as *charrettes*, warrant closer attention from humanitarians, as do the lessons that arose post-Katrina with regard to the appropriate time frame in which to plan and where such planning should take place.

Implications for theory and policy

It is important to point out what this study is *not* advocating. It is not calling for humanitarian workers to fling open their compounds and walk into the far-flung regions of the world to live at one with the 'other'. In fact, it implies the opposite. Highlighting the material constraints, which are necessary for the practical application of contemporary humanitarianism to function, simultaneously identifies why humanitarianism is fundamentally flawed in its conception. To go to others, to tell them what they need, and to do so from a position of superior material power, can only be a form of domination. As long as the material power is so superior as to be unassailable, so great as to be completely overwhelming, humanitarianism may be seen to function. Those who are overpowered will accept what is being offered without question, without retort. But as the power differential lessens and the mechanisms of control become visible, those being dominated may begin to exert their own desires, opinions and approaches. This implies that the current displays of material force and securitization by humanitarianism cannot be read as extensions of Western power, but rather as its decline or relative absence. The need to retreat to the compound – both figuratively and physically – implies that an urgent and fundamental rethink about the objectives and possibilities of humanitarian assistance is required.

Ironically, the same space of the compound and its associated auxiliary space is the very thing that prevents such a revisioning. The rapacious demand from headquarters for field reports, best practices, lessons learnt and situation reports encourages a spectacle of development as constructed from within the humanitarian enclave. Here, local issues are framed in global terms. Recent trends towards the securitization of humanitarian space also suggest that local challenges to the humanitarian project (i.e. 'making do') are interpreted through global frames of reference. For example, increases in criminal activity and the prevalence of small arms and light weapons in many of the states where humanitarian workers live have become linked within the humanitarian imaginary to global terrorist threats. Rather than understanding increases in kidnappings or the theft of NFI shipments as acts which are motivated by local dynamics, humanitarian organizations frame these acts as explicit targeting as part of a larger anti-Western campaign. In turn, the retreat of humanitarians towards militarized spaces and the deployment of aid workers to overtly politicized territories such as Afghanistan and Iraq does link together local political dynamics and global demands, reinforcing the beliefs of the humanitarian imaginary.

It is possible that it is too late to redress the situation: that the dynamic put in place through previous modes of spatial domination (Smirl 2009) has reconfigured the landscape to such a degree that new, hybrid approaches to development and conflict have emerged. Hoffman (2004) examines the transformation of warfare within the context of West Africa. In Sierra Leone, the targeting of civilians by combatants was a tactic adopted by rebel groups seeking to maximize their political leverage vis-à-vis the international community. According to Hoffman, this tactic was subsequently adopted by Liberian rebel groups, in the context of their own civil war. While the targeting of civilians was originally the perverse result of humanitarian assistance in Sierra Leone, it has become disjoined from its origins and has been further developed and adapted to suit the needs of Liberian political forces. Similarly, it is possible that the political project of humanitarianism as embodied in the bodies and built environments of aid workers has become irrelevant (if this was ever not the case). Their significance stems only from the political and economic resources that they bring with them. Insofar as the kidnapping, ambushing and hijacking of humanitarian aid are a tangible rejection of the humanitarian project, they are political.

But step out of the compound, and these acts are perhaps no more than the tactics of battle to which aid workers are at best incidental, at worst an unwitting revenue stream (Munkler 2005).

In the context of already existing humanitarianism (Hoffman 2004), this work also points to the need for further work on aid workers' experiences and perceptions in the field. As mentioned in the introduction, initially the focus on the material aspects of aid work is often met with suspicion and defensiveness: that what is being critiqued is not the aid worker's relative wealth but the aid worker's *morality*. Examining the larger structures which shape and constrain the aid worker's experience in the field moves the discussion away from the level of personal accusation and individual failings and into a realm where measured critique and analysis can be undertaken. Such a critique points to the need for further work on issues of access and remote management, most notably by rethinking what constitutes 'the field'. As a marker of the structural pathologies of the postwar aid architecture, the spatial distribution of headquarters and the field points to the need for a radical reconfiguration of the way in which aid is delivered. Ultimately, this will challenge the underlying principles of sympathy (Rutherford 2009), assistance and relief. To recognize that what is given cannot be extracted from the material, spatial and historical processes in which it is embedded changes the parameters of and possibilities for humanitarianism. At a broader level, the consideration that material form needs to be considered for its potential agency (Miller 2005a; Latour 1993) challenges the fundamental positivist assumptions of humanitarian intervention; a project which puts at its centre the potential of the individual agent to change the direction of world history.

Future research directions

This study has been a first step towards applying a spatial and material lens to humanitarian intervention. As a first attempt, an intentionally wide scope was adopted. Not only were the spatial and material environments of the aid workers themselves considered, but the material and spatial qualities of the interventions were also assessed. As well as addressing these issues within a traditional North/South context, the dynamic of post-crisis reconstruction was also explored within a North/North context. Because of this broad scope, certain areas inevitably could not be investigated. Ideally one or two more cases would have been undertaken. Initially, I was interested in including South Sudan and/or Darfur as an in-depth case study. This would have allowed for further testing of the hypothesis that the material approach of the international community is similar, regardless of whether it is in a post-conflict or a post-natural-disaster context. However, constraints of time and funding precluded this possibility. Through this book and my previous work (Smirl 2008), I have exhausted the research potential of the Aceh case. The unexpected arrival of Hurricane Gustav, in August 2008, and the mandatory evacuation of New Orleans curtailed my field research on the Gulf Coast. However, I am undertaking further research on new architectural approaches to post-disaster housing there.[1]

Additional work should also be done on the compounding tendency of humanitarian intervention and the increased securitization of humanitarian personnel. Exploring the spatial history of contemporary humanitarianism in more depth could provide insight into current trends in the rapprochement between military and humanitarian interventions. Buchanan and Muggah's (2005) findings that perceptions of insecurity were highest in not only de facto active conflict situations but also in places like Nepal and Angola imply the possibility for a larger research project which would explicitly explore the potential link between levels of physical securitization and perceptions of insecurity. Ideally this would be done under the auspices of a supporting organization with a significant field presence, as it is almost impossible to obtain information on staff security as an independent researcher.

---

1 Editors' note: this research was never finished.

The results of this research would be of relevance not only to humanitarian intervention but also to broader understandings of the affective significance of the built environment. For example, what are the impacts of new housing developments with insurance requirements and building codes, which stress security (Minton 2009)?

There is also a crucial need for sustained research work on the impact of the material and spatial aspects of humanitarianism on surrounding communities (Carnahan et al. 2006; Pouligny 2006). Part of the reason that this has not been done is the practical difficulties involved in this type of research (translation, establishing the validity of responses, establishing a sufficiently long time horizon). However, such research could be an excellent locus for a critical re-evaluation of the humanitarian project. Together, aid workers and national and local actors could elaborate a full-spectrum account of how aid as a process, an act and a space reworks and has reworked the communities in which it operates. Such a project could also integrate the tactics and approaches that beneficiaries and their associated communities and networks have deployed in the context of aid missions. This might move aid work away from the construction of imaginary subjects (and objects) of development and towards partnership that might be recognized as such by the 'partners' themselves.

The issue of time horizons also deserves further attention. Insufficient attention has been paid to the pernicious effect of short-term consultants on humanitarianism at large. Forensic work on the monetary investment alone would be revealing in its scale and scope. Historical investigation of the role of experts and consultants in humanitarianism would arguably be destabilizing for the entire aid industry. Some of these areas I intend to pursue in my own work. Others, I hope, will be picked up by other researchers.

BIBLIOGRAPHY

Afrida, N. (2006) 'Two BRR officials named suspects in corruption case', *Jakarta Post.com*, 14 September.

Agamben, G. and D. Heller-Roazen (1998) *Homo Sacer: Sovereign power and bare life*, Stanford, CA: Stanford University Press.

Age, L. (2005) 'IDPs confined to barracks in Aceh', *Forced Migration Review* (Special Issue: 'Tsunami, learning from the humanitarian response'), July, pp. 22–3.

Agnew, J. A. (1987) *Place and Politics: The geographical mediation of state and society*, London: Allen and Unwin.

— (1997) *Political Geography: A reader*, London: Arnold.

Ahmed, S. (2004) *The Cultural Politics of Emotion*, Edinburgh: Edinburgh University Press.

Alagappa, M. and T. Inoguchi (1999) *International Security Management and the United Nations*, New York: United Nations University Press.

Alesina, A. and D. Dollar (2000) 'Who gives foreign aid to whom and why?', *Journal of Economic Growth*, 5: 33–63.

Alexander, C., S. Ishikawa and M. Silverstein (1977) *A Pattern Language: Towns, buildings, construction*, New York: Oxford University Press.

Anderson, J. (1982) 'Untitled', United Press International, 1 October.

Anderson, M. B. (1999) *Do No Harm: How aid can support peace – or war*, Boulder, CO: Lynne Rienner Publishers.

Ansell, N. (2008) 'Third World gap year projects: youth transitions and the mediation of risk', *Environment and Planning D: Society and Space*, 26: 218–40.

Appadurai, A. (1986) *The Social Life of Things: Commodities in cultural perspective*, Cambridge: Cambridge University Press.

— (1997) *Modernity at Large: Cultural Dimensions of Globalization*, Public Worlds vol. 1, Minneapolis: University of Minnesota Press.

Armas, E. B. et al. (2008) *Aceh Poverty Assessment: The Impact of the Conflict, the Tsunami and Reconstruction on Poverty in Aceh*, Jakarta/Washington, DC: World Bank.

Aspinall, E. (2007) 'The construction of grievance: natural resources and identity in a separatist conflict', *Journal of Conflict Resolution*, 51(6): 950–72.

— (2009) 'Combatants to contractors: the political economy of peace in Aceh', *Indonesia*, 87: 1–34.

Atkinson, R. and S. Blandy (2005) 'Introduction: International perspectives on the new enclavism and the rise of gated communities', *Housing Studies*, 20(2): 177–86.

Atkinson, R. and J. Flint (2004) 'Fortress UK? Gated communities, the spatial revolt of the elites and time–space trajectories of segregation', *Housing Studies*, 19(6): 875–92.

Augé, M. (1994) *Pour une anthropologie des mondes contemporains*, Paris: Aubier.

— (1995) *Non-Places: Introduction to an anthropology of supermodernity*, London: Verso.

— (1998) *A Sense for the Other: The timeliness and relevance of anthropology*, Stanford, CA: Stanford University Press.

Australian Government Development Cooperation in Indonesia (2008) *Review of the Aceh Reconstruction Phase* (draft).

Bakker, K. (2005) 'Katrina: the public transcript of "disaster"', *Environment and Planning D: Society and Space*, 23: 795–809.

Ball, I. (2005) Presentation for Engineers without Borders, Leiston Abbey, UK, 25 November.

Ball, W. (2008) *The Monuments of Afghanistan: History, archaeology and architecture*, London: I. B. Tauris.

Barakat, S. (2003) 'Housing reconstruction after conflict and disaster', Humanitarian Practice Network Paper, London: ODI.

Barakat, S., M. Chard, T. Jacoby and W. Lume (2002) 'The composite approach: research design in the context of war and armed conflict', *Third World Quarterly*, 23(5): 991–1003.

Barenstein, J. D. (2008) 'From Gujarat to Tamil Nadu: owner-driven vs. contractor-driven housing reconstruction in India', Paper read at the 4th International i-Rec Conference at Christchurch, New Zealand.

Barlow, C. A. (2007) 'In the Third Space: a case study of Canadian students in social work practicum in India', *International Social Work*, 50(2): 243–54.

Barnes, T. J. (2003) 'The place of locational analysis: a selective and interpretive history', *Progress in Human Geography*, 27(1): 69–95.

Barnett, M. (2005) 'Humanitarianism transformed', *Perspectives on Politics*, 3(4), December.

Barnett, M. N. and M. Finnemore (1999) 'The politics, power, and pathologies of international organizations', *International Organization*, 53(4): 699–732.

Barron, P. (2007) 'Getting reintegration back on track: problems in Aceh and priorities for moving forward', Paper read at 'The peace process in Aceh: the remainders of violence and the future of Nanggroe Aceh Darussalam', Harvard University, 24–27 October.

BBC (2005a) 'Aceh rebels refuse to give names', BBC, 27 October.

— (2005b) 'Indonesia restricts Aceh aid work', BBC, 11 January.

Beck, U. and M. Ritter (1992) *Risk Society: Towards a New Modernity*, London: Sage.

Bendelow, G. and S. Williams (1998) *Emotions in Social Life: Critical Themes and Contemporary Issues*, London: Routledge.

Bergdoll, B., P. Christensen and R. Broadhurst (2008) *Home Delivery: Fabricating the modern dwelling*, New York: Museum of Modern Art.

Berger, M. W. (2005) 'The American hotel', *Journal of Decorative and Propaganda Arts*, 25: 6–9.

Bergman, C. (2003) *Another Day in Paradise: Front line stories from international aid workers*, London: Earthscan.

Bergson, H. (1988) *Matter and Memory*, New York: Zone Books.

Besio, K. (2007) 'Depth of fields: travel photography and spatializing modernities in Northern Pakistan', *Environment and Planning D: Society and Space*, 25: 53–74.

Bhabha, H. (1990) 'The Third Space: interview with Homi Bhabha', in Jonathan Rutherford (ed.), *Identity: Community, culture, difference*, London: Lawrence and Wishart.

— (2004) *The Location of Culture*, Routledge Classics, Oxford: Routledge.

Birch, E. L. and S. M. Wachter (2006) *Rebuilding Urban Places after Disaster: Lessons from Hurricane Katrina*, The City in the Twenty-first Century, Philadelphia: University of Pennsylvania Press.

Biswas, S. (2008) 'Trail of destruction at Mumbai hotel', *BBC News*, 29 November.

Blakely, E. J. and M. G. Snyder (1997) *Fortress America: Gated communities in the United States*, Washington, DC: Brookings Institution Press.

Blunt, A. and R. M. Dowling (2006) *Home*, Key Ideas in Geography, London: Routledge.

Boddy, T. (2008) 'Architectural emblematic: hardened sites and softened symbols', in M. Sorkin (ed.), *Indefensible Space: The Architecture of the National Insecurity State*, London: Routledge.

Bourdieu, P. (1984) *Distinction. A social critique of the judgement of taste*, London: Routledge and Kegan Paul.

— (1990) *The Logic of Practice*, Cambridge: Polity.

Bourdieu, P. and R. Nice (1977) *Outline of a Theory of Practice*, Cambridge Studies in Social Anthropology, vol. 16, Cambridge: Cambridge University Press.

Bowie, F. (2006) *The Anthropology of Religion: An introduction*, 2nd edn, Oxford: Blackwell.

Bradsher, K. (2003) *High and Mighty: The dangerous rise of the SUV*, New York: Public Affairs.

Brahimi, L. (2000) *Report of the Panel on United National Peace Operations*, New York: United Nations (DPKO).

— (2008) *Towards a Culture of Security and Accountability*, New York: United Nations.

Bridge, G. (2004) 'Pierre Bourdieu', in P. Hubbard, R. Kitchin and G. Valentine (eds), *Key Thinkers on Space and Place*, London: Sage.

Brinkley, D. (2006) *The Great Deluge: Hurricane Katrina, New Orleans, and the Mississippi Gulf Coast*, New York: HarperCollins.

Brown, B. (2006) 'Katrina Cottage unveiled: affordable cottage a hit at builder's show', 11 January, www.mississippirenewal.com/info/dayJan-11-06.html, accessed 5 April 2007.

BRR (2007) *Agency of the Rehabilitation and Reconstruction for the Region and Community of Aceh and Nias*, 8 February, www.e-aceh-nias.org.

Buchanan, C. and R. Muggah (2005) *No Relief: Surveying the Effects of Gun Violence on Humanitarian and Development Personnel*, Geneva: Centre for Humanitarian Dialogue.

Buchanan, I. (2000) *Michel de Certeau*, (pub. with Theory, Culture & Society), London: Sage.

Bull, M. (2004) 'Automobility and the power of sound', *Theory, Culture & Society*, 21: 243–60.

Burke, A. and Afnan (2005) 'Aceh: reconstruction in a conflict environment: views from civil society, donors and NGOs', Indonesian Social Development Paper 8, London: DfID.

Burnett, J. (2005) *Where Soldiers Fear*

to Tread: At Work in the Fields of Anarchy, London: Heinemann.

Cain, K. (2004) *Emergency Sex (and other desperate measures): A true story from hell on earth*, New York: Miramax Books/Hyperion.

Calhoun, C. (2004) 'A world of emergencies: fear, intervention, and the limits of cosmopolitan order', Paper read at the 35th Annual Sorokin Lecture, University of Saskatchewan.

Campbell, D. (1998) *National Deconstruction: Violence, identity, and justice in Bosnia*, London: University of Minneapolis Press.

— (2005) 'The biopolitics of security: oil, empire, and the Sports Utility Vehicle', *American Quarterly*, 57(3): 943–72.

Carnahan, M., W. Durch and S. Gilmore (2006) *Economic Impact of Peacekeeping*, Peace Dividend Trust.

Carrier, J. (1991) 'Gifts, commodities, and social relations: a Maussian view of exchange', *Sociological Forum*, 6(1): 119–36.

Carter, P. (2004) *Material Thinking: The theory and practice of creative research*, Carlton, Victoria: Melbourne University Publishing.

Casey, M. (2006) 'Agencies under fire for tsunami failures', *washingtonpost.com*, 23 September.

Castells, M. (2000) *The Rise of the Network Society*, 2nd edn, Information Age, Oxford: Blackwell.

Castoriadis, C. (1987) *The Imaginary Institution of Society*, trans. K. Blamey, Oxford: Polity/Blackwell.

Chandler, D. (2006) *Empire in Denial: The politics of state-building*, London: Pluto.

Chandrasekaran, R. (2006) *Imperial Life in the Emerald City*, New York: Knopf.

Chesterman, S. (2001) *Just War or Just Peace?: International law and humanitarian intervention*, Oxford Monographs in International Law, Oxford: Oxford University Press.

— (2004) *You, the People: The United Nations, transitional administration, and state-building*, Oxford: Oxford University Press.

Christian Science Monitor (2005) 'In tsunami's spindrift, a calming peace', *Christian Science Monitor*, 30 December.

Clarke, G. (2009) 'Brad Pitt makes it right in New Orleans', *Architectural Digest*, 66: 60–72.

Cocks, C. (2001) *Doing the Town: The rise of urban tourism in the United States 1850–1915*, Berkeley: University of California Press.

Coleman, S. (2002) 'Do you believe in pilgrimage?: Communitas, contestation and beyond', *Anthropological Theory*, 2(3): 355–68.

Collier, P. (2007) *The Bottom Billion: Why the poorest countries are failing and what can be done about it*, Oxford: Oxford University Press.

Collins, R. (2004) *Interaction Ritual Chains*, Princeton Studies in Cultural Sociology, Oxford: Princeton University Press.

Consultative Group On Indonesia (2005) *Indonesia: Notes on Reconstruction. The December 26, 2004 Natural Disaster*, 19/20 January, BAPPENAS.

Corbridge, S. (2007) 'The (im)possibility of development studies', *Economy & Society*, 36(2): 179–211.

Corsellis, T., A. Vitale, Y. Aysan and I. Davis (2006) *Exploring key changes and developments in post-disaster settlement, shelter and housing, 1982–2006: scoping study to inform revision of 'Shelter after*

Disaster: Guidelines for Assistance',
United Nations/OCHA.

Courtemanche, G. and P. Claxton
(2003) A Sunday at the Pool in
Kigali, Toronto: Knopf Canada.

Courtney, M. (lead), H. Riddell,
J. Ewers, R. Linder and C. Cohen
(2005) In the Balance: Measuring
Progress in Afghanistan, July Post-
Conflict Reconstruction Project,
ed. F. Barton and B. Crocker (co-
directors), CSIS.

Coward, M. (2001) Urbicide and the
Question of Community in Bosnia-
Herzegovina, Electronic resource,
University of Newcastle-upon-
Tyne.

— (2002) 'Community as heterogeneous ensemble: Mostar and
multiculturalism', Alternatives,
27(1): 29–38.

— (2009) Urbicide: The politics of
urban destruction, New York:
Routledge.

Crain, C. (2008) 'Good at being gods',
London Review of Books, 30.

Crang, M. (2000) 'Relics, places and
unwritten geographies in the work
of Michel de Certeau (1925–86)', in
M. Crang and N. Thrift (eds), Thinking Space, Critical Geographies, ed.
G. Valentine and T. Skelton, London
and New York: Routledge.

Crang, M. and N. Thrift (2000) Thinking Space, Critical Geographies,
ed. G. Valentine and T. Skelton,
London and New York: Routledge.

Cresswell, T. (2004) Place: A short
Introduction, Short Introductions
to Geography, Oxford: Blackwell.

CSIS (2004) Progress or Peril:
Measuring Iraq's Reconstruction,
Post-Conflict Reconstruction
Project, ed. F. Barton and B.
Crocker (co-directors), Center for
Strategic and International Stud-
ies, December.

Cuny, F. C. and S. Abrams (1983) Disasters and Development, New York:
Oxford University Press.

Cupples, J. (2007) 'Gender and Hurricane Mitch: reconstructing subjectivities after disaster', Disasters,
31(2): 155–75.

Currier, N. (2003) '"Protecting the
protectors". Strengthening staff
security: priorities and challenges',
UN Chronicle.

Cusato, M. (n.d.) www.marianne
cusato.com/Site_3/Marianne
Cusato.com.html, accessed
15 April 2009.

Cusato Cottages (n.d.) www.cusato
cottages.com/index_content.html,
accessed 30 June 2007.

Cutter, S. (2006) The Geography of
Social Vulnerability: Race, Class
and Catastrophe, Social Science
Research Council, understanding
katrina.ssrc.org/Cutter/, accessed
31 May 2007.

Czarniawska, B. and C. Mazza (2003)
'Consulting as a liminal space',
Human Relations, 56(3): 267–90.

Da Silva, J. and Z. Zubkowski (2006)
The People of Aceh: Aceh and Nias
Post-Tsunami Reconstruction, Review
of Aceh Housing Program, London:
Ove Arup & Partners Ltd, April.

Dallaire, R. and B. Beardsley (2003)
Shake Hands with the Devil: The
failure of humanity in Rwanda,
Toronto: Random House Canada.

Dant, T. (2004) 'The driver-car', Theory,
Culture & Society, 21(4/5): 61–79.

Davis, I. (1978) Shelter after Disaster,
Oxford: Oxford Polytechnic Press.

Davis, M. (2006) City of Quartz: Ex-
cavating the future in Los Angeles,
New York: Verso.

De Certeau, M. (1988) The Practice
of Everyday Life, trans. S. Rendell,
Berkeley: University of California
Press.

De Certeau, M., F. Jameson and C. Lovitt (1980) 'On the oppositional practices of everyday life', *Social Text*, 3: 3–43.

De Man, P. (1979) 'Autobiography as de-facement', *MLN*, 94(5): 919–30.

Deleuze, G. and F. Guattari (2004) *A Thousand Plateaus: Capitalism and schizophrenia*, London: Continuum.

Denby, E. (1998) *Grand Hotels: Reality and illusion: an architectural and social history*, London: Reaktion Books.

Dercon, B. (2009) *Post-Tsunami Aceh-Nias Settlement and Housing Recovery Review*, UN-Habitat, April.

Destries, M. (2009) 'Brad Pitt's Make It Right intros new green duplex designs', www.ecorazzi. com/2009/07/02/brad-pitts-make-it-right-intros-news-green-duplex-designs/, accessed 4 August 2009.

Deutsche Presse Agentur (2006) 'Radical Sharia police raid UN diplomatic compound in Indonesia', Deutsch Presse Agentur, 23 August.

Dieter, H. and R. Kumar (2008) 'The downside of celebrity diplomacy: the neglected complexity of development', *Global Insights*, 14: 259–64.

Donais, T. (2002) 'The politics of privatization in post-Dayton Bosnia', *Southeast European Politics*, 3(1): 3–19.

Doty, R. L. (1996) *Imperial Encounters: The politics of representation in North–South relations*, Minneapolis: University of Minnesota Press.

Douglas, M. (2002) *Purity and Danger: An analysis of concepts of pollution and taboo*, Routledge Classics, London: Routledge.

Dovey, K. (1999) *Framing Places: Mediating power in built form*, Architext Series, London: Routledge.

Drury, A. C., R. S. Olson and D. A. van Belle (2005) 'The politics of humanitarian aid: US foreign disaster assistance, 1964–1995', *Journal of Politics*, 67(2): 454–73.

Duany, Plater-Zyberk and Company (2009) *Smart Code Version 9.2.*

Duffield, Mark R. (2001) *Global Governance and the New Wars: The merging of development and security*, London: Zed Books.

— (2007) *Development, Security and Unending War: Governing the world of peoples*, Cambridge: Polity.

— (2009) 'Architectures of aid', Lecture, University of Cambridge.

Dufour, C., V. Geoffroy, H. Maury and F. Grenewald (2004) 'Rights, standards and quality in a complex humanitarian space: Is Sphere the right tool?', *Disasters*, 28(2): 124–41.

Duncan-Jones, R. (1990) *Structure and Scale in the Roman Economy*, Cambridge: Cambridge University Press.

Duvall, S. (2007) '"Ambassador mom": Angelina Jolie, celebrity activism, and institutional power', Paper read at the annual meeting of the International Communication Association, San Francisco, CA, 23 May.

Dyson, M. E. (2006) *Come Hell or High Water: Hurricane Katrina and the color of disaster*, New York: Basic Civitas.

Eade, D. (1997) *Capacity-building: An approach to people-centred development*, Oxford: Oxfam.

Eade, J. and M. J. Sallnow (2000) *Contesting the Sacred: The anthropology of pilgrimage*, Urbana: University of Illinois Press.

Easterly, W. (2002) 'The cartel of

good intentions: the problem of bureaucracy in foreign aid', *Policy Reform*, 5(4): 223–50.

— (2006) *The White Man's Burden: Why the West's Efforts to aid the rest have done so much ill and so little good*, Oxford: Oxford University Press.

Edensor, T. (2001) 'Performing tourism, staging tourism: (re)producing tourist space and practice', *Tourist Studies*, 1(1): 59–81.

— (2004) 'Automobility and national identity: representation, geography and driving practice', *Theory, Culture & Society*, 21(4/5): 101–20.

Edkins, J. (2000a) 'Sovereign power, zones of indistinction and the camp', *Alternatives*, 25: 3–25.

— (2000b) *Whose Hunger?: Concepts of famine, practices of aid*, Borderlines, vol. 17, Minneapolis/London: University of Minnesota Press.

Eide, E. B., A. T. Kaspersen, R. C. Kent and K. von Hippel (2005) *Report on Integrated Missions: Practical Perspectives and Recommendations*, May.

Ek, R. (2006) 'Giorgio Agamben and the spatialities of the camp: an introduction', *Geografiska Annaler, Series B*, 88(4): 363–86.

Elden, S. (2006) 'Spaces of humanitarian exception', *Geografiska Annaler, Series B*, 88(4): 477–85.

English, L. M. (2005) 'Third-Space practitioners: women educating for justice in the global South', *Adult Education Quarterly*, 55(2): 85–100.

Escobar, A. (1994) *Encountering Development: The making and unmaking of the third world*, Princeton Studies in Culture/Power/History, Princeton, NJ: Princeton University Press.

— (2001) 'Culture sits in places: reflections on globalism and subaltern strategies', *Political Geography*, 20(2): 139–74.

European Commission Humanitarian Aid Office (2004a) *Generic Security Guide*, Brussels: ECHO.

— (2004b) *Report on Security of Humanitarian Personnel: Standards and Practices for the Security of Humanitarian Personnel and Advocacy for Humanitarian Space*, Brussels: ECHO.

— (2006) *NGO Security Collaboration Guide*, Brussels.

Fast, L. (2007) 'Characteristics, context and risk: NGO insecurity in conflict zones', *Disasters*, 31(2): 130–54.

Fearon, J. D. and D. D. Laitin (2003) 'Ethnicity, insurgency, and civil war', *American Political Science Review*, 97(1): 75–90.

Featherstone, M. (2004) 'Automobilities: an introduction', *Theory, Culture & Society*, 21(4/5): 1–24.

Featherstone, M., N. J. Thrift and J. Urry (2005) *Automobilities*, London: Sage.

Ferguson, J. (1990) *The Anti-Politics Machine: 'Development', depoliticization, and bureaucratic power in Lesotho*, Cambridge: Cambridge University Press.

— (2006) *Global Shadows: Africa in the neoliberal world order*, Durham, NC/London: Duke University Press.

Fiske, J. (1989) *Reading the Popular*, London: Unwin Hyman.

Forced Migration Review (2004) *House: Loss, refuge and belonging*, Trondheim: FMR.

Foucault, M. (1995) *Discipline and Punish: The birth of the prison*, 2nd edn, New York: Vintage Books.

Frey, D. (2008) 'Crowded house', *New York Times*, 8 June.

Friedman, T. L. (1984) 'Lebanese meet with the Israelis about a pullout', *New York Times*, 9 November.

Frow, J. (1991) 'Michel de Certeau and the practice of representation', *Cultural Studies*, 5(1): 52–60.

George, A. L. and A. Bennett (2005) *Case Studies and Theory Development in the Social Sciences*, BCSIA Studies in International Security, London: MIT.

George, T. (writer) (2004) *Hotel Rwanda*, UK, USA, Italy, South Africa: Lions Gate Entertainment and United Artists.

Giddens, A. (1984) *The Constitution of Society: Introduction of the theory of structuration*, Berkeley: University of California Press.

— (1990) *The Consequences of Modernity*, Cambridge: Polity/ Blackwell.

— (1993) *New Rules of Sociological Method: A positive critique of interpretative sociologies*, 2nd edn, Oxford: Polity.

— (1995) *Politics, Sociology and Social Theory: Encounters with classical and contemporary social thought*, Cambridge: Polity.

Gillem, M. L. (2007) *America Town: Building the outposts of empire*, Minneapolis: University of Minnesota Press.

Gilroy, P. (1993) *The Black Atlantic: Modernity and double consciousness*, Cambridge, MA: Harvard University Press.

Giroux, H. A. (2006) *Stormy Weather: Katrina and the politics of disposability*, The Radical Imagination Series, London: Paradigm.

Glancey, J. (2009) 'The architecture of diplomacy', *Guardian*, 9 January.

Glover, L. (2000) 'Driving under the influence: the nature of selling Sport Utility Vehicles', *Bulletin of Science Technology Society*, 20(5): 360–5.

Goffman, E., C. C. Lemert and A. Branaman (1997) *The Goffman Reader*, Oxford: Blackwell.

Goldsworthy, A. K. and J. Keegan (2000) *Roman Warfare*, London: Cassell.

Goodwin, J., J. Jasper and F. Polletta (2001) *Passionate Politics: Emotions and Social Movements*, Chicago, IL, and London: University of Chicago Press.

Gottdiener, M. (1994) *The Social Production of Urban Space*, 2nd edn, Austin: University of Texas Press.

Gournay, I. and J. C. Loeffler (2002) 'Washington and Ottawa: a tale of two embassies', *Journal of the Society of Architectural Historians*, 61(4): 480–507.

Government of Canada (2009) *Foreign Affairs and International Trade Canada, Pre-Departure Course in Intercultural Effectiveness*, www. international.gc.ca/cfsi–icse/cil– cai/predeparture–predepart–eng. asp, accessed 5 September 2009.

Graft (artist) (2003) *Brad Pitt Studio (House of Brad)*, www.graftab.com.

Graham, S. and S. Marvin (2001) *Splintering Urbanism: Networked infrastructures, technological mobilities and the urban condition*, London: Routledge.

Grosz, E. A. (1995) *Space, Time, and Perversion: Essays on the politics of bodies*, London: Routledge.

— (1999) *Becomings: Explorations in time, memory, and futures*, Ithaca, NY, and London: Cornell University Press.

Gunder Frank, A. (1971) *Capitalism and Underdevelopment in Latin America*, Revised edn, Pelican Latin American Library, Harmondsworth: Penguin.

Gupta, A. and J. Ferguson (1997a)
*Anthropological Locations: Bounda-
ries and grounds of a field science*,
Berkeley: University of California
Press.

— (1997b) 'Discipline and practice:
"the field" as site, method and location in anthropology', in A. Gupta
and J. Ferguson (eds), *Anthropological Locations: Boundaries and
grounds of a field science*, Berkeley:
University of California Press.

Hales, L. (2005) 'In Mississippi, the
reshape of things to come', *Washington Post*, 15 October.

Harmer, A. (2008) 'Integrated missions: a threat to humanitarian
security?', *International Peacekeeping*, 15(4): 528–39.

Harrell-Bond, B., E. Voutira and
M. Leopold (1992) 'Counting the
refugees: gifts, givers, patrons and
clients', *Journal of Refugee Studies*,
5(3/4): 205–25.

Harrow, K. W. (2005) '"Un train peut
en cacher un 'autre'"': narrating
the Rwandan genocide and Hotel
Rwanda', *Research in African Litera-
tures*, 36(4): 223–32.

Harvey, D. (1973) *Social Justice and the
City*, London: E. Arnold.

— (2000) *Spaces of Hope*, Edinburgh:
Edinburgh University Press

— (2001) *Spaces of Capital: Towards
a critical geography*, Edinburgh:
Edinburgh University Press.

Hattori, T. (2001) 'Reconceptualizing
foreign aid', *Review of International
Political Economy*, 8(4): 633–60.

— (2003) 'Giving as a mechanism of
consent: international aid organizations and the ethical hegemony
of capitalism', *International Relations*, 17(2): 153–73.

Hayden, D. (2003) *Building Suburbia:
Green fields and urban growth,
1820–2000*, New York: Pantheon.

Hays, K. M. and D. Miller (eds) (2008)
*Buckminster Fuller: Starting with
the Universe*, New Haven, CT: Yale
University Press.

Hedren, J. and B.-O. Linner (2009)
'Utopian thought and the politics
of sustainable development',
Futures, 41(4).

Helmig, J. and O. Kessler (2007)
'Space, boundaries, and the problem of order: a view from systems
theory', *International Political
Sociology*, 1: 240–56.

Henderson, J. C. (2001) 'Conserving
colonial heritage: Raffles Hotel in
Singapore', *International Journal of
Heritage Studies*, 7(1): 7–24.

Heron, B. (2008) *Desire for Develop-
ment: Whiteness, Gender, and the
Helping Imperative*, Waterloo,
Ontario: Wilfrid Laurier University
Press.

Higate, P. (2007) 'Peacekeepers,
masculinities, and sexual exploitation', *Men and Masculinities*, 10(1):
99–119.

Higate, P. and M. Henry (2004)
'Engendering (in)security in peace
support operations', *Security
Dialogue*, 35(4): 481–98.

Hillier, J. and E. Rooksby (2002) *Habitus: A sense of place*, Urban and
Regional Planning and Development, Aldershot: Ashgate.

Hirst, P. Q. (2005) *Space and Power:
Politics, war and architecture*,
Cambridge: Polity.

Hirst, P. Q. and G. Thompson (1999)
*Globalization in Question: The
international economy and the
possibilities of governance*, 2nd edn,
Cambridge: Polity Press.

Historic Green (n.d.) 'Historic Green',
www.historicgreen.org/historic_
green.php, accessed 24 April
2009.

Hitchcott, N. (2009) 'Travels in

inhumanity: Veronique Tadjo's tourism in Rwanda', *French Cultural Studies*, 20(2): 149–64.

Hochschild, A. R. (1983) *The Managed Heart: Commercialization of Human Feeling*, Berkeley: University of California Press.

— (1997) *The Time Bind: When Work Comes Home and Home Becomes Work*, New York: Metropolitan Books.

— (2003) *The Commercialization of Intimate Life: Notes from Home and Work*, Berkeley: University of California Press.

Hodge, J. M. (2007) *Triumph of the Expert: Agrarian doctrines of development and the legacies of British colonialism*, Ecology and History Series, Athens: Ohio University Press.

Hoffman, D. (2004) 'The civilian target in Sierra Leone and Liberia: political power, military strategy, and humanitarian intervention', *African Affairs*, 103(411): 211–26.

— (2005) 'The Brookfields Hotel (Freetown, Sierra Leone)', *Public Culture*, 17(1): 55–74.

— (2008) 'The city as barracks: Freetown, Monrovia, and the organization of violence in postcolonial African cities', *Cultural Anthropology*, 22(3): 400–28.

Hoge, W. (2007) 'Sudan flying arms to Darfur, panel reports', *New York Times*, 18 April.

Holder, P. A. (1980) *Studies in the Auxilia of the Roman Army from Augustus to Trajan*, British Archaeology Reports.

Hoogvelt, A. (2006) 'Globalization and post-modern imperialism', *Globalizations*, 3(2): 159–74.

hooks, b. (1990) *Yearning: Race, gender, and cultural politics*, Boston, MA: South End Press.

House of Commons (2009) *Department for International Development: Operating in insecure environments*, London: House of Commons, 9 March.

Hubbard, P., R. Kitchin and G. Valentine (2004) *Key Thinkers on Space and Place*, London: Sage.

Hughes, R. (2007) 'Through the looking blast: geopolitics and visual culture', *Geography Compass*, 1(5): 976–94.

— (2008) 'Dutiful tourism: encountering the Cambodian genocide', *Asia Pacific Viewpoint*, 49(3): 318–30.

Humanitarian Accountability Partnership (2007) *The 2007 Humanitarian Accountability Report*, ed. HAP, Geneva: HAP.

Hutchinson, J. F. (1996) *Champions of Charity: War and the rise of the Red Cross*, Oxford: Westview.

Hyndman, J. (2000) *Managing Displacement: Refugees and the politics of humanitarianism*, London: University of Minnesota Press.

— (2007) 'The securitization of fear in post-tsunami Sri Lanka', *Annals of the Association of American Geographers*, 97(2): 361–72.

— (2009) 'Siting conflict and peace in post-tsunami Sri Lanka and Aceh, Indonesia', *Norwegian Journal of Geography*, 63(1): 89–96.

IASC Working Group (2006) *Saving Lives Together: A Framework for Improving Security Arrangements among IGOs, NGOs and UN in the Field (Amended Version)*, New York: Inter-Agency Standing Committee, 15–17 November.

Ibelings, H. (1998) *Supermodernism: Architecture in the age of globalization*, Rotterdam: NAi.

Inayatullah, N. and D. L. Blaney (2004) *International Relations and* the *Problem of Difference*, New York: Routledge.

Independent Panel on the Safety and Security of UN Personnel in Iraq (2003) *The Independent Panel on the Safety and Security of UN Personnel in Iraq*, New York: United Nations.

International Court of Justice (1949) 'Reparation for injuries suffered in the service of the United Nations', ed. International Court of Justice, Leiden: A. W. Sijthoff's.

International Crisis Group (2007) *Aceh: Post-Conflict Complications*, Asia Report 139, 4 October.

— (2008) *Crisis Group, the Responsibility to Protect (R2P), and Sri Lanka*, www.crisisgroup.org/home/index.cfm?id=5421, accessed 28 May 2008.

International Federation of the Red Cross and Red Crescent Societies (2007) *Stay Safe: The International Federation's guide to a safer mission*, Geneva: IFRC.

Iveson, K. (2006) 'Strangers in the cosmopolis', in J. Binnie, J. Holloway, S. Millington and C. Young (eds), *Cosmopolitan Urbanism*, Abingdon: Routledge.

Jacobs, J. (2000) *The Death and Life of Great American Cities*, London: Pimlico.

Jakarta Post (2009) 'Aceh govt backs BRR against criticism', *Jakarta Post*, 16 April.

James, W. and F. Burkhardt (1981) *The Principles of Psychology*, The Works of William James, Cambridge, MA: Harvard University Press.

Jameson, F. (1990) *Postmodernism, or, the Cultural Logic of Late Capitalism*, Durham, NC: Duke University Press.

Jones, R. and C. Fowler (2007) 'Placing and scaling the nation', *Environ-ment and Planning D: Society and Space*, 25: 332–54.

Kaplan, A. (2005) 'Where is Guantanamo?', *American Quarterly*, 57(3): 831–58.

Katz, J. (2000) *How Emotions Work*, Chicago, IL: University of Chicago Press.

Katz, M. (1999) 'The Hotel Kracauer', *Differences: a Journal of Feminist Cultural Studies*, 11(2): 134–52.

Kaufman, G. (1997) 'Watching the developers: a partial ethnography', in R. D. Grillo and R. L. Stirrat (eds), *Discourses of Development: Anthropological Perspectives*, Oxford and New York: Berg.

Keen, D. (2008) *Complex Emergencies*, Cambridge: Polity.

Kell, T. (1995) *The Roots of Acehnese Rebellion, 1989–1992*, Ithaca, NY: Cornell Modern Indonesia Project, Southeast Asia Program, Cornell University.

Kenny, S. (2005) 'Reconstruction in Aceh: building whose capacity?', *Community Development Journal*, 42(2): 206–21.

Kent, R. C. (1987) *Anatomy of Disaster Relief: The international network in action*, London: Pinter.

Kern, S. (1983) *The Culture of Time and Space 1880–1918*, London: Weidenfeld and Nicolson.

Kertzer, D. I. (1988) *Ritual, Politics and Power*, New Haven, CT, and London: Yale University Press.

Keteylan, A. (2008) 'CDC suppressed toxic trailer warnings', *CBS News*, 28 January.

Khan, S. (1998) 'Muslim women: negotiations in the Third Space', *Signs*, 23(2): 463–94.

Killing Memory (1995) *Killing Memory: The Targeting of Bosnia's Cultural Heritage*, Testimony presented at a hearing of the Commission on Security and Cooperation in Europe, 4 April.

King, A. D. (1990) *Urbanism, Colonialism, and the World-Economy: Cultural and spatial foundations of the world urban system*, International Library of Sociology, London: Routledge.

— (2004) *Spaces of Global Cultures; Architecture, Urbanism, Identity*, Architext Series, London: Routledge.

Klein, N. (2007) *The Shock Doctrine: The Rise of Disaster Capitalism*, London: Allen Lane.

Kleinfeld, M. (2007) 'Misreading the post-tsunami political landscape in Sri Lanka: the myth of humanitarian space', *Space and Polity*, 11(2): 169–84.

Koshar, R. (2004) 'Cars and nations: Anglo-German perspectives on automobility between the world wars', *Theory, Culture & Society*, 21(4/5): 121–44.

Kostof, S. (1999) *The City Shaped*, London: Thames and Hudson.

Kracauer, S. and T. Y. Levin (1995) *The Mass Ornament: Weimar essays*, Cambridge, MA: Harvard University Press.

Krause, K. and M. C. Williams (1997) *Critical Security Studies: Concepts and cases*, Minneapolis: University of Minnesota Press.

Kusno, A. (2000) *Behind the Postcolonial: Architecture, urban space, and political cultures in Indonesia*, Architext Series, London: Routledge.

Lacey, M. (2009) 'Mexican police make arrest in killing of candidate and his family', *New York Times*, 7 September.

Land Rover (n.d.) 'Technical specifications', www.landrover.co.uk/gb/en/vehicles/defender/ features-and-specifications/technical-specifications.htm, accessed 13 August 2009.

Lange, A. (2007) 'Don't call David Adjaye a starchitect', *New York Magazine*, 15 July.

Lange, S. (2007) *Bernd and Hilla Becher: Life and work*, London: MIT.

Latour, B. (1993) *We Have Never Been Modern*, New York and London: Harvester Wheatsheaf.

— (2005) *Reassembling the Social: An introduction to actor-network-theory*, Clarendon Lectures in Management Studies, Oxford: Oxford University Press.

Laugier, M. A. and S. D. Wale (1755) *An Essay on Architecture; in which its true principles are explained*, London: T. Osborne & Shipton.

Laurier, E. (2004) 'Bruno Latour', in P. Hubbard, R. Kitchin and G. Valentine (eds), *Key Thinkers on Space and Place*, London: Sage.

Lausten, J. (2008) 'Energy efficiency requirements in building codes, energy efficiency policies for new buildings', IEA Information Paper, Paris: OECD/IEA.

Le Billon, P. and A. Waizenegger (2007) 'Peace in the wake of disaster? Secessionist conflicts and the 2004 Indian Ocean tsunami', *Transactions of the Institute of British Geographers*, 32(3): 411–27.

Le Corbusier (1967) *The Radiant City: Elements of a doctrine of urbanism to be used as the basis of our machine-age civilization*, London: Faber.

Leach, F. (2006) 'Researching gender violence in schools: methodological and ethical considerations', *World Development*, 34(6): 1129–47.

Leapman, B. (2004) 'Huge security upgrade for US embassy', *Evening Standard*, 28 May.

Lefebvre, H. (1991) *The Production of Space*, Oxford: Basil Blackwell.

— (2004) *Rhythmanalysis: Space, time, and everyday life*, London and New York: Continuum.

— (2008) *Critique of Everyday Life*, Special edn, London: Verso.

Lesle, T. (writer) (2008) 'China: Green Dreams, a not so model village', in T. Lesle (producer), *Frontline World: Stories from a Small Planet*, PBS.

Lewis, D. and D. Mosse (2007) 'Development brokers and translators: the ethnography of aid and agencies', *Development in Practice*, 17(2): 307–9.

Lewis, J. (2006) 'Battle for Biloxi', *New York Times*, 21 May.

Lipsitz, G. (2007) 'The racialization of space and the spatialization of race', *Landscape Journal*, 26(1): 10–23.

Lischer, S. K. (2007) 'Military intervention and the humanitarian "force multiplier"', *Global Governance*, 13: 99–118.

Liu, A. (2008) *The State of New Orleans: An Update*, Washington, DC: Metropolitan Policy Program, Brookings Institution, 30 August.

Liu, A. and A. Plyer (2008) *The New Orleans Index: Special 3rd Anniversary Edition*, Washington, DC: Metropolitan Policy Program, Brookings Institution, August.

Liu, L. Y. (2008) 'Blank slates and disaster zones', in M. Sorkin (ed.), *Indefensible Space: The Architecture of the National Insecurity State*, London: Routledge.

Loeffler, J. C. (1998) *The Architecture of Diplomacy: Building America's embassies*, New York: Princeton Architectural Press.

— (2000) 'The identity crisis of the American embassy', *Foreign Service Journal*, June, pp. 19–20.

Los Angeles Times (2007) 'Environment – New Orleans: two years later – cheap, clean and green – 21st century neighborhood takes shape in the 9th Ward', *Los Angeles Times*, 29 August.

Low, S. M. (2001) 'The edge and the center: gated communities and the discourse of urban fear', *American Anthropologist*, 103(1): 45–58.

— (2003) *Behind the Gates: Life, security, and the pursuit of happiness in fortress America*, London: Routledge.

Lowe's (n.d.) www.lowes.com/lowes/lkn?action=pg&p=2006_landing/Katrina_Cottage/KatrinaCottageGallery.html, accessed 6 August/2007.

Luttwak, E. (1976) *The Grand Strategy of the Roman Empire from the First Century AD to the Third*, Baltimore, MD, and London: Johns Hopkins University Press.

Luymes, D. (1997) 'The fortification of suburbia: investigating the rise of enclave communities', *Landscape and Urban Planning*, 39(2/3): 187–203.

MacLeod, G. and K. Ward (2002) 'Spaces of utopia and dystopia: landscaping the contemporary city', *Geografiska Annaler, Series B: Human Geography*, 84(3/4): 153–70.

Marcus, L. (1994) *Auto/biographical Discourses: Theory, criticism, practice*, Manchester: Manchester University Press.

Marriage, Z. (2006) *Not Breaking the Rules, Not Playing the Game: International assistance to countries at war*, London: Hurst & Co.

Martin, E. (1995) 'Working across the human–other divide', in L. Birke and R. Hubbard (eds), *Reinventing*

Biology: Respect for life and the creation of knowledge, Bloomington: Indiana University Press.

Martin, S. (2007) 'The role of the stoa in the topography of the ancient Athenian agora: the Stoa Basileios, Stoa Poikile and Stoa of Zeus Eleftherios', PhD thesis, University of Cambridge.

Maslow, A. H. (1943) 'A theory of human motivation', *Psychological Review*, 50(4): 370–96.

Massey, D. (2006) *For Space*, London: Sage.

Massumi, B. (2002) *Parables for the Virtual: Movement, affect, sensation*, Post-Contemporary Interventions, Durham, NC: Duke University Press.

Mate, D. (2007) *Community Housing Assessment and Monitoring Program (CHAMP) Overview and Key Finding of CHAMP Housing Assessment Activities*, Banda Aceh: LOGICA/Australian Government, AusAID, 13 December.

Mauss, M. (1969) *The Gift: Forms and functions of exchange in archaic societies*, London: Cohen and West.

McDonough (n.d.) 'Projects – Huangbaiyu', www.mcdonoughpartners. com/projects/huangbaiyu/default. asp?projID=huangbaiyu, accessed 11 January 2009.

McDonough, W. and M. Braungart (2002) *Cradle to Cradle: Remaking the way we make things*, New York: North Point Press.

McFarlane, C. A. (2004) 'Risks associated with the psychological adjustment of humanitarian aid workers', *Australian Journal of Disaster and Trauma Studies*, 2004-1.

McKee, B. (2005) 'Gulf planning roils residents', *New York Times*, 8 December.

McNeill, D. (2008) 'The hotel and the city', *Progress in Human Geography*, 32(3): 383–98.

Mehaffy, M. (2008) 'Venezuela's new socialist cities', *Urban Land*, May, pp. 106–9.

Merleau-Ponty, M. (1962) *Phenomenology of Perception*, International Library of Philosophy and Scientific Method, London: Routledge & Kegan Paul.

Merry, S. E. (1981) *Urban Danger: Life in a neighborhood of strangers*, Philadelphia, PA: Temple University Press.

Michael, M. (2001) 'The invisible car: the cultural purification of road rage', in D. Miller (ed.), *Car Cultures*, Oxford: Berg.

Miller, D. (2001) *Car Cultures*, Oxford: Berg.

— (2005a) *Materiality*, Durham, NC: Duke University Press.

— (2005b) 'Materiality: an introduction', in D. Miller (ed.), *Materiality*, Durham, NC: Duke University Press.

Minca, C. (2006) 'Giorgio Agamben and the new biopolitical nomos', *Geografiska Annaler, Series B: Human Geography*, 88(4): 387–403.

Minion, L. (2004) *Hello Missus: A girl's own guide to foreign affairs*, Sydney: HarperCollins.

Minton, A. (2009) *Ground Control*, London: Penguin.

MIR (n.d.) 'Make it right', www. makeitrightnola.org/preview/ MIR_Oct_2008/MIR_video_update. php, accessed 8 January 2009.

Mississippi Renewal Forum (2005a) *Mississippi Renewal Forum Pre-Event Paper*, Fall.

— (2005b) *The Bulletin*, Biloxi: Mississippi Renewal Forum, 13 October.

Mitchell, D. (2005) 'The S.U.V. model of citizenship: floating bubbles, buffer zones, and the rise of the "purely atomic" individual', *Political Geography*, 24(1): 77–100.

Morris, T. (1991) *The Despairing Developer: Diary of an aid worker in the Middle East*, London: I. B. Tauris.

Moule, E. (2005) 'Challenges to the Gulf Coast', *New York Times*, 22 December.

Mouzon, S. A. (2006) *Gulf Coast Emergency House Plans: The First Book of Katrina Cottages*, Miami Beach: New Urban Guild Foundation.

Mowforth, M. and I. Munt (2009) *Tourism and Sustainability: Development, globalization and new tourism in the Third World*, 3rd edn, London: Routledge.

MSF (n.d.) 'About us', www.msf.org/msfinternational/aboutmsf/, accessed 5 February 2009.

Multi Donor Fund (2007) *Three Years after the Tsunami: Delivery Results, Supporting Transition*, December Progress Report (IV), Jakarta: Multi Donor Fund for Aceh and Nias Banda Aceh.

Munkler, H. (2005) *The New Wars*, Oxford: Polity.

Musa, E.-T., I. Scott, J. Hutton, J. Ievers et al. (2008) *Learning about Transition Programming in Aceh and Nias: Drivers and Inhibitors of Transition from Emergency to Recovery and Development in Oxfam International's Ache and Nias Programme*.

MVRDV (n.d.) 'MRVDV', www.mvrdv.nl., accessed 11 January 2009.

Nas, P. J. M. (2003) 'Ethnic identity in urban architecture', in R. Schefold, P. Nas and G. Domenig (eds), *Indonesian Houses*, vol. 1, Leiden: KITLV Press.

National Audit Office (2008) *Department for International Development: Operating in insecure environments*, London: NAO, 13 October.

New Urban Guild (n.d.) www.new urban.guild.com, accessed 29 June 2007.

New York Times (1975) 'Newswire', *New York Times*, 7 June.

Newman, D. (2003) 'Boundaries', in J. A. Agnew, M. Katharyne and G. Ó Tuathail (eds), *A Companion to Political Geography*, London: Blackwell.

Nexon, D. H. (2009) *The Struggle for Power in Early Modern Europe: Religious conflict, dynastic empires, and international change*, Princeton, NJ: Princeton University Press.

Ó Tuathail, G. (1996) *Critical Geopolitics: The politics of writing global space*, London: Routledge.

O'Beirne, E. (2006) 'Mapping the non-lieu in Marc Augé's writings', *Forum for Modern Language Studies*, 42(1): 38–50.

Odgers, J., F. Samuel and A. Sharr (2006) *Primitive: Original matters in architecture*, London: Routledge.

Oliver-Smith, A. (1996) 'Anthropological research on hazards and disasters', *Annual Review of Anthropology*, 25(1): 303–28.

Olson, L. (1999) *A Cruel Paradise*, Toronto: Insomniac Press.

Ouroussoff, N. (2008) 'Reflections: New Orleans and China' *New York Times*, 14 September.

— (2009) 'At a border crossing, security trumps openness', *New York Times*, 26 July.

Oxfam Inter-Agency Meeting (2008) *Inter-Agency Workshop on Transitions in Aceh: Further down the road*, Oxfam.

Painter, J. (2000) 'Pierre Bourdieu', in M. Crang and N. Thrift (eds), *Thinking Space*, Critical Geographies, ed. G. Valentine and T. Skelton, London and New York: Routledge.

Pandolfi, M. (2002) '"Moral entre-preneurs", souverainetés mou-vantes et barbelés: le bio-politique dans les Balkans postcommun-istes', *Anthropologie et Sociétés*, 26(1): 29–51.

— (2003) 'Contract of mutual (in)difference: governance and the humanitarian apparatus in con-temporary Albania and Kosovo', *Indiana Journal of Global Legal Studies*, 10: 369–82.

Paris, R. (2006) *At War's End: Build-ing Peace after Civil Conflict*, Cambridge: Cambridge University Press.

Parry, J. (1986) 'The Gift, the Indian gift and the "Indian Gift"', *Man*, 21(3): 453–73.

Penrose, J. and P. Jackson (1994) *Constructions of Race, Place and Nation*, Minneapolis: University of Minnesota Press.

Piazza, T. (2008) *City of Refuge*, New York: HarperCollins.

Plan Aceh (2007) *Ranub Lampuan Plan Aceh*, Banda Aceh: Plan.

Pogrebin, R. (2007) 'Brad Pitt com-missions designs for New Orleans', *New York Times*, 3 December.

Polidori, R. (artist) (2005) *2732 Orleans Avenue*, Photograph.

Pollock, N. R. (n.d.) 'Ban-Aid', *Architectural Record*, archrecord. construction.com/features/ humanitarianDesign/0810banaid. asp, accessed 7 January 2009.

Pouligny, B. (2006) *Peace Operations Seen from Below: UN missions and local people*, London: Hurst & Co.

Power, S. (2008) *Chasing the Flame: Sergio Vieira de Mello and the fight to save the world*, London: Allen Lane.

Pritchard, A. and N. Morgan (2006) 'Hotel Babylon? Exploring hotels as liminal sites of transition and transgression', *Tourism Manage-ment*, 27(5): 762–72.

Pupavac, V. (2005) 'Human security and the rise of global therapeutic governance', *Conflict, Security & Development*, 5(2): 161–81.

Ravetz, A. and R. Turkington (1995) *The Place of Home: English domestic environments, 1914–2000*, Studies in History, Planning and the Environment, London: Spon.

Reid, A. (2006) *Verandah of Violence: The background to the Aceh problem*, Singapore: Singapore University Press in association with University of Washington Press.

Reid-Henry, S. (2007) 'Exceptional sovereignty? Guantanamo Bay and the re-colonial present', *Antipode*, 39(4): 627–48.

Renner, M. (2006) 'Aceh: peacemak-ing after the tsunami', www.world watch.org/node/3930, accessed 8 February 2008.

Report of the Secretary General (2000) *Scope of legal protection under the Convention on the Safety of United Nations and Associated Personnel*, A/55/637, New York: United Nations.

— (2003) *Safety and security of humanitarian personnel and protec-tion of United Nations personnel*, A/58/344, New York: United Nations.

Republic of Indonesia (2005) *Master Plan for the Rehabilitation and Reconstruction of the Regions and Communities of the Province of Nanggroe Aceh Darussalam and the Islands of Nias, Province of North Sumatra*.

Reuters (2008) 'World Bank consult-ant kidnapped in Indonesia's Aceh', Reuters, 25 September.

Richey, L. A. and S. Ponte (2008)

'Better (red) than dead? Celebrities, consumption and international aid', *Third World Quarterly*, 29(4): 711–29.

Risen, C. (2005) 'Wrong way home', *Morning News*.

Rizal, F. (2007) *Methodology of Surveying Approach and Validity of Outputs*, Banda Aceh: LOGICA/ Australian Government, AusAID, 13 December.

Rozario, K. (2003) '"Delicious horrors": mass culture, the Red Cross, and the appeal of modern American humanitarianism', *American Quarterly*, 55(3): 417–55.

Rubenstein, J. (2007) 'Distribution and emergency', *Journal of Political Philosophy*, 15(3): 296–320.

Rubinstein, R. A. (2005) 'Intervention and culture: an anthropological approach to peace operations', *Security Dialogue*, 36(4): 527–44.

Rutherford, D. (2009) 'Sympathy, state building, and the experience of empire', *Cultural Anthropology*, 24(1): 1–32.

Rybczynski, W. (2005) 'There's no place like home: the historical problems with emergency housing', *Slate*, 31 July.

Saco, D. (1998) *Cyberspace and Democracy: Spaces and Bodies in the Age of the Internet*, Minneapolis. University of Minnesota.

Said, E. W. (1995) *Orientalism*, Penguin History, reprinted with a new afterword, London: Penguin.

Sandoval-Strausz, A. K. (2007) *Hotel: An American history*, New Haven, CT, and London: Yale University Press.

Sassen, S. (2000) *Cities in a World Economy*, 2nd edn, Sociology for a New Century, London: Pine Forge Press.

Schaper, D. (2005) 'New Urbanism advocated in Gulf Coast rebuilding', National Public Radio.

Schefold, R., P. Nas and G. Domenig (2003) *Indonesian Houses*, Leiden: KITLV Press.

Scheper-Hughes, N. (1992) *Death without Weeping: The violence of everyday life in Brazil*, Berkeley and Oxford: University of California Press.

Schmid, K. A. (2008) 'Doing ethnography of tourist enclaves: boundaries, ironies, and insights', *Tourist Studies*, 8(1): 105–21.

Schmitt, C. and G. L. Ulmen (2003) *The Nomos of the Earth in the International Law of the Jus Publicum Europaeum*, New York: Telos Press.

Schulze, K. E. (2003) 'The struggle for an independent Aceh: the ideology, capacity, and strategy of GAM', *Studies in Conflict and Terrorism*, 26: 241–71.

Scott, J. C. (1985) *Weapons of the Weak: Everyday forms of peasant resistance*, New Haven, CT, and London: Yale University Press.

— (1998) *Seeing like a State: How certain schemes to improve the human condition have failed*, Yale ISPS Series, New Haven, CT, and London: Yale University Press.

Shapiro, M. J. (1997) *Violent Cartographies. Mapping cultures of war*, London: University of Minnesota Press.

Sheik, M., M. I. Gutierrez, P. Bolton, P. Speigel et al. (2000) 'Deaths among humanitarian workers', *British Medical Journal*, 321, 15 July.

Sheller, M. (2004) 'Automotive emotions: feeling the car', *Theory, Culture & Society*, 21(4/5): 221–42.

Shields, R. (1999) *Lefebvre, Love and Struggle: Spatial dialectics*, International Library of Sociology, London: Routledge.

— (2004) 'Henri Lefebvre', in P. Hubbard, R. Kitchin and G. Valentine (eds), *Key Thinkers on Space and Place*, London: Sage.

Sibley, D. (1988) 'Survey 13: Purification of space', *Environment and Planning D: Society and Space*, 6: 409–21.

Siegel, J. T. (2003) *The Rope of God*, Ann Arbor: University of Michigan Press.

Slater, D. (1997) 'Geopolitical imaginations across the North–South divide: issues of difference, development and power', *Political Geography*, 16(8): 631–53.

Smillie, I. (2001) *Patronage or Partnership: Local capacity building in humanitarian crises*, Bloomfield, CN: Kumarian Press.

Smirl, L. (2008) 'Building the Other, constructing ourselves: spatial dimensions of international humanitarian response', *International Political Sociology*, 2(3): 236–53.

— (2009) 'Plain tales of the reconstruction site', in M. Duffield and V. Hewitt (eds), *Development and Colonialism*, London: James Currey.

Smith, N. (2006) 'There's no such thing as a natural disaster', Social Science Research Council, understandingkatrina.ssrc.org/Smith/, accessed 31 May 2007.

Smith, R. (2008) 'In Katrina's wake, a new biennial', *New York Times*, 5 September.

Smith, S. and J. Watson (2001) *Reading Autobiography: A guide for interpreting life narratives*, London: University of Minnesota Press.

Smyth, M. and G. Robinson (2001) *Researching Violently Divided Societies: Ethical and methodological issues*, Tokyo: United Nations University Press.

Snyder, M. (2007) 'Mississippi communities hope to avoid sprawl in rebuild', *HoustonChronical.com*, 3 June.

Soja, E. W. (1996) *Thirdspace: Journeys to Los Angeles and other real-and-imagined places*, Oxford: Blackwell.

Sonne, W. (2003) *Representing the State: Capital city planning in the early twentieth century*, Munich and London: Prestel.

Spees, P. (2004) *Gender, Justice and Accountability in Peace Support Operations*, London: International Alert.

Spivak, G. C. (1988) 'Subaltern studies: deconstructing historiography', in R. Guha and G. C. Spivak (eds), *Selected Subaltern Studies*, Oxford: Oxford University Press.

Spivak, G. C. and S. Harasym (1990) *The Post-Colonial Critic: Interviews, strategies, dialogues*, London: Routledge.

Stamp, J. (2008) 'Brad Pitt's Make it Right homes now under construction', 9 September, lifewithoutbuildings.net/2008/09/brad-pitts-make-it-right-homes-now-under-construction.html, accessed 11 January 2009.

Stansbury, N. (2005) 'Exposing the foundations of corruption in construction', in *Global Corruption Report*, London: Pluto Press.

Stengers, I. (1997) *Power and Invention: Situating science*, Theory out of Bounds, Minneapolis: University of Minnesota Press.

— (2000) *The Invention of Modern Science*, Theory out of Bounds, Minneapolis: University of Minnesota Press.

Stewart, K. (1988) 'Nostalgia – a polemic', *Cultural Anthropology*, 3(3): 227–41.

Stewart, R. (2007) *The Places In Between*, Rearsby: W. F. Howes.

Stoddard, A., A. Harmer and K. Haver (2006) *Providing Aid in Insecure Environments: Trends in policy and operations*, Humanitarian Policy Group, Overseas Development Institute, September.

— (2009) *Providing Aid in Insecure Environments: 2009 update*, Humanitarian Policy Group, Overseas Development Institute, September.

Stohr, K. (ed.) (2006) *Design Like You Give a Damn: Architectural Responses to Humanitarian Crisis*, London: Thames & Hudson.

Streeter, A. (2006) 'Big trouble in rural China?', *Sustainable Industries*, 28 April.

Sturdy, A., M. Schwarz and A. Spicer (2006) 'Guess who's coming to dinner? Structures and uses of liminality in strategic management consultancy', *Human Relations*, 59(7): 929–60.

Sudjic, D. (2005) *The Edifice Complex: How the Rich and Powerful Shape the World*, London: Allen Lane.

Sudjic, D. and H. Jones (2001) *Architecture and Democracy*, London: Laurence King.

Sufi, R. and A. Budi Wibowo (2004) *Aceh Nan Kaya Budaya*, Banda Aceh: Dinas Pariwisata, Provinsi Nanggroe Acch Darussaam.

Suhrke, A. and I. Samset (2007) 'What's in a figure? Estimating recurrence of civil war', *International Peacekeeping*, 14(2): 195–203.

Susanka, S. and K. Obolensky (1998) *The Not So Big House: A blueprint for the way we really live*, Newtown, CN: Taunton Press.

Swope, C. (2009) 'Road to Katrinaville', *Governing*, April.

Talen, E. (2005) *New Urbanism and American Planning: The conflict of cultures*, Planning, History, and

the Environment Series, London: Routledge.

Taylor, C. (2002) 'Modern social imaginaries', *Public Culture*, 14(1): 91–124.

— (2005) *Modern Social Imaginaries*, Public Planet Books, Durham, NC, and London: Duke University Press.

Taylor, R. B. (1988) *Human Territorial Functioning: An empirical, evolutionary perspective on individual and small group territorial cognitions, behaviors, and consequences*, Environment and Behaviour Series, Cambridge: Cambridge University Press.

Teather, E. K. (ed.) (1999) *Embodied Geographies*, London: Routledge.

Telford, J. and J. Cosgrove (2006) *Joint Evaluation of the International Response to the Indian Ocean Tsunami: Synthesis Report*, London: Tsunami Evaluation Coalition.

Thrift, N. (2004) 'Driving in the city', *Theory, Culture & Society*, 21(4/5): 41–59.

— (2008) *Non-Representational Theory: Space, politics, affect*, International Library of Sociology, London: Routledge.

Tilly, C. (2005) *Identities, Boundaries, and Social Ties*, Boulder, CO: Paradigm.

Tomlinson, J. (1999) *Globalization and Culture*, Chichester: Polity.

Traub, J. (2008) 'The celebrity solution', *New York Times*, 9 March.

Tsunami Global Lessons Learned Project Steering Committee (2009) *The Tsunami Legacy: Innovations, Breakthroughs and Change*, UNORC.

Tuan, Yi-fu (1977) *Space and Place: The perspective of experience*, Minneapolis: University of Minnesota Press.

Turner, V. W. (1969) *The Ritual Process: Structure and anti-structure*, Lewis Henry Morgan Lectures, London: Routledge & Kegan Paul.

— (1975) *Dramas, Fields, and Metaphors; symbolic action in human society*, Ithaca, NY: Cornell University Press.

— (1977) 'Chapter III: Variations on a theme of liminality', in S. Falk Moore and B. G. Myerhoff (eds), *Secular Ritual*, Assen: Gorcum.

UN Development Group (2008a) *Priority Business Practice Issues Identified by Resident Coordinators from 'Delivering as One' Pilots*, UNDG.

— (2008b) *Task Force on Common Premises/Working Group on Joint Funding Mechanisms, Financial and Audit Issues Common Premises (One Office) Funding Position Paper*, UNDG.

— (n.d.) UN House/UN Common Premises Programme website, www.undp.org/unhouse/popups/dbot.htm, accessed 13 May 2009.

UN Secretary General (1997) *Renewing the United Nations: A Program for Reform*, New York: United Nations.

UN-HABITAT (2007a) *Anchoring Homes: UN-Habitat's People's Process in Aceh and Nias after the Tsunami*, Nairobi: UN-HABITAT.

— (2007b) *Field Report: Building Back Better in Pakistan*, Nairobi: UN-HABITAT, 16–20 April.

UNAMID (2009) *Information Circular No. 2009/042*, El Fasher: UNAMID.

UNDP (2003) *Malicious Acts Insurance Policy*, New York: Office of Human Resources Bureau of Management, 4 February.

UNDRO (1982) *Shelter after Disaster: Guidelines for Assistance*, New York: United Nations.

United Nations (n.d.) *Security in the Field: Information for all staff members of the United Nations system*, New York: United Nations.

— (1946) *Privileges and Immunities of the United Nations*, 22 (I) A, New York: United Nations.

— (1994) *Convention on the Safety of United Nations and Associated Personnel*, New York: United Nations, 9 December.

— (2002) *Minimum Operating Security Standards*, New York: United Nations.

— (2006a) *Delivering as One: Report of the Secretary General's High Level Panel*, New York: United Nations.

— (2006b) *United Nations Integrated Missions Planning Process (IMPP) Guidelines Endorsed by Secretary-General on June 13 2006*, New York: United Nations, June.

UNORC/BRR (2007) *Tsunami Recovery Indicators Package (TRIP): For Aceh and Nias*, Banda Aceh: UNORC/BRR, March.

— (2009) *Tsunami Recovery Indicators Package (TRIP): The third report for Aceh and Nias*, Banda Aceh: UNORC/BRR, January.

Upton, D. and J. M. Vlach (eds) (1986) *Common Places: Readings in American Vernacular Architecture*, Athens and London: University of Georgia Press.

Urban Design Associates (n.d.) *Louisiana Speaks: Pattern Book*.

Urry, J. (2007) *Mobilities*, Cambridge: Polity.

US Department of State (1997–2005a) *Country Reports on Human Rights Practice*.

— (1997–2005b) *Country Reports on Terrorism and Patterns of Global Terrorism*.

— (n.d.) 'Bureau of Overseas Building Operations', www.state.gov/obo, accessed 8 September 2009.

Vale, L. J. (1992) *Architecture, Power,*

and National Identity, New Haven, CT, and London: Yale University Press.

Vale, L. J. and T. J. Campanella (2005) The Resilient City: How modern cities recover from disaster, Oxford: Oxford University Press.

Van Brabant, K. (2000) Operational Security Management in Violent Environments (Good Practice Review), ed. ODI, London: HPN, June.

Van Gennep, A. (1960) The Rites of Passage, trans. G. L. Caffee and M. B. Vizedom, London: Routledge & Kegan Paul.

Van Zoonen, L. (2005) Entertaining the Citizen: When politics and popular culture converge, Lanham, MD: Rowman & Littlefield.

Venturi, R., D. Scott Brown, K. Rattenbury and S. Hardingham (2007) Learning from Las Vegas, SuperCrit, Abingdon: Routledge.

Vesely, D. (2004) Architecture in the Age of Divided Representation: The question of creativity in the shadow of production, London: MIT Press.

Virilio, P. (1994) Bunker Archeology, New York: Princeton Architectural Press.

— (2006) Speed and Politics, Semiotext(e) Foreign Agents Series, Los Angeles: Semiotext(e).

Vltchek, A. (2005) 'Aceh abandoned: the second tsunami', Guernica: A magazine of art and politics, May.

Voegelin, E. and M. Franz (2000) The Ecumenic Age, Order and History, London: University of Missouri Press.

Wagner, P. L. and M. W. Mikesell (1962) Readings in Cultural Geography, ed. with introductions and translations by P. L. Wagner and M. W. Mikesell, London and Chicago, IL: University of Chicago Press.

Waizenegger, A. (2007) 'Armed separatism and the 2004 tsunami in Aceh', Canadian Asia Commentary, 43, February.

Walker, B. (2003) 'Another kind of science: Christopher Alexander on democratic theory and the built environment', Canadian Journal of Political Science, 36(5): 1053–72.

Wall, I. (2006) The Right to Know, Office of the UN SG's Special Envoy for Tsunami Recovery.

Warf, B. (2004) 'Anthony Giddens', in P. Hubbard, R. Kitchin and G. Valentine (eds), Key Thinkers on Space and Place, London: Sage.

Waterson, R. (1990) The Living House: An anthropology of architecture in South-East Asia, Oxford: Oxford University Press.

Weinberger, S. (2007) 'Building a fortress on the Hill: welcome to the U.S. embassy in Baghdad (bumped and updated)', War Update, 20 November, blog.wired.com/defense/2007/05/building_a_fort.html.

Weiss, T. G. and C. Collins (2000) Humanitarian Challenges and Intervention, 2nd edn, Dilemmas in World Politics, Oxford: Westview Press.

Weizman, E. (2007) Hollow Land: Israel's Architecture of Occupation, London: Verso.

Wernle, B. (2000) 'Land Rover eyes aid market', Automotive News, 4 September.

Wharton, A. J. (2001) Building the Cold War: Hilton International hotels and modern architecture, Chicago, IL: University of Chicago.

Wheeler, N. J. (2000) Saving Strangers: Humanitarian intervention in international society, Oxford: Oxford University Press.

Whitehead, A. N. (1956) Modes of

Thought, Cambridge: Cambridge University Press.

Whitehead, A. N. and N. Frye (1960) *Process and Reality: An essay in cosmology*, New York: Harper & Row.

Whitworth, S. (2004) *Men, Militarism, and UN Peacekeeping: A gendered analysis*, Critical Security Studies, London: Lynne Rienner.

Wilson, D. (ed.) (2004) *The Sphere Project: Humanitarian Charter and Minimum Standards in Disaster Response*, The Sphere Project.

Wilson-Doenges, G. (2000) 'An exploration of sense of community and fear of crime in gated communities', *Environment and Behavior*, 32(5): 597–611.

Woods, C. A. (1998) *Development Arrested: The blues and plantation power in the Mississippi Delta*, Haymarket Series, London: Verso.

World Bank/DSF (2007) *Aceh Conflict Monitoring Update*, World Bank/Decentralization Support Facility, 1 June–31 July.

— (2008) *Aceh Conflict Monitoring Update*, World Bank/Decentralization Support Facility, May/June.

— (2009) *Aceh Conflict Monitoring Update*, World Bank/Decentralization Support Facility, 1 December 2008–28 February 2009.

Yacobi, H. (2004) *Constructing a Sense of Place: Architecture and the Zionist discourse*, Design and the Built Environment, Aldershot: Ashgate.

— (2007) 'The NGOization of space: dilemmas of social change, planning policy, and the Israeli public sphere', *Environment and Planning D: Society and Space*, 25(4): 745–58.

Yamashita, H. (2004) *Humanitarian Space and International Politics: The creation of safe areas*, Burlington, VT: Ashgate.

Yamba, C. Bawa (1995) *Permanent Pilgrims: The role of pilgrimage in the lives of West African Muslims in Sudan*, International African Library, London: Edinburgh University Press for the International African Institute.

Yang, G. (2000) 'The liminal effects of social movements: Red Guards and the transformation of identity', *Sociological Forum*, 15(3): 379–406.

Yeoh, B. S. A. (1996) *Contesting Space: Power relations and the urban built environment in colonial Singapore*, South-East Asian Social Science Monographs, Oxford: Oxford University Press.

Yudhoyono, S. B. (2009) 'Opening address at the 42nd ADB Annual Meeting of the Board of Governors', Paper read at the 42nd ADB Annual Meeting of the Board of Governors, Bali, 4 May.

Žižek, S. (1989) *The Sublime Object of Ideology*, Phronesis, London: Verso.

INDEX

logging, illegal, as source of revenue for GAM, 158
Louis Berger company, 161
Louisiana, reconstruction of, 17
Louisiana Speaks: Pattern Book, 194
Lowe's company, 189, 198
Lower Ninth Ward (New Orleans), 18, 205; not suitable for residential building, 173; reconstruction of, 169–79
lying by aid workers, 34

Maas, Winy, 172
maison basse house form, 193
Maison Dom-ino, 166
Make It Right project, 166, 170–4, 178, 191
'making do', 93, 106, 112, 147, 164, 204, 207
Malicious Acts Insurance Policy (MAIP), 59, 67
Manaf, Muzakkir, 158
mapping of disaster *see* cartography
marginal characters, definition of, 40
martial law, imposed in Aceh, 122
Marxism, 86
material environment, causality/agency of, 79
material theory, i, ii, 11, 82
materiality, 9, 163; importance of, 82–7; of humanitarian intervention, 47, 202–3, 208–9
Mauss, M., 18, 163; *The Gift*, 132; theory of exchange, 132–3, 139
May, Shannon, 174
means, financial, of end-users, 177
measurable results, demonstration of, 124–5
Médecins sans Frontières (MSF), 27, 30, 64
memoirs of aid workers, 107; process of writing of, 38; used as source, 16, 20–46
Mennonite Central Committee, 134
Merhamets organization, 34
methodology, 13–15; use of interviews, 115

middle classes, travelling of, 41
military and humanitarian mandates, conflated, 48–50
military aspects of missions, 50, 72–3
military backgrounds of aid staff, 71
military presence, at compounds, 81
Minimum Operating Residential Security Standards (MORSS), 60, 61, 64, 67
Minimum Operating Security Standards (MOSS), 60–1, 64, 67, 71
Mission Aviation Fellowship (MAF), 123
Mississippi, reconstruction of, 17
Mississippi Emergency Management Agency (MEMA), 185–6
Mississippi Renewal Forum (MRF), 179–80, 183, 187, 190
mistiming of funding, 11
mobile phones, use of, 80
mobility, 16, 93, 123; differing rates of, 11, 119; of aid workers, constrained, 123
model-based solutions, 169
Mogadishu ('the dish'), 27
moments, concept of, 89
moral frameworks of international assistance, 163, 208
Morel, Adrien, kidnapping of, 158
Morphosis company, 172
Multi Donor Fund (MDF), 116, 154
Museum of Modern Art (New York), 171, 194
MVRDV company, 171–2

national and expat teams, relationships between, 30
National Audit Office (UK), 48
National Development Planning Agency (BAPPENAS) (Indonesia), 118, 127, 149–54
national–international divide, 71
nationless figures, 22
native, construction of, 136
natural disasters, reconstruction after, 14
Ndembu tribe (Zambia), 21